When Angels
Fooled the World

RESCUERS OF JEWS
IN WARTIME HUNGARY

When Angels Fooled the World

RESCUERS OF JEWS
IN WARTIME HUNGARY

Charles Fenyvesi

THE UNIVERSITY OF WISCONSIN PRESS / DRYAD PRESS

The University of Wisconsin Press
1930 Monroe Street, 3rd Floor
Madison, Wisconsin 53711-2059
www.wisc.edu/wisconsinpress/

Dryad Press
Post Office Box 11233
Takoma Park, Maryland 20913

3 Henrietta Street
London WC2E 8LU, England

Copyright © 2003 Charles Fenyvesi

5 4 3 2 1

Printed in the United States of America

Cover art by Susan Due Pearcy titled "Fire Storm"
Book and cover design by Sandy Rodgers

The publishers are grateful to the United States Holocaust Memorial Museum for providing historical photographs and granting permission for their use (see page 301 for complete acknowledgments).

Text is typeset in
Adobe Garamond 12 on 15.5

The paper used in this publication meets the minimum requirements of American National Standard for Information Sciences — Permanence of paper for Printed Library Materials, ANSI Z39.48

Library of Congress Cataloging-in-Publication Data
Fenyvesi, Charles, 1937–
    When angels fooled the world: rescuers of Jews in wartime Hungary /
    Charles Fenyvesi.
      p. cm.
    ISBN: 0-299-18840-X (alk. paper)
      1. Righteous Gentiles in the Holocaust—Hungary. 2. World
    War, 1939–1945—Jews—Rescue—Hungary. 3. Holocaust, Jewish
    (1939–1945)—Hungary. 4. Hungary—Ethnic relations. I. Title
    D804.65F46   2003
    940.53′1835′09439—dc21   2003045831

Acknowledgments

Sketching the portraits of rescuers of Jews, I relied on two kinds of sources, those who knew particular rescuers and authors including historians who wrote about one or another rescuer and their times. I thank first members of my family whose memories persuaded me that I should write this book: my mother Anna Schwarcz, her brother Samuel (Shumi) Schwarcz, their sister Mara Schwarcz Thury, and her son Levente Thury. For insights into the lifelong humanitarian devotions of Pastor Gabor Sztehlo, I am beholden to his daughter Ildiko Sztehlo Sundheim, his cousin Sara Sztehlo, his co-workers Magda and Emil Koren, as well as individuals Pastor Sztehlo rescued: Andras Rac, Balint Fuzeki, Pal Foti, Otto Orban, and Gabor Vermes. Grappling with the enigma of Raoul Wallenberg, I was inspired by my colleague Victoria Pope. The bibliography at the end of the book lists the authors whose work I drew on.

Two rabbis whose brilliant arguments illuminated the theology of angels in Jewish tradition are Michael Berenbaum and Max Ticktin. My children — Shamu, Danny, and Malka — as well as cousins Andrea Szego and Laszlo Kadar, along with friend Helen Epstein, offered questions and criticisms that were invaluable. My wife Lizou, the first to scrutinize the manuscript, fought valiantly to rein in my sentimental impulses.

I am also grateful for my literary agent F. Joseph Spieler who did not lose his faith in the project even after several publishers rejected the idea as a commercial no-win. Similarly, my editor Merrill Leffler's sympathetic magic saved me from giving up.

In memory of my mother Anna Schwarcz
who wanted me to write this book and
who left me a legacy of protest
against the iniquity of forgetfulness.

Contents

Prologue

I live a contented life on seven and a half acres of tawny Maryland clay we keep improving with mounds of withered leaves and manure from our goats and sheep. The farm offers, for family and friends, such crops as thornless blackberries and plump hazelnuts, and I am inordinately proud of our goat cheese and wild-pear cider, each pungent in its own way, and our celandine poppies and black-eyed Susans, the former in the shade and latter in the sun, both of them luminescent with petals of a solar gold.

What I have kept to myself is that at night I am often elsewhere. In my dreams the Nazis again have all the guns, and once more I am on the run with a forged document that bears a stranger's name. Getting caught is only a matter of time; a bullet through the heart would be a relief. After nearly sixty years, the nightmare is as familiar as the last scene in *Hamlet*. Won't it ever fade away? Or will the ghosts always circle around me, regardless of where I am, anchored at home near the Potomac or talked into a visit by the Danube?

I try not to react to individuals I dislike with conjectures about how they might react if ordered to shoot defenseless people. On the other hand, it is unreasonable to think of my closest Gentile friends as the kind of individuals who would surely hide my family in their attics in the unlikely event — and such an event is implausible, even unthinkable, until it happens — that a need presented itself one day. I did not choose them as friends because they reminded me, if only in some small way, of those exceptional few who rescued Jews in Hungary during World War II. Or did I? They were known as angels. They fooled the killers.

When will I stop resenting analysts who pronounce judgments on foreign invasions and local resistance, swings of personal loyalty and clashes of ideological wills, yet have never had to fear for their lives when occupation troops checked identity papers? Whether casual or cynical, their observations have the ring of French phrases picked up from a guidebook for tourists. Often they miss the evil heart of a story — or they see nothing else but that — and they cannot imagine themselves as part of it. They are professional bystanders whose resumés do not include entries such as "targeted in a roundup by thugs in uniforms." They have not cowered in a city under siege, fearing to step out of their rooms, scraping through without any food in the pantry, and surrendering to the mind-numbing probability that whether by bullet or by bomb, getting killed is only a question of time. Nor did they have tears in their eyes when listening to a Gypsy violinist's lament for an old, lightning-struck sycamore tree now nodding to its fall that inspired the sweetest daydreams of our youth.

The day ought to come when I can take an afternoon's stroll under the walnut trees I have planted and forget to congratulate myself for having evaded deportation to a *Konzentrationslager*. But will wisps of smoke rising from the far end of a meadow — most likely from a farmer's leafpile or a family barbecue — always remind me of a crematorium? I did not see those chimneys, said to be as tall as church spires. Yet they became my memories through my cousins' stories: how the acrid, gritty fumes and darker than a thunderhead billowed day and night, and clung to the earth till lifted by a wind. When at last the smoke rose, it canceled the sun. Heaven choked on the smoke.

Those billowing dark clouds hovered over the stories my family would tell well past midnight, holding back the most gruesome details until after my parents sent me to bed in the adjacent room, the door shut tight. But I could still hear nearly every word. Fighting sleep, I kept up with the narrative about a loaf of bread stolen or a fist-size cache of potato peels found by Agi or Kati, Gizel or Chibi. Agi was ebullient and Kati melancholy, Gizel intense and Chibi easygoing. I loved each of them wholly and unconditionally as "our blood," the proud plural possessive cherished within my extended family, then as now. Images from their deportation imprinted on my retina, and their phrases stayed with me like lines from a poem memorized in school. In my dreams I accompanied them, and at times I still do, as a child once more. When I wake, the skeletal figures of prisoners that slipped in and out of my dream seem as real as my parents telling me to hurry up for school; on the street the morning crowds are as insubstantial as puffs of smoke. The part of the dream that stays with me for hours, even days, is the reassuring grip of a relative's hand, a grip stronger than death.

I was as happy as a puppy new to the household when my parents allowed me in the living room with the grownups to listen to slender, dark-eyed cousin Agi Bekes, a fast talker with expressive hands and thick mobile eyebrows, as she recalled the last days of the war.

Agi's Story

With the sounds of shelling and bombing coming closer and closer, Agi and her fellow inmates in Bergen-Belsen were lined up and herded into cattle cars, which optimists interpreted as just a transfer to another concentration camp. For eight days the train crept along, stopping often and at times reversing its course. Gunfire and explosions could be heard from every direction. Bullets rattled and sometimes pierced the thick wooden planks of the wagon. At one point the sounds of war quieted, and the train stopped. Suddenly, the guards slid the doors open and ordered the prisoners to line up by what some recognized as the river Elbe a hundred meters away. They saw machine gun nests all around and knew that this was it — the fusillades would begin momentarily and the current would carry away their bodies.

As two thousand prisoners began marching down toward the water, one screamed, "The Americans are here!"

On the other side of the train tracks, a column of soldiers in unfamiliar uniforms came into view. They were riding motorcycles. Agi knew English. Her friends pleaded, "Go tell them they mustn't shoot at us Jews." Summoning all her strength, Agi broke out of the line, ran toward the soldiers, and cried out as loud as she could: "Don't shoot! We are Jewish prisoners!"

After some seconds, or maybe half a minute that only seemed to stretch out to an hour, a soldier at the head of the column stopped his motorcycle and shouted in her direction. Agi could not make out the words, but she knew from the big friendly smile on his young face that he had to be an American. She was still running when suddenly she understood what he kept shouting: *"Sholem aleichem!"*

Agi found herself sobbing so convulsively that it took some time before she could return the soldier's traditional Jewish greeting, "Peace be with you."

In the Wilderness of Kaddish

Since those days I have coached myself. I learned not to ask acquaintances and strangers, either provocatively or conversationally, "Where were you *then?*" Holding back offers advantages. A smile dams tears; silence plugs a burst of emotions. But meeting someone who was an adult during the war happens less and less frequently. The last time I checked with a survivor's organization — and that was quite a few years ago — the average age of its membership was nearly seventy-five. Or at least this is what I was told by one of the leaders, a rough-hewn block of a Warsaw Jew who distrusted everyone, including himself. He told me that at least once a week he had been attending a camp inmate's funeral. "I am not lying to you," he said, wagging his forefinger an inch from my nose that I could not help noticing had the same curvature as his. "This is *emes.*" He had the chutzpah to translate the word from the Yiddish: "*Emes* means the truth." Seeing me smirk, he added with a smirk, "I know you know *emes.* Good. But you Hungarians don't know nothing."

Nowadays what amazes me is how many people born since V-E Day travel to see Auschwitz or Babi Yar or other sites in Poland or Ukraine, Germany or Hungary, where brick walls are nicked by bullets from firing squads, the soil is laced with human ashes, and sagging warehouse roofs let rain leak into rooms filled with shorn hair that the authorities cannot decide what to do with. Miles away, in hotels built for the tourist trade, investment bankers and sensitive thirteen-year-olds awaken at night to the cries of someone, perhaps a restless spirit. They could have gone to Paris or Rome or Vienna. With tears and prayers they pay homage to the dead — *our* dead. I cannot do more than that myself, except to drop my survival tools of evasion: stop tending and poetizing the six-pointed stars of daffodils and the whirligigs of daisies, and waste no more time on whittling those tight little journalistic items that lose their value faster than a daylily's bloom.

I could let myself sink ever deeper into memories — some of them mine and others inherited from family members — as if there were no bountiful earth under my spade and no life-sustaining sun above, nothing to harvest and no purpose to planting, and no reason to continue a stone retaining wall that is now eighty feet long. After all, what else merits attention besides that one intractable fraction of the past which demands total concentration and undivided loyalty and which beckons at the terminal for every train of thought. Still, temperamentally I am unsuited to live in the wilderness of perpetual Kaddish.

Listening and reporting have been my downtown job, and I know that it must be done patiently, and with an open mind. With a bit more than due diligence, I track down people on both sides of a controversy, telling myself that Nazis would do no such thing — and then I feel foolish for entertaining such a thought. Interviewing a Serbian intellectual, supposedly Westernized and liberal, justifying ethnic cleansing and sympathizing with Slobodan Milosevic's burdens of leadership, I sat poker-faced and fussed over the exact wording of his direct quotes. Day after day in the spring of 1999, I watched on television Kosovo Albanians fleeing Yugoslavia. Their pageantry of grief seemed the same on every film clip and ever so familiar; only the faces changed. Writing about their exodus, several times I typed "Jews" instead of "Albanians" on the computer, then paused, superstitiously reluctant to hit the delete button.

But of course the circumstances and the dimensions of the two genocides are as different as the landscapes and the languages. Historical parallels are forced, as no event can be the replica of another. Yet like a clever rhyme, an echo can snare the mind. It is only human to think of the past as the template for the present.

In the 1960s and 70s, I did not wince when crowds of demonstrators screamed "Hitler" and "Sieg Heil" at Lyndon Johnson or Richard Nixon or Ronald Reagan. I reminded myself that this is another generation and another continent; for both, Nazi Germany is ready-made rhetoric that offers the most effective synonyms for evil. Is it really inexcusable then that to some people "Holocaust" was a series they either caught or missed on TV and that Auschwitz has become a convenient metaphor? A city's roundup of stray cats, for example, animal lovers call "Cat

Auschwitz." Thank God, I tell myself, I live in the New World where such references to Old World conflicts are taken as seriously as advertising jingles. Oh well, I can't be on the watch all the time, scanning the horizons for infractions of good taste and historic truth.

Offered a tip by a State Department official in 1982 about the Pentagon quietly preparing to ship back to Germany more than 6,000 works of captured Nazi war art — despite a postwar agreement not to do so unless all four allies consented — I first thought of it as just another Washington story, a back-room shenanigan involving a few American officers who thought they had a smart idea and a congressman or two who fell in with the wrong people while visiting Germany. But my heart did beat a little faster when I filed the report, and my throat tightened when I got up the next morning and saw the scoop on the front page of my paper then, *The Washington Post.*

On assignment in the White House I once muttered, "Oh, shut up, already," listening to Israeli Prime Minister Menachem Begin toasting President Jimmy Carter with a fifteen-minute lecture on the meaning of the Holocaust. At other times I could smile at the familiarity of his posture, as stiff as the barrel of a gun, and his Polish-Austrian-Hungarian histrionics of hand-kissing, performed with the vigor of a stapler stapling documents. But in the White House he made me cringe when he cited the massacre of six million European Jews as an argument to justify his policy of annexing the West Bank of the Jordan River. Should the appeasement-in-Munich card be pulled out whenever someone suggests a diplomatic compromise? Must every opponent be automatically labeled a Nazi, or at least a collaborator? How long will the bully ghosts of Hitler and Chamberlain haunt the Middle East? When will the Second World War end?

On another occasion I was as courteous as my colleague, a Southern gentleman originally from Mississippi whose desk was next to mine at *The Post*, when, just after an eight p.m. deadline — usually a time of relief, a call for a drink in the bar around the corner — a stranger on the telephone insisted on reciting for me excerpts from her book-length epic poem titled "Auschwitz." It was in Hungarian, her mother tongue and mine. In one neat couplet after the other, she mourned her twin babies she was forced to give up for Dr. Josef Mengele's medical experiments. As she caught her breath between two stanzas, I gently interrupted and asked if she had had other children since then. Yes, she had given birth to one, and he was now in his late thirties, still unmarried, living in a Maryland suburb, always busy with his motorcycle. She would not say more about him. Solemnly, she cited her duty to remember — and mine.

That conversation happened more than a decade ago, but only recently have I begun to understand the woman's knife-in-the-heart need to pass along what she called the lessons of her life. As the years sneaked up behind her, she told me, so did her fear that what she valued the most would be buried with her: memories that were her own and no one else's.

She assured me that she labored long and hard on her lines, meticulously matching the words of a rhyme-rich language. I thought I heard her chuckle when she agreed with my suggestion that writing poetry should be an analgesic. Oh yes, counting syllables, picking synonyms, and especially getting a bull's-eye rhyme help the mind to rise above the terrors described. But, she insisted, her purpose was not only literary. She wanted to make sure that years after she is gone a reader could still learn the precise hue of her twins' chestnut-brown eyes and the timbre of the Hungarian gendarme's husky voice offering to hide her and her babies if she only agreed to quit her husband and live with him. On the telephone, her voice went from a rasp to a tinkle when she said, "I was a pretty young girl then."

From Generation to Generation

No one from my Grandmother Roza's generation came home from the camps. My grandmother was then in her seventies, and none of my relatives over the age of fifty-five — or under eighteen — survived deportation to Germany. In the 1990s, the remnant of those left from my mother's generation passed away, one by one. A series of strokes silenced the last of my uncles, Anti, once a wiry song-and-dance comedian whom his favorite sister, my mother Anna, apple-cheeked and chubby, had always tried to "fatten up." When I went to take farewell of him in Beersheba in 1993, that jaunty storyteller from my childhood had to rely on his daughter, Zhuzhi, to complete a word he began to pronounce. The following year he died, but no one had the heart to tell his one remaining sibling, my mother Anna. By then she could barely recognize those closest to her, and she was no longer aware of the year, or even the decade, printed on the calendar.

Signaling the beginning of her descent into dementia was her frequent comment — which family members at first shrugged off as a conversational gambit — that whenever someone pressed the buzzer to her apartment, she thought it would be one of her brothers or sisters who had died ten or twenty years earlier. Week after week, her once firm grip on what she used to call "the strictly real" loosened a little more. Soon after she was taken to the hospital she got into the habit of complaining that she did not understand what she could have possibly done wrong so that none of her brothers and sisters would come to see her. "I have always been a good sister," she said. "It's not right that they forget about me."

Mortified when unable to recall the name of Cousin Agi accompanying me on a visit, Mother beamed when twenty minutes later she remembered — or at least she addressed Agi by the name of *her* mother, my mother's first cousin dead for some twenty years and admired in the family for her agile mind. Agi, so pleased that her eyes misted over, would not think of making a correction.

In Mother's lucid moments, increasingly infrequent, she surprised us by saying that of her parents' seven children, she was the only one still alive. In the same authoritative, now-let-me-tell-you-the-latest tone she had used for years in reporting on our far-flung family, she added that all her first cousins, numbering more than fifty before the war, were gone as well.

Knowing that in the hospital she had no access to a telephone and she received no letters, family members asked: But how could Anna know? *How?* No visitor would tell her, and no one did. Yet she knew — she *knew*, and she was shaman-sure — what the rest of us found out through a relay of phone calls and letters.

From the time she was a little girl, my mother kept mental files on family births and deaths; the successes and failures of marriages and business ventures; one cousin's weakness for redheads and the scent of money and a nephew's collection of wives and children and stepchildren. She gathered details avidly, as if she had sought them for a family saga. She would not rest until she ferreted out why in the course of the welcoming embrace by the front door, someone furtively slipped an envelope into a relative's pocket. (It was, as I happened to hear in a conversation years later, a stipend to a needy cousin whose late grandfather had once similarly helped his sister, the donor's mother.)

In the hospital she surmised what visitors so carefully kept from her: that she was the last of her generation. She was not grateful for her longevity. She said she had complained to God directly why He was so cruel to her as to choose her as "the one to close the ledger." (Mother spoke to God freely and without hesitation, with the kind of respect due to an older relative, such as a great-uncle with many direct descendants claiming his primary attention. But she expected to be remembered by God, and she referred to earlier appeals, some of them successful.) She felt lonely; she felt abandoned. At times she said that she was the last person alive who had walked with her father through the fields of their native village and who had felt the grip of his hand — and that grip is a sensation immeasurably precious that will be lost, irretrievably, once she is gone. She argued that a witness's memory and memory passed down do not have the same weight as evidence. (Was she jealous of those of us in the family, myself included, who cite her father and rely on him as our lawgiver?) "I am the last witness who can testify what my father was really like," she insisted. "Once I am dead, no one can speak for him."

On occasion she would conjure up the past with chilling precision. The last time I saw Mother she recalled her last attempt to visit her mother Roza, in the summer of 1944, in an internment camp in the outskirts of Budapest where a trainload of Jews allegedly arrived from Debrecen, Grandmother's hometown. Mother's source of information was a Gentile acquaintance sympathetic to Jews — and therefore trustworthy — who in turn heard it from someone whose brother-in-law worked for the railroad. Though Mother's younger sister Mara, a hardened skeptic, dismissed the tip as an unreliable wartime rumor, Mother latched onto it, and she hurried off to the internment camp as soon as she put together a food packet. I tagged along; I wouldn't miss a chance to see my grandmother.

More than fifty years later, Mother reenacted rather than told the story. She set the stage by citing the torrential downpour, and she called the rain "drunken," a phrase from her village, suggesting a rage beyond reason and control. She left clauses dangling in mid-air and substituted gestures for the words that failed to come to her, as her tongue no longer responded to the summons of her mind. But her diction was fluent when she interjected the cry, again and again, "Do you still remember?" Each time I replied, "I do, I do."

The two of us arrived at the internment camp's gate just as the rain's fury reached a new peak. The guards, who had taken shelter inside their office by the gate, made it clear, first with wrists crossed tight over the stomach and then with forefingers aimed at us like pistols, that entry was forbidden and that unless we left forthwith, we would end up in handcuffs and then with bullets in the head.

But nothing could stop Mother. We walked along the fence until we reached a secluded spot out of the guards' hearing. Clutching the barbed wire, Mother shouted, "I am looking for my mother, Roza Schwarcz from Debrecen," and I too shouted as loud as I could, "I am looking for my grandmother, Roza Schwarcz."

At last one prisoner ventured outside, and he agreed to call out in the barracks, "Is Roza Schwarcz here from Debrecen?" Others took up his cry, and the words sounded like echoes in a crevasse.

After a long while a tiny, very old woman with a face as wrinkled as the bark of a locust tree made her way over to us. "My name is Roza Schwarcz," she said. However, she added, she came not from Debrecen but Miskolc, another town east of Budapest. Softly, she cautioned, "I don't think anyone is here from Debrecen."

"I brought you a little something to taste," Mother said brightly, holding back her tears. The lilt of her voice and her choice of words carried over from countless tea times when she used to offer cakes symmet-

The author's grandparents, Roza (Ruchl) and Karl (Akiba) Schwarcz in the early years of the twentieth century.

The Schwarcz family in 1934 at the wedding of Mara Schwarcz and Levente Thury (in the center) between those seated: Roza Schwarcz (on the left) and her eldest daughter Elza. Standing (from left to right) are Roza's children Mishi, Anna, Anti. On the far right: her eldest son Shumi, and to his left is his wife Agnes.

rically arranged on a silver tray. But for that one time in her life she did not ask questions to explore whether Roza Schwarcz from Miskolc might be related to us. Wordlessly she lifted me up, and I carefully lowered over the fence the basket of food intended for my grandmother.

Throughout the long ride home on a relay of streetcars, Mother, though a devout member in the congregation of perennial hope, kept muttering to herself, "I will never see my mother again."

In Remembrance Is the Secret of Redemption

In the hospital in 1995, three weeks before her ninetieth birthday, Mother presented her account of our visit to the internment camp as if it had happened earlier that day. "Look outside, it's still pouring," she said, though the sky was cloudless and the sun brilliant. "But why didn't Mara come?" she asked, still angry with her sister. Her voice bristled with thorns.

Suddenly the words flowed: "Tell me, where has my mother gone, and where are my four brothers and two sisters? And my many first cousins? Where are they now?" Then in a calm, matter-of-fact tone she asked if I could please check after nightfall whether the stars too vanished from the sky.

One bleak moment between Uncle Anti's death and Mother's hospitalization, I called on the Angel of Death in my synagogue in Frederick, Maryland: *Malach Hamaves*, stop! Please, our God of Justice and Compassion, restrain Your Angel of Death! (I was speaking on Holocaust Remembrance Day, and the congregation did not seem to object to my outburst.) I said it was unfair and unreasonable that the few who outsmarted Hitler's legions should decline like everyone else, with their minds and bodies falling apart little by little. I pleaded: stop taking them away!

To remember them by telling stories about their lives is to reassure ourselves that they are still with us. The motto I find myself repeating comes from the Baal Shem Tov, the gentle rabbi born some three hundred years ago in a small village in the eastern Ukrainian foothills of the Carpathian mountain range. "Forgetfulness prolongs our exile," he said, and his words should be added to the Kaddish. "In remembrance is the secret of redemption."

By exile the Baal Shem Tov meant estrangement: our lives and thoughts drifting farther away from life's core meaning which he derived from the burning bush of I-am-who-I-am in the Sinai desert and the thunderstorm of the thou-shalt and thou-shalt-not at Mount Sinai. He did not try to set on fire the souls of his followers, my ancestors among them, by promising the imminence of redemption, that ever-receding fantasy pledge of Jewish theology hinged to the arrival of the Messiah who will not only bring peace and justice but will make all barren trees bear fruit, cease the labor pains of women, and announce the End of Time.

Instead, the Baal Shem Tov invited us to do what is within everyone's reach: look for treasures of buried memories, our own or our family's. He understood that a mortal's greatest triumph is over time, as in the instance of saving from the iniquity of oblivion the individuals who brought us into life or kept us alive or offered luminous moments. A joyous spirit, he would have cheered the words – or was it a toast? — attributed to William Faulkner: "There is no such thing as *was* — only *is*."

The Baal Shem Tov suggested that we overcome the fearful belief that it is dangerous to visit with the dead or it is wrong to risk disturbing their peace — and ours — by talking too much about how they lived and died. He reminded us that a *meisele* — a simple or not so simple little story that took place the morning of its telling or when our grandparents were still young — can make us smile or leave us with the gift of a small piece of truth, or both, or throw light on how we lost or found our way, preferably both, yet in the end we returned where we had started. After we tell a favorite story a few times, or a story becomes a favorite through repetition, we begin to wonder if the mysterious stranger who leads us to the hidden treasure or lets us in on the secret we must know is someone close to us, perhaps Grandfather. Then one morning we may wake up and think that in so many ways Grandfather is *us*, and *was* is indeed *is*.

No, my mother Anna in her decline did not make a mistake in calling Cousin Agi by her mother's name years after Agi's mother passed away, and decades earlier Mother was right on the mark in delivering that food packet to Roza Schwarcz of Miskolc as if it had been prepared for her. What matters is not the correctness of the names entered on our birth certificates, or the legal truth of a government document replete with signatures and stamps, or even whether someone is dead or alive. What counts is the enduring strength of the filaments finer than silk that bind a family by plying past and present together and make us shuttle back and forth between roles patterned generations ago. Unknowingly, we could be tracing an old plot that requires completion or revision or rectification, and such a job is waiting for us. Or telling that story well so our audience takes pleasure in it is all that we need to do.

The Baal Shem Tov believed that a good story should be as familiar as the road, muddy in the spring and dusty in the summer, which leads to the market, and as sweet or as tearful as Grandmother's voice. To him, a story worth repeating conceals several layers of meaning, as does every word in the holy Torah.

The stories the Baal Shem Tov himself told prove that darkness hides sparks and that darkness too can be made to light up and illuminate the firmament. Reading his stories reminds me that an incandescent flame fed by pallid wax does more than sit atop a candle's charred wick: it is a splendid little jewel which is to be cherished. He taught us what we always knew or could have known: we should be grateful heirs.

I think of the Baal Shem Tov, ironically enough, when reading the high-toned xenophobe T.S. Eliot: how in his ancestors' "draughty church" in Somersetshire, at "the still point of the turning world," he discovered that "Only through time time is conquered." As stealthily as day turns to night, eternity — which is the time the poet thought he could conquer — buries our childhood even before our parents die. Nevertheless, we can clear the debris which covers the past so relentlessly by remembering another kind of time: times of special validity and the individuals who mastered them, such as the impulsive janitor who stopped the Nazis attempting to enter our apartment building, and the peerless civil servant who violated her oath of office in forging Christian identity documents for Jews, including my mother and me.

Though parts of us die with the dying, we survive by summoning the dead. If we forget them, we are smoke from a fire that did not burn. The Baal Shem Tov would nod in assent with Eliot's lines, "We are born with the dead:/ See, they return, and bring us with them."

Rustling Leaves by the Blue Danube

The idea of summoning times past put me on a squeaky Budapest streetcar chugging across the Danube bridge named after Saint Marguerite, daughter to a thirteenth century Hungarian king. I scanned the embankment, a miles-long rampart of square-cut granite and poured concrete engineered to defend the city from floods. Soon my eyes locked in on the section where I had witnessed in 1944 a group of Jews thrust into the water by rifle shots shattering the napes of their necks. They vanished as if they had never been born. Their executioners dissolved into the swirling crowds of the metropolis as if they had done nothing, certainly nothing worth talking about. No detective could track down nameless gunmen in complicit alleys or identify their faceless targets in deep waters.

I jotted down some lines:

> A river of life, a river of refuse.
> Its hidden cargo is time,
> a contraband no one will buy.
> Only the ferryman turns a profit,
> plying his trade at cross-purpose.
> Bones tile the riverbed.
> Above, gulls dressed in white keen their Kaddish.

I could hear a voice much like the rustling of dry leaves recount ances-tral beliefs: the earth opens to a dead body as a lock opens when its key is turned. Unless the body is laid to rest in the ground where it belongs, the spirit may return to wander among the living. Like thorn into skin or burr into wool, a homeless spirit can hook into this man or that woman, whether frail and vulnerable or strong and independent; an impressionable student or a wizened accountant; Gentile or Jew. A rancorous spirit causes eruptions of unwarranted anger. A trickster torments its host, then snaps free abruptly, only to leave behind a void that aches. A gentle spirit inspires tears that flood the eyes, seemingly without any reason or no reason that we can account for.

O my God, King of Kings and God of Our Mothers and Fathers, why didn't You stop the killers loose across the land? *Adonoi, Riboyno shel Oylam*, why did You let our little world perish? Did we feast too often on the goose-liver we craved? Were we too proud of our monogrammed silver, their luster assured by unlettered maids? Did You think that we came to love our comfort more than we loved You, *Dayan Emes*?

Adonoi, You tricked us. You had us believe that we are Your chosen people and You and we are bound together in an everlasting covenant. You tricked us more than we tricked ourselves when we believed that You would protect us. (Or maybe it is the other way around.) This time You didn't stop our enemies pursuing us. The waters did not part. This time *we* ended up drowning.

I got off the streetcar and walked over to the railing of the bridge. I stared at the waves, rootless yet sprouting again and again, and I was hypnotized by the eddies, a field of funnel-shaped, unfading blooms, independent of the current hurtling southward. For a long time I watched the flow of the river the color of a wine bottle, both infamous for their indifference to the cargo they carry.

But the heart can hold only so much sorrow. I had to walk. I had to get away from the river and its phantoms. Crossing one street, I saw faces as familiar as if they had been neighbors or schoolmates. But they ignored me. At the next intersection, people looked as foreign as if they had been tourists from an unknown country or another century, and they stared at me. I quickened my pace. I walked briskly, with eyes fixed on the asphalt the color of a rat's tail and just as smooth. My feet took me to an old Jewish neighborhood I had never been to. Recognizing the street's name, I made up a verse:

> Must memory be the only plot
> and the echo time's master?

Then I hummed a variation on the theme:

> Must time rhyme
> and the past plot our path?
> Can't a newborn start again
> and inherit no hoarded grief?

Wafting through the arched portals of an apartment building was Johann Strauss Jr.'s "Blue Danube" waltz, the unofficial anthem of the late Austro-Hungarian monarchy. I was ready to be buoyed by the trills coming from the center of a sunless courtyard, from a battered hurdy-gurdy. Its copper belly groaned and grunted while grinding out the tune born less than two hundred miles upriver, in Vienna. Looking up, I saw no one on the tiers of sagging galleries all around that seemed as if they might give way and come crashing down at any moment. Stucco, mortar, and brick no longer fused as the builders had planned; they began reverting to sand, lime, cement, and clay. But the building was not abandoned. The fragrances of fried onion and boiled cabbage attested to the presence of life bound to this earth, as did the coins clinking on the courtyard's mustard-colored tiles that started splintering before the waltz's seduction of the civilized world.

The melody was irresistible, as always. Its echoes skittered back and forth and around the courtyard, and its metallic twang mocked the depredations of time and teased Old Man Death himself. "Take a partner for a whirl, and love will come, again and again," Strauss' Danube cooed. "Forget what you left behind and forgive everyone, including yourself. Happy is the man who forgets what he cannot change."

"But what is the meaning of what happened on the riverbank in 1944?" a harsh, impatient rabbinic voice called out, from a house of study built of tightly-fitted stone, somewhere in Jerusalem. "Mourning is not enough. Memory must have a purpose. You must learn, analyze, and draw your conclusions."

"I will," I replied in the language of rustling leaves, "I will."

What the Medium Said

Another day my cousin Levente Thury drove me to Obuda, an ancient quarter of Buda named after a brother to Attila the Hun whose army camped there 1,500 years ago and slaughtered much of the indigenous population, who were Celts or Slavs, or both. On the narrow, twisting streets the houses seemed to be dropping to their knees, confirming their submission to the Roman Catholic church spires thrusting upward.

In a baroque palace reincarnated as an art museum, Levente put on an exhibit of his ceramic sculptures. Each had its own story. One piece, "My Ancestors' Spirits," combined two faces sprouting out of lustrous blue-green spheres that suggested casks in a wine cellar. The spirits Levente coaxed into clay felt robust yet kind and wise, and as approachable as two chess players hunched over their board astride a park bench around the street corner.

Levente's enterprise made me think of his mother Mara, a lifelong nonbeliever whose friend, the writer Rozsa Ignacz, a Presbyterian pastor's daughter, had insisted on taking her a few months after the war's end to visit Obuda's famous medium, Maria Irtzl. An ethnic German and a pious Roman Catholic, Maria Irtzl asked her regular clients, Christians who believed in communicating with the dead, to pass the word that she was "besieged" by the spirits of murdered Jews rising from their unmarked graves and "imploring" her to serve as a channel to their relatives still alive. In her tiny apartment, crudely printed icons of the Virgin Mary, Hungary's patron since its conversion to Christianity, and multicolored plaster saints rubbed shoulders with Jews from diverse segments of society who waited for hours for their turns, shaken yet speechless when they heard through the walls a succession of voices, each of them different though suffused with the same familiar genre of affection, recalling the last hours of their lives, and dispensing advice about spouses, children, and assets.

As soon as Aunt Mara entered the medium's presence, Maria Irtzl fell into a trance, while her face, which seemed molded out of pastry dough, remained expressionless. Aunt Mara trembled when she heard the voice of her mother Roza speaking in the dialect of her native Carpathian mountains, warning about grave dangers facing Mara's husband and urging her to take their son to a doctor immediately. She did, and son Levente was diagnosed with a virulent form of juvenile diabetes. And hard times for the three of them came again soon enough.

"My children, you must watch your steps," were the last words pronounced by the voice. "Watch out for your lives."

The Most Wonderful Child in the World

The one euphoric postwar moment I like to recall for my children followed the birth in 1949 of Cousin Zhuzhi, daughter of Aunt Clara and Uncle Anti. She was the first child born in our family after the war, and the assembled relatives passed her around, each of them holding her up for a close look, then hugging her for minutes, and kissing her plump little hands again and again. Tears glistened in everyone's eyes. For once, a very verbal group of individuals could not find words to match the occasion, a ritual that remained strangely silent.

At age eleven I did not have to be told that Zhuzhi was more than just another baby, splashed a bit too generously with Eau de Cologne and swathed in layers of seraphic lace composed by her mother. Nor was she just one more cousin to love and to cherish as a sister — which is what Levente and I called her, of course — but proof that our family, though with many limbs and branches chopped off, was still alive and still capable of bringing forth new life.

No one asked the question that must have troubled everyone: why those present lived to see this day, while others, especially Grandmother Roza, did not. No one needed to say aloud what the sparkling eyes all around the room said: despite the tragedy behind us, we will endure as a family, and nothing could be more important than that. Zhuzhi was, God willing, a future mother, given our grandmother's Hebrew name, Rachel. She was a healthy, happy, beautiful baby — the most wonderful child in the world.

My tribal heart pounds and life is filled with meaning whenever I see Zhuzhi and her husband and their three children nowadays and I know that my children think of her much the way I do: not only in the

Polaroid present as a warm-hearted, cheerful cousin everyone loves instantly but also through the zoom lens of the past as a much-awaited newborn whose photographs launched a new family album.

The Sad Dancer and the Crippled Reaper

Visiting Hungary over the past three decades I looked for stories that portray the land I had left in 1956, a week before my nineteenth birthday.

During one visit, out for a midnight walk in Budapest, I caught sight of a tall, bear-like figure of a man dancing a dignified village dance on a quiet side street, alone in the damp moonlight, confining himself to one square yard on the cobblestones. The steel heel-plates of his boots kept perfect rhythm, and his posture suggested pride in his artistry. I thought of calling out "well done!" or clapping, but I changed my mind when walking past him I noticed tears coursing down the creases of his middle-aged face. They were not tears of joy.

He paid no attention to me. Absorbed in his art and grief — and I wondered which came first — he fixed his eyes on the sky. Long after turning into another street, I could still hear his heel-plates hammer the cobblestones, keeping up the pace of an eighteen-year-old who doesn't know how to slow down.

Another day I saw a muscular man mowing waist-high grass on a vacant lot where a house had been leveled in an air raid during the war. The gleaming steel of his scythe splattered sunlight over the surrounding buildings stained by coal dust. Swinging the long curved blade in identical arcs, he left behind a swath as even as a carpet, even though the terrain was steep and treacherous. The sequence of his deceptively effortless motions was as precisely balanced as metrical verse, neither of which I could ever master.

When he stopped to sharpen the blade with a whetstone he whisked from a sheath looped to his belt, I was astonished to discover that he had only one arm. To steady the scythe, he put a foot on the snath's projecting handle that his missing hand would have gripped.

I asked the janitor from a nearby house sweeping the sidewalk if she had seen the laborer before.

"Sure," the janitor replied, "the same man cuts the grass there every summer."

"But don't you think," I asked, "that it is an incredible achievement for a one-armed man to learn to wield a scythe?"

The janitor shrugged. "I haven't found any fault with the fellow's work," she replied, her face as morose as if she had.

From time to time the one-armed reaper enters my dreams. He keeps swinging his scythe and does not even stop to sharpen his blade. The scythe goes on cutting down all that is green on a slope that is endless.

Rumbles from Underground

Limestone steps, each dented like a pillow after a sleepless night, led from the street to a cellar tavern where cigarette smoke swaddled the crowd and a scattering of 25 watt bulbs yielded a viscous twilight.

Customers, many of them working-class, some perhaps half-drunk, confided to their friends (or whoever happened to sit or stand near them) why they detested (or, in one case, admired) old communists still in power trying hard to conduct themselves like ordinary folks, or former dissidents unable to figure out how to take charge of the country in the current, so-called post-communist era; the genial old gentry or the unchangeable peasantry; Jews or Gypsies; Romanians or Slovaks or Serbs; Germans or Russians or Americans; winners or losers in the Second World War and in the recent collapse of the peace settlements that came in its wake.

I eavesdropped on a boothful of intellectuals locked in argument, their faces ruddy with patriotic passion. Probably not for the first time, they portioned out blame among politicians and soldiers — either fools or traitors — for the tragedies that history so persistently conferred on the Hungarian people, always the victim and never the aggressor.

One burly polemicist in his sixties with a full head of spiky hair declared that in the thirteenth century Hungarians should have joined rather than fought their kinsmen, the Tatar hordes of Genghis Khan. "What good has the West ever done for us," he thundered, striking the table with his fist. "The West brought us the Catholic Church and Roman law, both speaking in Latin, a foreign language imposed on us.

It also trained us to lie and to deceive, and we ourselves were our first victims."

Others dismissed his argument as "archaic" and "absurd." One critic, tall, thin, and with sunken cheeks, weighed each word of his as if on a pharmacy scale and was careful not to give offense: "More than two centuries before the Tatar invasion, Hungary pledged its fealty to the West by wading into the waters of baptism. Intellectually and politically, it is wistful romanticism to ignore the transformation of our nomadic ancestors into sedentary farmers, or to dismiss our progress from Asians to Europeans."

The rise of a communal sigh was almost audible: if we could only reverse the flow of time, undo a single battlefield defeat, be it in 955, 1241, 1526, 1711, or 1849, or rewrite the peace treaty signed in Paris in 1920! Why can't an invading army march backwards and guns suck back the bullets they fired? Could history be as irreversible as Marxists insist it is? The consensus sounds like a whine: "Must we always cave in to the demands of progress, time's pushy, arrogant bastard?"

Left uncontested was one young nihilist's brief: whether for a nation or an individual, to keep losing or "just messing up" requires a special talent, though it helps when one can draw on the patient, piecemeal work of generations. "At least our Hungarian tradition of failure is consistent," he intoned in a stage whisper, his dark eyes smoldering, his complexion the color of faded newsprint, "so it compares favorably with the chaos of the forever successful West. And we love and cherish our failures, and we distrust our successes."

Scar across the Sky

From high up on a balcony overlooking the verdant hills of Buda, I sat with an old friend, spellbound by the spectacle of a crimson sunset spilling across the horizon. We agreed that the clouds that scuffed the solar disk looked like blood-soaked bandages.

A respected member of the new, multi-party Parliament, my host offered his thoughts along with slices of an incomparable hazelnut torte.

Hungarian soldiers look at the corpses of eight Jews they shot on the bank of the Danube in 1944. Photo credit: U.S. National Archives.

Conscripts of Hungarian Labor Battalion VIII/2 laying track in 1942 in Huszt, Hungary (now Chust in Ukraine). Photo credit: Adalbert Feher.

"In this country everything is up for sale," he said, "and it is our tradition to sell ourselves cheap, preferably below cost."

A communist believer before 1956, he was an important personality in the revolution against the Stalinist dictatorship. Since the collapse of the Berlin Wall, he has opposed the equivalent of denazification or a South Africa-style Truth Commission. "Communism was imposed here by brute force, then some of the enforcers themselves were killed by fellow communists," he has argued. "Sure, you can still track down many torturers and killers, as well as those who signed the papers ordering torture and murder. But do you want to jail every communist party bureaucrat, every informer and collaborator, every accessory to the crimes committed, which would mean hauling into court every tenth person in the country at the very least? Where do you stop the reckoning, the chase after scraps of paper and personnel files, many of which the guilty parties have altered or burned? As my dear friend, the President of the Republic, says: 'All of us have been at least splattered with mud, and some more than others.'"

He talked about his recent lunch — which he described as "completely normal, even cordial" — with the Stalinist judge who had given him a stiff jail sentence after the 1956 revolution. (He said he had feared life imprisonment.) Courteous with a most thoughtful man and a friend inherited from my uncles, I said I was impressed with his equanimity.

"I live in this country," he responded curtly, his face a mask of papier-mache.

With the sun no longer visible, a vast scar spread over the sky like a pagan omen. Behind us, on the other side of the next hill, flowed the Danube, the river of oblivion.

The Sunday of Eternal Life

What lifted my spirits on a November morning of soiled snow and mouse-gray skies was a sermon on the Lutherans' Sunday of Eternal Life, delivered in their church, a simple, modest structure on Castle Hill and a mid-nineteenth century latecomer to the city's acropolis.

The pastor, praised by my friends, the two congregants who invited me to the service, was a shy man in his early thirties, squeezed into a threadbare black suit that looked as if he might have borrowed it from his father. With fists pounding the air, he pleaded that one must listen to the call of "a higher conscience" and "practice heroism" in everyday life. "Do not fear death," was his refrain, "because eternal life is waiting for you." He spoke from his earnest heart, and I pondered his words as I joined his congregation in singing Bach's chorale, "A Mighty Fortress Is Our God," inspired by King David's psalms.

After the service, the midday sun felt chillier on the skin than the morning mist. Congregants saying their goodbyes in front of the church weighed the odds for more snow by the evening. One lady, whose wisps of gray hair wreathed a blue beret which she might have worn half her life, told a stylish, fur hat-crowned contemporary whose silence bespoke skepticism that she was sure of "lots and lots of snow coming" and that "snow will make the city beautiful again. I love freshly fallen snow the way I love a pure soul — like our pastor."

A close friend, Eniko Bollobas, lives in a house a short walk uphill. A professor of American literature at Budapest's main university and a small child in 1956, she has an independent view of the recent past, unaffected by personal scores that need settling. Her sympathies are with the pastor's honesty, and she disagrees with "the messy argument" by the member of parliament perched on Rose Hill, only a cannon shot away. "Most Hungarians were not members of the communist party or the secret police, just as most people didn't belong to the Nazi Arrow Cross," she said. "That was so, not necessarily as a matter of political principle, but because of a moral inhibition, whether conscious or not. For most of the thinking people there was something wrong in joining those in power, even at the lowest levels where no power was shared. Of course, it was no fun joining the victims either, but at least the victims were the authentic people, not driven by selfish ambition or greed for power and recoiling from the thought of vulgar daily compromises with the dicta-torships. Why should the former victims now walk arm in arm with those who were guilty of collaboration, even if a snub splits Hungarian society? Actually, in the early 1990s many of the former victims thought they could do a lot to heal this split, by refusing the equivalent of a denazification process. The first post-communist prime minister, Jozsef

Antall, argued against denazification — but not because everybody was guilty one way or another. No, Antall insisted that differences did exist between the guilty and the innocent. But he believed that victors should be generous. I worked for him, and I thought he was right, even though at that time most of the country demanded revenge."

A few dozen steps from Bollobas's house stands a remnant of the rampart that girded the fortress of Castle Hill for most of the past millennium. Down below and across the river is Pest, a burgeoning metropolis on a defenseless plain. Further uphill on cobblestones as smooth as plums is the multicolored Roman Catholic church where Hungary's last king, Charles IV, was crowned in 1916, half-way through the First World War. In the plaza in front of the church, he mounted an immaculate white horse. As he thrust his sword in the four cardinal directions, symbolic of his resolve to defend the country against all enemies, his horse skidded, and the heavy gold crown, which Hungary's first king, Stephen, had received from Pope Sylvester II in the year 1000, very nearly slid off Charles' small head. The king had to use his left hand to keep the sacred relic from crashing to the ground. An ill omen, gasped the assembled lords spiritual and temporal, and the story of the near-disaster spread across the land with the speed of an ancient curse.

In two years the Habsburg monarchy lost the war, and Charles, deposed first in Vienna and then in Budapest, was packed off into exile. After nine centuries, no more king, no more kingdom. Hungary lost two thirds of its territory. Austria's empire was trashed like yesterday's newspaper.

Steep and solitary, and the undisputed first among the hills of Buda, Castle Hill rises from the riverbank like an image from a conqueror's dream the night before he sets out on his campaign. The terrain, now civilized by a serpentine road, inspired some of the fiercest battles between the Wehrmacht and the Red Army, among Ottoman Turk and Hungarian and Austrian, and deeper in time between spear-carrying tribes whose names we will never know because even those who vanquished the victors lacked a system of writing.

History is locked up in the earth, and the ashes of its passions feed the thistles and nettles that sprout from crevices in between the rocks. Sink a spade in the sienna clay of Castle Hill, and sooner or later your blade will clang against a bullet or a bone or a belt-buckle, or what is left of a necklace or a leg iron, any of which can turn you into a pilgrim to a time not your own.

Cellars crouch underneath cellars, and veils of mildew shroud the ceilings. Prying boulders out of floors, enterprising tenants found shards of a cauldron that had stewed dinner for Celts or Slavs tending grapevines on the hillsides two thousand summers ago. Other explorers came upon shreds of a prayer shawl that mantled a Jew who addressed his God in a synagogue built some five thousand years after Creation, or the fourteenth century according to the Christian calendar.

History cuts eternity into neat slices. Castle Hill says: history is an attack by communal memory that aims to conquer a sequence of time; yet time remains as indivisible as the wind.

Whatever is material dies and turns into something else, and then drifts back to the soil that is the final repository. Only the soul is imperishable and stays true to itself, wandering from body to body, though split into smaller segments with every generation and combining with other souls, much like puffs of smoke do. On his deathbed, the Baal Shem Tov consoled his followers: "You will carry my body out the door, but one day my soul will fly back through the window." With similar self-confidence, the Lutheran pastor told his congregation: "Death does not matter. But individual conduct does."

Cradled in the past, I am future-blind. I collect stories, each a fragment of a fragment, and in my head they add up as footnotes to history.

Another year my visit took place during a sweltering June that always surprises temperate-climate Budapest with its tropical intensity. It was the week of high school graduations, a rite of passage known across the European continent as "matriculation," or *matura* as Hungarians call it in Latin. At the streetcar terminal I had passed through every school day for four years, I saw a few dozen new graduates milling around, the boys sweating in their thick wool suits purchased for the occasion and the girls still looking freshly ironed in their white blouses and dark blue skirts. A smile settled on my face when I realized from their conversation that they came from the same high school I had attended, on the eastern slope of Castle Hill.

Their farewells went on and on. The boys traded silly jokes, laughed a lot, and shook hands; the girls hugged and kissed and cried. At the edge of the crowd, a short boy built like a weightlifter was talking earnestly to a girl as gangly as a hollyhock.

She interrupted. "But will we ever see each other again?" she asked.

"Whatever happens, I will love you forever," he said, and his face suggested surprise at letting such words slip off his tongue.

"Do you really mean that?" she asked, incredulous.

As solemn as his double-breasted dark blue suit, he replied, "I do. I do."

Historia Est Magistra Vitae

My graduation occurred in the fateful year of 1956. A few days later the Soviet Politburo at last ordered the dismissal of the communist party's secretary-general it had earlier acclaimed as "Stalin's best Hungarian disciple" and who was the country's most hated man, Matyas Rakosi. The adults whose opinion I respected were hopeful that it would be only a matter of time before Rakosi's successor, another mercenary of the Kremlin, would also be forced out. (Indeed, both fled to Moscow after the revolution broke out in October.)

Raucous and slapping each other's backs like schoolboys let out for the summer, my uncles agreed among themselves: finally the Kremlin understands that the oppression cannot continue indefinitely as it did under Stalin. The dictatorship must come to an end. In a matter of months, if not weeks, the communists will be cleared out, like the Nazis before them — two rival gangs spawned in the same poisoned streams of hate.

It felt good to believe in the symmetries of justice. At long last, the turn of events complied with what we liked to believe was the natural order, the very grammar of history.

Since then I have often asked myself: Who taught us to parse time?

Why do we insist on perceiving events as if they were driven by an internal logic or supervised by a higher consciousness?

One authority I still see in my mind's eye is my high-school teacher of Latin, stocky and bow-legged like a Tatar horseman. His chalk rode over the blackboard; his strokes were swift and decisive. The rounded letters were as gracefully looped as the calligraphy of a wedding invitation: "*Historia est magistra vitae.*" He called out the words, and then translated, enunciating each syllable while tapping the blackboard with his stumpy forefinger: "History is the master of life."

That was our first sentence in Latin, the mother tongue of law and civilization that parents and teachers promised will discipline our unruly minds.

The solemnity of the presentation awed the class into silence and stillness. Our stern teacher's face, as broad as an owl's, beamed. Ours was the thirtieth class of his career, he said. (We knew — Hungary is one gossipy village — that he had started out as a Roman Catholic priest but quit to marry a woman who walked with a limp.) He said he hoped that we would rank as his best class ever because we will be his last, as he planned to retire after our graduation. It seemed only right and fitting, he explained, that our class would outperform all his other classes before us, and not only in learning the Latin language but in serving "our beautiful homeland and our nation steeped in misfortune."

Three times a week he marched us along the hedgerows of Latin genitives and accusatives, and up through the steep, treacherous passes of irregular verbs. When one of us stumbled in the declension of a noun, we chanted in unison all of its five cases, first in the singular, then the plural. Our teacher led the chorus.

He did not need to pause before recollecting a word or composing a sentence. As a model citizen of the past perfect, he would never be guilty — and to our minds, he could not be guilty — of making a mistake in its language.

Sealed in a marble sarcophagus, Latin was gloriously dead; its grammar — the soul of a language — safe from innovation, decay, and error. That immutability pleased our teacher, as did the obedience it demanded of all of us. Neither a stuffy patrician nor a seedy plebeian could launch a trend by dropping a letter or two in a word, or inserting a convenient vowel to make it easier to pronounce a dense consonantal cluster. Nor was there a poet alive to champion a new meter or an alternative syntax.

When someone in class asked for an explanation why one verb had to be irregular while another conformed to the great majority, our teacher did not suggest that the inquirer was lazy or impertinent. Instead, he shared with us his *sub-rosa* surmise that we might well be facing a secret higher order encrypted in a code still unbroken, and he praised both that order and our eagerness in trying to pierce its mysteries.

Some fifteen years later, during a visit to his small apartment, dark with massive bookcases and wardrobes, he assured me that we did not disappoint him. "Your class was the best I taught," he said, and his once stentorian voice quavered. "But what I cannot understand is how your generation, born and raised at a time of the worst lawlessness and mendacity, turned October 1956 into the finest moment of our national history. How can disorder engender truth and beauty? Where is the logic? What would Horatius say? Or his friend Vergilius?"

He recited a few lines from each of the poets, and his cantillation had the same paced passion I remembered. But ashamed to admit that I forgot the Latin he had taught, I did not ask for a translation. Nor did I risk distracting his galloping thoughts by asking the questions that troubled me: Aren't we slaves to history, both to its masters and to the transcriptions of its details by partisan survivors? And after all is said and settled, isn't history what lies in ambush at the dark, wooded edge of the present, waiting to pounce on us, either with a gun or a grin?

A reporter is tethered to the here and now. The first time I chafed under that requirement was between the springs of 1994 and 1995 when I found it hard to focus on the events my colleagues called historic: President Bill Clinton's stumble at the polls, the Republican sweep of both houses of Congress, and House Speaker Newt Gingrich's rise as a rival to the president. But the passions of the day seemed pale and insubstantial as I found myself mesmerized by reports on the world commemorating the fiftieth anniversary of events such as the miraculous Allied landing in Normandy in June 1944 (which was followed by the large-scale deportation of Hungarian Jews, including most of my relatives), the liberation of Auschwitz in January 1945 (which coincided with the Red Army pushing the Wehrmacht out of Budapest), and the German capitulation in May 1945 (about the time the dozen or so of my relatives who survived the camps started drifting back to Budapest and told the rest of us — who had hidden in various locations with the help of Gentile friends — how the larger part of our family had perished).

Throughout that one year it seemed as if I had always had a call waiting: from half a century ago. As insistent as a ringing phone, childhood memories forced my attention on that one year when everything of enduring importance seemed to have happened and an unforgettable cast of vanished relatives and unpredictable angels defined a code to live by for the rest of my life.

CHAPTER ONE

Killers, Opportunists, Angels

... neither memory nor magic will save me.
The sky is laden with ill omens.
Turn around, my friend, and shrug.
Where an angel once kept watch with a sword
now perhaps no one stands.

Miklos Radnoti: "Neither Memory Nor Magic"

Witnessing German soldiers beat Ukrainian villagers with iron rods and drop children into wells, my Uncle Mishi could not bring himself to look at the victims. But when glancing at the perpetrators, he saw "something almost worse than the crimes": a glint of thrill in the eyes.

Mishi's tender heart was breaking because he could not help the villagers. As a chauffeur to a Hungarian colonel in charge of liaison with the Wehrmacht, he worried about keeping a most dangerous secret: he was Jewish. His Gentile friends had obtained documents that certified him as a one hundred percent Christian, with Szemes as his last name instead of Schwarcz. The colonel knew the truth because in the days of peace before the First World War, now as distant as the stars in the sky, the two fathers had been friends, and that old family connection — "a blessing from our father," as my mother Anna called it — secured for Mishi the job that offered better-than-average odds for survival. Had his secret been found out while Axis armies were advancing and regulations

1

were strictly enforced, Mishi could have been shot, and his colonel would have gotten into serious trouble. Had Mishi not disguised his identity, he would have had to join one of the so-called labor battalions set up for Jews and other politically unreliable males of conscription age. In many of the units, pro-Nazi officers made sure that most of their subordinates did not live to the war's end.

With a large aquiline nose, olive complexion, dark eyes, and dark wavy hair, Mishi looked stereotypically Semitic. Every day he served in the military he had to put on an actor's performance that made people ignore his physiognomy. Fortunately, he came from a family that had owned land for generations, and he inherited the carefree, jocular manners of the landed gentry, the class which set the nation's standards of deportment. Like the heroes in the operettas *Die Fledermaus* and *Csardas Princess* he loved so much, Mishi was handsome, debonair, and popular, and he had a way with women. He knew the best jokes and the liveliest anecdotes, and he mastered the art of telling them.

Other Hungarian veterans of the Russian front brought home bizarre stories about their encounters with ghostlike men dressed in layers of rags, hiding in the lunar whiteness of birch forests and begging for food, as well as with earthy women wrapped in black, who stayed behind in their village homes and on occasion invited soldiers to spend the night with them. (In one narrative a woman dropped to her knees in the morning, pleading that the soldier burn his uniform forthwith and stay with her; in another first-person account the woman woke the soldier at daybreak and threatened to kill him with a kitchen knife unless he cleared out immediately.) But Mishi, who had never before crossed the borders of his native land, could not be coaxed into talking about any of the foreigners he came across, the landscapes he admired, or the women he met.

After he returned from Russia fleeing from the victorious Red Army — he had walked hundreds of miles to his sister Mara's home in Budapest — Mishi sat in silence for days, smoking one cigarette after another. Again and again he stirred his coffee, which he sipped slowly, and he lit yet another cigarette, blowing rings of smoke ever so thoughtfully.

In the weeks and months to come, he courteously listened to the war stories of relatives and friends, but his eyes were fixed on his shoes. He asked no questions, looked for no familiar landmarks, and recalled no Russian phrase or village that would have served as a link, a shared souvenir of wartime camaraderie. Until the subject of the war was dropped, his friendly face, normally on the verge of a smile, remained somber. For once there was no entertainment offered by the inveterate raconteur who otherwise framed his life in anecdotes and who had a way of persuading his listeners that the characters he mimicked so well ought to be on stage.

When asked about the colonel he chauffeured, a nobleman from an illustrious family, Mishi would say that he was an exceptionally fine gentleman, one of the noblest who ever walked on the earth, even something of an angel, but he was probably no longer among the living.

Mishi did tell some of his relatives that one evening a Russian unit had attacked out of the blue, and both he and his colonel ran into a forest. "I never saw the colonel again," Mishi said with a sigh, and suggested that most likely he was captured by the Russians and shot on the spot or shipped to a forced-labor camp.

About his own participation in the war, Mishi would only say, "I have seen too much. I hate war." When someone he was fond of pressured him some more, he grunted: "I can't talk about killers. They don't belong in my stories. They are not from my world."

Relatives and friends told him "not to be a sphinx" and kept prodding him for specifics on how he passed off in the military as a Gentile, which seemed incredible to most people. Did anyone ever challenge the authenticity of his playacting? What ripostes and anecdotes worked best in allaying suspicion? Was there a moment when he lost his aplomb? Did anyone ever challenge his death-defying chutzpah?

Mishi kept his silence. But the family knew that for the rest of his life he often cried out in his sleep, again and again: "Don't shoot! I am a human being!"

Weeks or maybe months after his return home, he revealed to his older brother Shumi and his favorite brother-in-law Levente that on his arrival in Hungary with the defeated Hungarian army he was caught and "unmasked" as a Jew. He would not say anything about the circumstances, except that not getting shot right there and then was a stroke of luck he would never understand because his mind, he said with uncharacteristic solemnity, "was not equipped to understand matters such as miracles." Nor would he discuss what he did in the labor battalion he was shipped to as punishment. From his buddies — and of course he made lifelong friends in the labor battalion — our family learned that from dawn to dusk they dug trenches and set up tank traps. Their warm clothes were confiscated, and some of them died of pneumonia or froze to death in their sleep, which everyone believed was a merciful death because of the legend, cherished by different nationalities across Central Europe, that such an end comes without pain, accompanied by the sweetest of dreams. Still other members of labor battalions were shot for such transgressions as allegedly failing to give the proper salute to their Gentile officers.

Yet another capital offense was not marching fast enough when the Red Army's advance into Hungary prompted an order from headquarters to move westward, to Germany. That might have been the reason the poet Miklos Radnoti was shot, along with twenty-two members of his labor battalion unit. The massacre took place a few months after he completed his poem, now known to every high-school graduate in Hungary, "Neither Memory Nor Magic." As the poem predicted, the angel who had once stood guard over him suddenly disappeared. Radnoti's last poems were found in a small notebook in the pocket of his waterproof coat when a year after the war's end his mass grave was exhumed.

As the postwar judicial reckoning began, the wife of Mishi's labor battalion's commanding officer located him. Accompanied by her two small children, she begged him to say in court that her husband was not guilty of any cruelty. Mishi did testify, which helped the commander to get off with only a jail sentence.

When relatives and friends demanded to know why he agreed to defend a man who deserved to be hanged, Mishi stared vacantly into the air and would not answer beyond the suggestion, "Let's talk about something else." To those in the family closest to him, he explained that he could not bring himself to reject the tearful plea of a plain-looking woman in torn, dirty clothes who had come to see him with her two toddlers burying their faces in her skirt.

"I Followed Orders; I Did My Duty"

The killers were drunk with their freedom to kill. They were assisted by a multitude of impeccably sober opportunists.

"I followed orders, and I did my duty," opportunists have explained ever since, using nearly identical words, regardless of military rank, social class, and mother tongue. "I did nothing wrong, I didn't know what was going on elsewhere." A slightly more sophisticated self-justification gained currency throughout Eastern Europe after the collapse of communism: "Not everybody could be in opposition." No central office was responsible for the choice of words, yet the formulas that opportunists applied were as polished as the slogans, carefully crafted by the government's propaganda department, often painted in letters two feet tall on the walls of school buildings and factories, military barracks and concentration camps. One unforgettable example from the main gate of Auschwitz: *Arbeit macht frei.* (Work makes you free.) The communist equivalent: "Our highest value is the human being."

Opportunists made up a large force in Hungarian officialdom. They tended to be either embarrassed or modestly pleased with the deportation of Jews; some were privately troubled by what they called "excesses" in handling the victims but did nothing to alleviate them, and many worried about Allied threats of postwar reckoning — or both. A fair number seized the opportunities offered and took over a business or an apartment, furniture or silver or books left behind by the deportees, and claimed after the war that their purpose was the protection of those assets. When approached by people trying to ease the plight of Jews or to organize other types of resistance to the Nazis, the smartest opportunists voiced cautious sympathy for the anti-Nazi cause but then intoned, again in words that were nearly identical: "We can't do anything. The Germans are forcing our hand. Their power is immense, and their agents have penetrated every nook and corner of Hungarian society. We are helpless."

Long on dignity and short on smarts, Miklos Horthy, Hungary's head of state between 1920 and 1944, was an opportunist who pretended to have high principles. For instance, he claimed to be a monarchist loyal to the memory of Franz Josef, emperor of Austria and king of Hungary, whom he had served as an aide-de-camp prior to the First World War. He insisted on Hungary remaining a kingdom, one of the many instances of the ritualistic formalism which was to him fundamental, or, as he put it, "of the essence." Nevertheless, soon after taking over the reins of the country, rocked by revolutions and invasions by neighbors, under the historic relic of a title "Regent," Horthy twice blocked the return of the last Habsburg monarch, Charles, to whom he had once sworn "unswerving, eternal fealty," and sent him back into exile. A few years later, Charles died on the distant Atlantic island of Madeira. At no time during his regency could Horthy imagine that "the realities of the day" — a giveaway phrase of an opportunist — would permit a Habsburg restoration in Hungary, or even a public debate over the idea. Though historically the title "Regent" was conferred on a temporary surrogate while the kingdom awaited its king, usually a child, Horthy was determined to remain Regent-for-Life.

Tall, handsome, and stately, Horthy relished wearing elaborate uniforms and surrounded himself with aristocrats and former military officers. He took great pride in his flawlessly regal performances at ceremonial processions, and many of his subjects found him heroic, or at least impressive, in his efforts to construct a facade of baroque splendor for an impoverished, truncated, has-been kingdom which resembled grim, defeated Germany, as depicted in the post-First World War film *Grand Hotel* rather than the colorful fantasy realm in operettas such as The *Merry Widow*.

Though he titled his memoir in German *Ein Leben für Ungarn* — translated into English as *A Life for Hungary* — Horthy lived for the trappings of power and he reveled in exercising the highest privileges of the land. After Nazi Germany launched the Second World War and forced Hungary to join the Axis, Horthy, though a lifelong Anglophile, summarily dismissed suggestions that he follow the example of other European leaders who fled to London to inspire the anti-Nazi struggle at home. The idea was designed to improve Hungary's diplomatic position in a postwar settlement. Had Horthy become Regent-in-Exile, Hungary would have had a stronger argument for keeping at least some of the ethnic Hungarian areas it lost to neighbors after the First World War and regained in the course of the Second World War, thanks to its ally Germany. Horthy considered the recovery of those areas, particularly parts of Transylvania, the most significant achievement of his rule. But Hungary lost them all again in the postwar settlement of 1946, primarily because the Allies thought that Yugoslavia, Czechoslovakia, and Romania had better anti-Nazi records than Hungary, the country they put down as "Hitler's last ally."

A World War I admiral of the Austro-Hungarian navy, Horthy stubbornly maintained, from the mid-1930s on — and longer than other non-Nazi Hungarians — that the German military was unbeatable. One of his favorite quips about the Germans was that "no nation on earth could stand up to an army led by a thousand generals." But among his friends he allowed himself the luxury of looking down on Hitler who often summoned him on a humiliatingly short notice. Horthy referred to Hitler as "that former corporal I would not hire for guard duty" or as "that ambitious upstart house painter with coarse manners." In Hungary, snobbery has often been a substitute for policy.

At the same time, Horthy privately argued that as he was obliged to uphold Hungary's honor and he could not "desert" his German ally even if it headed for defeat.

Much like Janos Kadar, the communist apparatchik who agreed to serve as the Soviets' lead stooge after their suppression of the 1956 revolution, Horthy persuaded part of the nation, probably the majority, that he was the only Hungarian who could deal with a Great Power — Germany, in his case — from a position of strength, almost as an equal, and, most important, with the kind of honor and dignity that befits a state more than a thousand years old. Both Horthy and Kadar relied on smart propagandists presenting a strikingly similar argument: Hungary was preternaturally fortunate in having as its leader a thoughtful patriot and an experienced statesman — the only person who could stop a descent into chaos, avert a bloodbath by extremists, and prevent the collapse of whatever was left of national sovereignty. Oddly enough for a culture that takes pride in its legions of sharp wits and bold personalities, the two leaders who enjoyed the longest tenures in the twentieth century were mediocrities who caged themselves in their caution.

On June 30, 1944, following the mass deportations of Jews from the Hungarian provinces to concentration camps under German control, neutral Sweden's King Gustaf V protested "the extraordinarily harsh methods" and appealed to Horthy to "take measures to save those who still remained to be saved." Visibly shaken, Horthy attempted to persuade the Swedish diplomats who delivered the king's letter that no Hungarian authorities "could even imagine collaborating with the Germans." Recalling the meeting in his book about wartime Budapest, Sweden's Per Anger called the performance by Hungary's head of state "pathetic." Anger was too much of a diplomat to charge that Horthy, who had to know the truth, was lying: Hungarian authorities were indeed collaborating with the Germans.

Perhaps the most credible argument in Horthy's defense has been advanced by Professor Istvan Deak of Columbia University. His point of departure is that more Jews survived in countries that collaborated with Germany in varying measures — Hungary, Romania, and Bulgaria — than in those that fought it, notably Poland. Had Horthy resisted, the Germans would have eliminated him, and the country's Jews would have been liquidated as they were in Poland. Up to a point the Germans could rely on Horthy as an ally, Deak's argument concludes, and they grudgingly went along with his refusal, bolstered by his prime minister, Miklos Kallay, to hand over to the Reich the Jews of Budapest. But then came the German invasion, Kallay escaped arrest by fleeing to the legation of neutral Turkey, and the new, pro-Nazi prime minister did as he was told by Berlin.

However, the Germans knew that Horthy was too much of an anti-Semite — albeit an old-fashioned pre-Nazi one, as he liked to point out to those close to him — to make a strong, principled stand to defend Hungary's Jews. He did not try to shield the Jews of the countryside or those born in Poland or Romania because he considered them "scum." He sympathized with the Nazis' aim of curbing Jewish power, though he disagreed with the brutality of their methods. Or, to characterize his ambivalence in yet another way, he was opposed to the idea of killing innocent people even if they were Jews, and especially if he had met them socially.

After the Allies landed in Normandy in June 1944, Horthy finally realized that Germany was bound to lose the war and that he ought to pay attention to the warnings and threats the Allies were transmitting to him through neutral governments. (A similar recognition came to the Romanian dictator Ion Antonescu, both a national enemy of Horthy's and a fellow Axis member, and new policies led to some improvement in the situation of Jews in Romania.) When Horthy did at last order an immediate cessation of deportations in July 1944, it was in response to stern warnings from British and American leaders, including President Franklin Roosevelt. From the point of view of the nation he led and its Jewish citizens, that directive was Horthy's most laudable wartime decision. It might have been inspired by Horthy's calculation that in case the Allies defeated Germany, anything short of an order to stop the deportations would make him "a war criminal," a novel category that the Allies invented and applied, in this case successfully, as a form of political pressure.

As the summer of 1944 was drawing to an end, the Red Army entered Hungarian territory, which prompted Horthy to send a secret delegation to Moscow to negotiate an armistice. In the last days of September 1944, Horthy went down on his knees in an anguished letter that he himself composed in fractured English. Horthy begged Joseph Stalin "to spare" Hungary, an "unfortunate country" which nevertheless "has its own historic merits and whose people has so many affinities with the Russian people." Appealing to the Soviet dictator to exercise his "great influence" with his allies "to make conditions compatible with our peoples' interests and honor," the admiral who had originally seized power to save Hungary from communism explained to Stalin that his "poor country has been practically overrun by the German Fifth Column" — a reference to Hungary's own ethnic Germans who had indeed acquired key positions in the military and the civil service. Horthy pleaded that historically "the German colossus" always determined Hungary's fate, including "this unfortunate war with the Soviet Union."

A few weeks later, Horthy's much-postponed, ill-prepared, and half-hearted plot to cancel the alliance with Nazi Germany backfired. In retrospect, it looks as if Horthy knew that it would fail. (Perhaps he was more candid in a strange letter he penned in the early 1950s to Chancellor Konrad Adenauer, insisting that he had never contemplated "to stab in the back" his German ally.) A few weeks earlier, in August 1944, Romania's inexperienced, twenty-three-year-old King Michael surprised the Germans by canceling his country's pact with Berlin and, according to historians, accelerated the Wehrmacht's collapse in Central Europe and shortened the war by six weeks. But the veteran politician Horthy, supposedly unaware that German intelligence tracked every step of his, bungled his attempt to declare armistice. Many of the military officers he promoted ignored his orders. German tanks quickly surrounded his residence on top of Castle Hill, once Franz Josef's Royal Palace, and forced his resignation.

Besides saving his son, Miklos Jr. kidnapped by an SS commando unit, Horthy's main concern was that the Germans supply him, his family, and their servants with a residence "appropriate to his standing," which turned out to be a modest castle in Austria, surrounded by SS troops. Once the German ambassador in Budapest gave his solemn "word of honor" that Horthy's conditions would be met and he would be reunited with his son Miklos Jr. as soon as they arrived in Austria, the Regent resigned in favor of Ferenc Szalasi, the crazed Fuhrer of the Arrow Cross paramilitary thugs, a former professional army officer who lived in a malevolent fantasy world of the ninth century. That was the time of the Hungarian conquest of the Carpathian Basin, followed by a century of pillage of much of Western Europe by Hungarian horsemen lethally skillful with their short bows and long arrows.

By the time of his resignation Horthy lost his eldest son Istvan, a pro-Western, pro-Jewish engineer, and a professional pilot whose plane crashed on the Russian front because the Germans sabotaged its engine.

Ferenc Szalasi, the Fuhrer of the Arrow Cross movement, swears in as Hungary's new head of state on October 16, 1944. Photo credit: Magyar Zsido Muzeum es Leveltar.

In 1938 Hungary's Regent Miklos Horthy crosses a bridge on horseback. Photo credit: Yad Vashem Photo Archives.

Istvan's widow Ilona describes that when their special train arrived in Austria, the former Regent ran up and down the train, pleading in despair with the SS officers guarding them, "Where is my son?" No one seemed to know where Miklos Jr. was, and no one in the family wanted to say aloud what they feared: the vengeful Germans killed him because he was involved in the attempt to negotiate an armistice. In fact, he was sent to the concentration camp of Mauthausen and the U.S. Army eventually liberated him.

Horthy could feel vindicated when three months after his defiance of Hitler's demands to strengthen Germany's labor force with Hungarian Jews — the ostensible purpose of the deportations — the trains to the concentration camps were packed once again, on orders by his successor Ferenc Szalasi.

However, the suspension of deportations from early July until Horthy's replacement by Szalasi in mid-October also proved that even though the Wehrmacht occupied Hungary, Horthy as head of state did have enough power to protect its Jewish citizens. As in his pathetic appeal for Stalin's mercy, Horthy underestimated his freedom of action and overestimated the force of the great power facing him.

For an opportunist, miscalculation is usually fatal. However at the end of the war, it was the American army that captured Horthy. While President Josip Tito demanded that Horthy be handed over to Yugoslavia and put on trial there for his responsibility for wartime atrocities in that country, the Americans — and the British — remembered his contempt for Hitler and his attempts to switch sides. The unpredictable Stalin surprised everyone by taking pity on him — a unique instance of that tyrant's mercy. Though initially interned, in the end Horthy was not tried in Nuremberg or Budapest. He was allowed to live the remainder of his life in the calm and comfort of a villa in the picture-postcard Portuguese village Estoril, walking distance from the much grander residences of the former kings of Italy and Romania.

Rare for a man with an eye on the main chance, Horthy did not accumulate wealth, and he had no money stashed away in a Swiss bank. Perhaps he thought he would never need it. Or perhaps he was confident that in the unlikely event of his banishment, his bills would be discreetly taken care of by the Jewish industrialists with whom he socialized and who were able to escape from Hungary in 1944 by bribing the Gestapo. Indeed, they felt they owed that much to a man who agreed to be their friend when he was head of state. They also gave Horthy credit for stopping the deportations, thus saving the lives of many Budapest Jews. Whether Jewish or Gentile, his apologists agree with the assessment of General Bela Kiraly, an officer in Horthy's army and later a hero of the 1956 revolution: "The capital's Jews were protected under the Regent's voluminous cape."

In exile, Horthy exercised regularly and observed a strict diet because, he confided to an old friend, a Hungarian countess, he had to look fit riding a white horse when returning to power in Budapest. (In his ceremonial entrance to the historically Hungarian cities in Romania and Slovakia lost after the First World War and returned to Hungary by Hitler in the early 1940s, Horthy rode on a white horse, wearing the uniform of the long-defunct Austro-Hungarian Navy.) It was a matter of time, he assured the countess, before both the Americans and the Russians realized that restoring his rule was the one viable solution.

He died in Estoril in 1957, at the age of eighty-eight. Put down by most Hungarians at the time as a weak, luckless bungler, he nevertheless merited a front-page obituary in *The New York Times* that called him, unfairly, "the dictator of Hungary." He was never that. Had he acted like a dictator when confronting Hungary's extreme right and its German patrons — or his pro-German generals — he and the nation he headed might have fared better both during and after the Second World War. (On the other hand, as Professor Deak argues forcefully, the Germans would have speedily replaced him, had he followed such a policy.)

Those who knew Horthy well say that he never understood why anybody should have expected him to conduct himself differently during the war. He was the product of the Habsburg monarchy that rewarded men who would bend but not break and took pride in inventing the maxim, "the situation is critical but not serious." Behind his back, people called Horthy "The Old Ferryman," which referred to his skills in shuttling back and forth between two sides and in navigating in dangerous currents.

Hungary's Regent, whose highest praise for a person was "correct," strove to embody that ideal. He rated people he knew by the degree of their loyalty to him. He or his friends coined the adjective "Horthy-faithful" in Hungarian — which he applied as if it were synonymous with fidelity to the Hungarian nation, itself an exalted abstraction. To his way of thinking that nation did not include the masses of its Jewish citizens, especially those from the provinces. He perceived the protection of Jews from deportation to concentration camps — the ultimate purpose of which he stubbornly refused to believe for the longest time — as a concession to the Anglo-Americans, the Pope, and the Swedish king, and as a public relations exercise rather than his duty as head of state. He was genuinely baffled when asked what he had done to save those crushed by the German juggernaut. He believed he had lived up to the highest standards of morality by thinking of himself and his family first and last. To his mind, he *was* the state and the nation. But by the standards of the time and the region, he was a reasonably tolerant and flexible person — and a kind man who did not have what it takes to be a killer.

Defying Killers and Opportunists

Defying the killers and the opportunists were the angels, which was the word used by Jews to describe those who came to their rescue. In both Hungarian and Yiddish, "angel" means a blameless person of such quintessential goodness that he or she cannot believe evil exists. Indeed, what other order of beings could measure up to someone like Raoul Wallenberg? As an ordinary mortal, he failed. As second secretary at the Budapest legation of neutral Sweden, he could neither cajole, nor bribe, nor blackmail Lieutenant Colonel Adolf Eichmann of the SS even to slow down the liquidation of Hungarian Jewry, the last sizeable Jewish community still functioning in German-occupied Europe. So Wallenberg dreamed up the absurd but effective scheme of extending the protection of the Swedish crown for tens of thousands of Jews in Budapest.

Other angels, such as those who figure in the following chapters, invented other methods. Mr. Kanalas, a rough character who saved two families including mine, employed extreme verbal violence that turned back Arrow Cross thugs. Erzsebet David, a government official with the soul of a lyrical poet, supplied Jews with Christian birth certificates and cried when some Jews were afraid to accept them. Pastor Gabor Sztehlo organized a network of orphanages, ostensibly for Protestant children of Jewish origin. Journalist Levente Thury distributed an ingenious document that saved Jewish males of conscription age.

Among Hungarian government officials, standing up to Nazi pressures took subtle forms that nevertheless saved lives — the practice of bureaucratic delay in first issuing orders to round up Jews, then implementing those orders; setting up subterfuges that granted exemptions to "deserving" Jews such as decorated veterans of the First World War (Horthy's favorite category) and leading figures of industry, finance, and the arts; issuing patriotic protestations to the SS that Hungarian Jews must be interned on Hungarian soil and not sent abroad to Germany.

Strangely enough, the Hungarian government's highest-ranking active anti-Nazi was Ferenc Keresztes-Fischer, the Minister of Interior himself, holding a job traditionally reserved for a villain. "He stepped over his shadow," says Jeno Thassy, then an army lieutenant who rescued Jews and now a retired Voice of America broadcaster in New York as Eugene de Thassy. In his memoir, published in Hungarian under the title *Dangerous Land*, he described Fischer, whom he had met before the war socially, as a nondescript little bureaucrat "wringing his small dry hands" while listening intently to people who appealed to him knowing that he paid attention. During the war, he took on a different role. "Though the law was his Bible, he became a giant when he broke the law in saving lives," Thassy wrote. It was Fischer's responsibility to keep out enemy aliens such as refugees from German-occupied Poland whose ranks included many thousands of Jews. Instead, he let Jews enter Hungary by the tens of thousands, helped set up receiving centers for them, closed his eyes to Jews registering as Christians, and refused to hand them over to the Germans.

He was a not-so-secret ally of people representing diverse interests — from members of the Hungarian anti-Nazi underground to the eminent Hasidic rabbi from Poland, Aharon ben Yissachar of Belz, whom he assisted first during his stay in Budapest from 1942 to 1944 and then in his flight to Palestine. For those who knew him and his helpers — and they included Jozsef Antall, Sr., whose son became post-communist Hungary's first prime minister — an idea of a financial compensation for their efforts would have been unthinkable.

As soon as the German troops occupied Hungary, in March 1944, Fischer was relieved of his cabinet position, and after the Arrow Cross putsch in October, the Gestapo sent him to the Mauthausen concentration camp where his health quickly deteriorated. He died in Austria a few months after his liberation by American troops.

Fischer's was one of many individual cases of courage. Each stood out as a luminous exception which helped prove to patriotic Jews including most of my relatives that the Jewish experience in Hungary was unique, dramatically different from those in neighboring Romania, Russia, or Poland; that the bonds and the affinities nurtured in Hungary by several generations of Jews and Christians were real; and that, as many Jews phrased it, "the best people stood by our side and only the rabble turned against us." Though hiding or otherwise assisting a Jew carried the risk of imprisonment and, after the Hungarian Nazis replaced Horthy on October 15, 1944, summary execution, a significant minority of Gentiles believed that rescuing a Jewish friend was a matter of honor and that keeping one's honor was the better part of being Hungarian.

Those who saved Jews were not organized. While their activities were often impulsive, sporadic, and even episodic, the Nazis who made the killing machine run so efficiently were disciplined and coordinated, and their leaders competed in the number of Jews they eliminated. For instance, Eichmann's Hungarian equivalent, Laszlo Endre, bragged about having set "the world record" in arranging the transportation of close to half a million Hungarian Jews to the death camps in only two months. And both of them found plenty of volunteers to help them out with names and addresses of Jews in hiding.

The destruction of two-thirds of Hungarian Jewry was a tragedy of Hungarian history as well. Good intentions, smart bureaucratic tricks, and heroic efforts of individual defiance could not save the great majority. Large-scale rescue was yet another doomed enterprise of Hungarian history, echoing other conspiracies and revolutions that in the end were all crushed, their causes betrayed, and their protagonists — invariably the paragons of the national virtues — imprisoned, driven into exile, or killed. Only a small number of Hungarians, Gentile and Jewish, foresaw in 1944 how the deportations and the help provided by large numbers of the citizenry would tarnish the country's reputation for years to come.

From the vantage point of what Hungarians call "national destiny," the actions of angels rescuing Jews represented "fire made of straw," which is the favored local phrase only slightly less dismissive than the English "flash in the pan." At memorial gatherings since the war, the solemn metaphor is "a light in the darkness," or "*lux in tenebris*," as educated Hungarians like to say in Latin, the sacred language of liturgy and scholarship in earlier centuries. *Lux in tenebris* invokes the image of a lone, flickering flame of a candle that a gust of wind can easily extinguish. Such a flame invites admiration because it relieves, however symbolically, the gloom of total darkness.

Jews from other countries such as Poland who faced large-scale visceral hatred and received help from Gentiles only under the most exceptional circumstances are puzzled, if not incredulous, when hearing that, in one way or another, up to 200,000 Hungarian Jews who survived the Holocaust by dodging deportation owed their lives to Gentiles. Counting human beings is talmudically unacceptable, and our post-Holocaust ethic is wise in resisting comparisons based on tallies and percentage points. Nevertheless, that figure for Budapest Jewry is large enough to keep in mind, and it calls for an explanation.

Jewish among Hungarians, Hungarian among Jews

Studying the great equalizer, the Nazi killing machine, it is easy to lose sight of the fact that the millions of Europeans who were forced to wear the six-pointed yellow star had little in common, as they came from various national cultures. Jews born and raised in Hungary offered a salient example of being different which was — and is — a source of pride to some of them, exasperating to others while entertaining to a few.

For several generations, Hungarian Jews tended to think of themselves as "far more European" and "far more civilized" than the great masses of coreligionists living, "in misery and darkness," to the north, in Poland, and to the east, in Russia. They looked down upon fellow Jews in Romania and in the lands belonging to the South Slavs as "Balkan," which is a contemptuous term in the lexicon of Hungarian snobbery and a metaphor for all that mimics France (or Britain or Germany) on the surface, yet disguises Ottoman rot and fraud underneath. (Few prospects alarm Hungarians more than lapsing into "an Asiatic morass," be that Russian or Byzantine, Balkan or Levantine.) Only with their Austrian brethren did Hungarian Jews feel an affinity approaching equality, which was a sentiment reflecting a vestigial bow before the former imperial master. At the same time, they liked to ridicule Jews in the Czech lands for aping Austrian and German ways.

The ultimate Hungarian Jewish argument asserted (and still asserts) an historic deep rootedness in the country and in its ethos that coreligionists in neighboring lands could not match. Tombstones the color of mist excavated in the Roman outpost Aquincum, now part of Budapest, prove that Jews lived in the territory centuries before the Hungarian thrust into the Carpathian Basin, when it was known as Pannonia, a province of the Roman Empire inhabited mostly by Slavs and Celts.

There is a more intimate distant connection, and all the more alluring because it is so distant, linking the present to the cradling dark of origins. From the nineteenth century on, Hungarian scholars, both Gentiles and Jews, have contended that at least one but possibly two of the seven tribes that in the late ninth century galloped from the steppes of the east and conquered what later became the Kingdom of Hungary were Khazars who professed the Jewish faith.

It is a generally accepted fact that the Khazars, who were of Turkic origins, made history more than a hundred years earlier by rejecting Christianity and Islam, and converting to Judaism instead. The Khazars who joined the Hungarian tribes had broken away from their own tribal confederation.

The conquest of the land is Hungary's foundation myth, and the possible Jewish role in the historic exodus from the steppes into a western land promised in a dream to the matriarch of Hungarians has tantalized many Jews and philosemites. They have conjectured that after the pagan Hungarian royal house was christened at the turn of the first millennium, its kings must have forced the conversion of most of their Khazar subjects who were then gradually absorbed in the new, unified Christian state. But hints in chronicles and laws as late as in 1309 suggest that at least some Khazars in Hungary clung to Judaism and intermarried with Jews who had started wandering into Central Europe from the Holy Land even before the Roman destruction of the Temple in Jerusalem in the year 70 of the Common Era.

For several centuries the Khazars formed a powerful, rich empire incorporating what are now Ukraine and southern Russia and reaching as far south as the Black Sea and the Caspian Sea. By the eleventh century they vanished from history, as did earlier the ten lost tribes of Israel, which prompted Arthur Koestler, a Hungarian Jew and an inventive romancer, to write *The Thirteenth Tribe*, a few years before his death in 1983. Koestler claimed that the story of the Khazar converts' survival throughout Eastern Europe, though chiefly in Hungary, had been carefully concealed by embarrassed rabbis.

History can be putty in the hands of those practicing the narrative arts while shaping a thesis they wish to believe in. On the other hand, partisans of the Khazar connection (whose ranks include some of the finest people of Hungary) may well triumph one day, if someone ever stumbles upon an official document or a private letter — buried under a fencepost in an iron box or perhaps re-used to strengthen the spine of an old tome — that will substantiate the hypothesis about Khazar genes in both Christian and Jew in Hungary.

But historians who chronicle the symbiosis of the two communities need not go that far back in antiquity. Beginning in the first part of the nineteenth century something in the Jewish spirit resonated with the solemn sustaining myths of Hungarian patriotism: a stubborn isolation of a God-given separate identity, a tragic vulnerability to the imperial ambitions of great powers which tried every means to expunge that identity, an irrepressible yearning for a return to the grandeur of ancient virtues, and a quixotic predilection to live in the alternative reality of a mythic past. By the end of the nineteenth century, many if not most Hungarian Jews came to agree with the swagger of the Latin dictum, minted at a time when high Latin was still an official language of the state: *Extra Hungariam non est vita; si est vita, non est ita*. Translation: Outside Hungary there is no life; and if there is, it is not the same.

What made Jews, many of them wanderers from country to country only a few generations earlier, feel at home in Hungary, so much so that by the twentieth century only the ultra-Orthodox continued to speak of "exile," the classic description of living outside the Holy Land? A fundamental fact was the prosperity and social acceptance achieved by the majority of Jews by the end of the nineteenth century. But was that a cause or an effect? Perhaps more importantly, at about the same time Jews also became aficionados of the romance of everyday life in a country where a bouquet of fragrant violets costs less than a mug of beer, and both are offered frequently and sometimes with inimitable grace. Jews learned to shed tears along with the rest of the citizenry when listening to Gypsy songs that mourn the end of a summer or a betrayal by a lover. They embraced a national ethos that guaranteed that the most popular songs would be invariably sad — and the more sad the more popular.

Jews also joined the melancholy national cult of marking the passage of time with elaborate farewells, and especially funerals. They enthusiastically adopted the thousand and one local customs, such as reaching a critical decision during a stroll under an allee of linden trees, fragrant when in bloom. Of course, they came across anti-Semites, including some virulent specimens, but they found sympathy and assistance in a sizeable and influential liberal community whose members would argue freely and often eloquently on subjects such as whether it is perennially Jewish or quintessentially Hungarian that an eminent scholar or a good poet commands more respect than a prime minister or a bank president, albeit that scholar or poet is expected to be as poor as a church mouse. I cannot decide whether it was evasive or assertive, or perhaps only crafty, that so many in my grandparents' generation chose to identify themselves as "one hundred percent Jewish and one hundred percent Hungarian."

An early Jewish triumph was the mastery of the daunting Hungarian language, a gift of shamanistic Asia yet declaimed in the borrowed cadences of judicious Latin. That odd mix lent itself to poems as melodious as Italian and as supple as French, the best of which the nation has cherished as if they comprised the Torah. The secrets of writing such poetry were unlocked by Jews, some of them grandchildren of refugees from pogroms in Poland and Russia who had crossed the Carpathian mountains innocent of Hungarian, albeit often with entire tractates of the Talmud committed to memory.

With a collector's passion, Hungary's Jews hoarded the kind words they received from Gentiles and bequeathed them to the succeeding generations, along with Grandmother's candlesticks. For instance, the chief executive of my ancestral Szabolcs County — whose official title, "head steward," is older than the oldest walnut tree and has a connotation similar to "viceroy" — publicly embraced an Orthodox Jew like my grandfather and intoned in that plangent theatrical voice of his: "You are such a good Hungarian." He meant it, and the two of them were close friends — or so we, descendants and disciples, believe, just as we have been taught to believe, just as we want to believe. Regardless of the cynics' snicker, we have no reason to question motives. My grandparents' youth was Hungary's halcyon time of faith in ethnic harmony, and evidence suggests that Head Steward Andras Kallay, from one of the country's leading families, was far more of a passionate believer than a smart politician.

To explain the wonder of assimilation, sympathetic Gentile writers have employed sentimental metaphors, such as Jews drinking from a sorcerer's potion containing the germs of the national infection of melancholy: one sip and a metamorphosis took place; never again could the soul be at peace.

A vernacular version claims that assimilation began with the celebrated local dish stuffed cabbage, in which a cabbage leaf the shape of one's palm usually swaddles bony, chewy, inferior beef rather than a better cut — and almost never the best — yet the taste is all the more irresistible. At a turning point in the lives of many Hungarian Jews came a violation of the rabbinical ban on mixing meat and milk: sour cream was allowed to seep into the sauce, and the seduction by the resulting superior flavor was instant. There seemed to be no way back to keeping the dietary laws that originated with Moses and were elaborated by the rabbis. The next experiment often involved pork sausage, another culinary icon of Hungary.

Throughout the land, sensitive Gentiles with thatch-like, straw-colored hair and souls tantalized by the exotic kept falling in love with dark, curly-haired Jewish women whose laugh suggested the cooing of turtle doves. The romance seemed to have the signature of fate, and at the very least it was undoubtedly fashion, a puff from the warm breezes of the liberal *Zeitgeist*.

Early in this century, Hungary's preeminent writer, the Roman Catholic Gyula Krudy, described one of his literary alter-egos as living with a Jewish woman who would cook the traditional fish every Friday night and whose Hebrew blessings over wine and bread he memorized and recited along with her. By the time the First World War ended and the Habsburg monarchy crumbled after seven centuries, the descendants of cunning Jacob speckled the pedigrees of the country's so-called historic families, both the aristocracy and the intelligentsia, and a new breed known as "part-Jew" emerged, famously ambitious, in some cases preposterously arrogant, and on occasion going to great lengths to conceal a Jewish ancestor. Nevertheless, the secret got out sooner or later. Hungary is one large village, and villagers naturally conspire in exposing a conceit and laugh the laugh of their lives when a lie is punctured.

Scholars faithful to the covenant of Abraham as well as others beholden to the Enlightenment or to a Christian tradition have often spoken of "the love affair" between Jew and Gentile in Hungary. (Zionists on the other hand have decried the bitter mystery of such a misplaced infatuation.) In one memorable poem, Agnes Gergely, a prominent contemporary poet in Budapest and a rabbi's dutiful daughter, has declared her "hopeless love" for Hungary. The poem is a much-quoted favorite of Arpad Goncz's, a playwright once active in the anti-Nazi underground and elected as the first president of the post-communist republic in 1990.

But the idyll turned into tragicomedy featuring the fatally impractical Hungarian posture of pride — oh well, let jealous critics condemn it as intolerable snobbery — when flaunted by Dezso Szomory, born Moshe Weisz, a writer who critics have often compared to Proust. In 1944 a fellow writer from an aristocratic Gentile family offered the safe haven of his country estate to Szomory, then seventy-five years old and ailing, spending sleepless nights while waiting for deportation in a tiny room in the Budapest ghetto. Szomory said, no thanks, which he explained to a friend a few days before a stroke felled him, that the noble Gentile was "not a good enough writer to save my life."

Nimble on their feet and cunning in their schemes, Hungarian Jews have been overachievers not only as Magyar patriots and Hollywood movie moguls but as Olympic swordsmen, world-class mathematicians, and nuclear physicists, as financiers and inventors, painters and poets, and, most recently, as communist henchmen and anti-communist dissidents. Though they tend to be compulsively verbal and ostentatiously multilingual, those who know or use Yiddish or Hebrew have been the exceptions. They can be conceited and chivalrous, contrary and compassionate. Also stubborn and irreverent. Tell them that you have a crazy, absurd idea, and you have their undivided attention.

When not assimilated, Hungarian Jews can be so ultra-observant that they will drink slivovitz only if no Gentile hand touched the plums at any stage of their progress from bud to bottle. And drink they will, in a quantity that amazes a Jew from other communities accustomed to sobriety and moderation, and even in Jerusalem they dance at weddings in the styles of the Gentile peasants who had once lived next door to their great-great-grandparents.

It is unlikely that Jewish leaders from any of the countries neighboring Hungary would have approved a public statement as passionately nationalistic as the one signed in 1939 by the heads of the organizations representing Hungary's observant Jewry, ranging from Orthodox and Hasidic to the equivalent of Reform: "No man-made law can deprive us of our Hungarian homeland, just as no man-made law can deprive us of our love for the one God. Just as through the thousands of years of misfortune we remained unswerved by fire, water, beheading and auto-dafe, slavery on a galley ship and imprisonment in shackles, we will remain steadfast in our attachment to our Hungarian homeland, whose language is our language and whose history is our life. Just as our coreligionists preserved the old Spanish language and culture of their homeland through centuries of exile, we will keep waiting for the dawn of our vindication and Hungary's resurrection."

A cynical analyst may argue that the statement had an ulterior motive and was composed to help fight a law then being debated in parliament that aimed "to limit Jewish gains in public and economic life." The proposed limitation was drastic, Nazi-like, and its opponents believed that it had to be countered with strong protest while one could still raise one's voice in opposition, while there was still hope to keep the Nazis at bay.

But when reading the statement in the original, I hear the cry of a spurned lover and recognize the heartfelt echoes of romantic poetry, Hungarian rather than Hebrew. I am moved rather than embarrassed by the piling up of historical misfortunes, and by the coupling of precedent and prophecy when citing the Spanish Jewish tragedy. The statement's cadences suggest the lament of Hungarian Jewish melodies which fuse the tremolo of Galician synagogue chants with the amoroso of the Gypsy violin. I shudder, feeling the anguish of my people, a peculiar tribe within not one tribe but two, whose members find themselves Jewish among Hungarians and Hungarian among Jews.

The Stretch of a Poet's Rhyme

Until the last part of the Second World War, the great majority of Hungarian Jews believed that they were sheltered from the mad winds that uprooted communities in the rest of Europe and that what happened elsewhere could not happen to them. "Hungary is different from other European countries," they kept saying to foreigners, including fellow Jews, with the kind of serene self-assurance that, like the finest silverware, should be inherited from grandparents, if not from someone farther back on the family tree. "And we, Hungarian Jews, too, are different from Jews elsewhere." After all, they added with a smug little smile, where else in Europe does a Jewish industrialist — the textile magnate Leo Goldberger — play bridge with the head of state, Regent Horthy, every Thursday evening? Does anything more need to be said about the unique advantages enjoyed by Jews living under the protection of St. Stephen's sacred crown? And, by the way, didn't that first Christian king of Hungary declare a thousand years ago that a nation is weak when consisting of only one tribe and speaking only one language? (Unfortunately, Stephen did not add "following one religion," but, after all, he was forcefully baptizing his pagan nation and could not be expected to endorse religious diversity.) Wasn't Hungary for generations a safe haven for Jews fleeing Galicia and other eastern lands plagued by pogroms? Didn't tens of thousands of Jews from surrounding countries crushed by Hitler find asylum in Hungary in the first five years of the Second World War?

Professor Randolph Braham writes in his *Politics of Genocide* that while the Nazis systematically destroyed neighboring communities, "Hungarian Jews were developing a false sense of security." He charges them with self-delusion, "constantly rationalizing that they would somehow survive the war, although under less favorable economic conditions."

Indeed, somewhere deep within their souls many Hungarian Jews expected that a noble Gentile, a true Hungarian hero, would eventually appear and come to their defense: a high school classmate or a cousin's one-time lover now in a position of power would materialize and offer protection. Or help would come from a complete stranger whose "heart is in the right place." But whether self-confident or paralyzed with fear, or swinging back and forth between the two, the great majority of Jews regarded themselves as forming an inseparable part of the Hungarian landscape, and it seemed to them unthinkable that they could be uprooted.

Speaking from the second-story balcony of his Budapest hideout in January 1944, the venerable Belzer rebbe, Aharon ben Yissachar, reassured a crowd in Yiddish, "*Bleibt in shtilerkayt!*" — or stay quiet. The phrase was interpreted to mean that the country that gave the Galician rabbi asylum was safe for Jews. Later, after the rabbi fled to Palestine and the rabidly Nazi Arrow Cross seized power in Budapest, there were wistful rumors among Orthodox Jews about saintly rabbis reaching the conclusion that God must have decided He could not watch any more the destruction of His people and that the Messiah was on the way.

The Jewish confidence in being at home in Hungary suggested the stretch of a poet's rhyme rather than the chicanery of a bookkeeper cooking the books. The large majority of Jews living in Hungary *were* at home in a country whose language and civilization, plains and hills, dynasties and revolutions were theirs from birth, and whose myths they subscribed to. They were loyal Hungarians. As a Radnoti poem gives it:

> I can't tell what this landscape means to someone else;
> to me, this little country ringed by flames is my homeland.
> . . . I grew from it as a twig grows from a branch,
> and I hope that my body will sink into its soil.

That feeling of belonging warmed the heart, though in the end the Nazis proved it a lie. Nevertheless, even as a form of self-deception, that belonging helped many Jews keep their self-respect, or at least their sanity. Giving up such an illusion and dumping it on history's trash heap would have conceded victory to the Nazis. It would have meant throwing away a most precious possession. It would have amounted to the ultimate treason of disowning one's self.

When a Hungarian soldier guarding Radnoti's labor battalion demanded that he state his occupation, he answered: "Hungarian poet." The guard screamed at Radnoti that he was "a stinking Jew — not a poet and certainly not a Hungarian."

My aunt Clara recalls that when her Auschwitz-bound train stopped at the border and a Hungarian military officer formally announced to the deportees that after the train crossed into German territory they would no longer be under the protection of Hungarian law, nearly everyone on the train broke out in tears even though such protection meant nothing by then. The tears flowed freely over the solemn cutting of that last shred of belonging, however fictitious. The deportees mourned the end of the cherished illusion of having a country, a culture, and a legal system they could call their own; they mourned for the proud people they had once been.

The Banality of Evil, the Banality of Good?

During Eichmann's trial in Jerusalem in 1961, the German-born New York social philosopher Hannah Arendt coined the term "the banality of evil," a phrase she first used when filing her report for *The New Yorker*.

Eichmann was not banal but a resourceful, indefatigable, and compulsive killer whose resolve to kill could not be deflected. Appeals to his humanity, threats of postwar punishment, and offers of bribes rolled off him. Hearing daily reports on the Red Army moving closer and closer to Budapest and facing the imminent collapse of the Third Reich, he worked around the clock to make sure that the murder machinery he set up so expertly would go on functioning. Until the last minute, with the Russians surrounding Budapest and advancing toward Vienna, he used his high SS connections to override the Wehrmacht's urgent demands for trains, which he insisted on filling with Hungarian Jews destined for death camps in the Reich. In an interview with a Dutch Nazi journalist in Argentina in 1957 and intended for publication after his death, he extolled "the magnificent way" the transports rolled into Auschwitz and expressed regret only over his failure to kill even more Jews. He denied that he had been only a recipient of orders from above; he declared himself an idealist determined to destroy the enemy, the Jew.

Arendt's label of banality is an intellectual's putdown of evil as a life force too simplistic and thus undeserving of serious inquiry. (Dante, another exile, might have called Arendt's choice of word "haughty," which was his condemnation of overweening pride.) A superior intellect such as Arendt would not stoop to analyze someone banal; in her judgment, Eichmann was a humdrum bureaucrat — and thus as unworthy of serious analysis as an accountant absorbed in his job or a poet unable to rise above mediocrity.

Others who studied various forms of resistance to the Nazis have suggested the existence of a mirror image of the Nazi frenzy of pillage and murder. Was there indeed such a phenomenon as righteous drunkenness in those exceptional individuals who challenged the militarily superior forces of evil? For instance, did Raoul Wallenberg become as reckless in his efforts to save Jews as the Nazis were relentless in organizing their extermination? Could there have been something of a parallel between such incarnations of good and evil, both of them blind to what opportunists placed on a pedestal as concrete reality?

Then, could it be that ultimate good is also banal?

"With fear and trembling, I suggest that we look at the banality of the good," writes Michael Berenbaum, a thoughtful American-born student of the Holocaust. Working on oral history interviews with rescuers and the people they helped, he and his students were struck by "the ordinariness of good, its routineness, its naturalness, its simplicity, and its banality." But then Berenbaum checks himself and declares that in those days "the ordinary was extraordinary. The sum total of banal deeds is not banality, but nobility." His conclusion is couched in fine talmudic singsong: "We cannot let the nobility of the circumstance obscure the banality of the deed, nor can we allow the banality of the deed to obscure its nobility."

Rescuers have been known to spurn suggestions for public recognition, and many of them would rather not part the curtains on the high drama of their lives — except perhaps for the right person, and at a time and under circumstances of their choosing. But even among those rescuers who do talk willingly, the sameness of the questions that earnest interlocutors feel they must pose takes its toll. Only the most patient heroes fail to tire of giving the same answers. Asking a rescuer to explain why he or she did something as noble as saving a life is likely to inspire diffidence and distance, rather than an expansive soliloquy, let alone an epiphany of an interview.

The rescuer I knew best, my Uncle Levente Thury, spoke of the experience of having to account for his motives as "deeply embarrassing." Suddenly, he decided he needed to brew another pot of coffee when someone proposed to rummage in his unconscious in an earnest effort to find "the well-springs of heroism." He muttered curses under his breath and asked his wife not to let his interlocutor cross the threshold ever again.

For once, our confrontational protocol — shared by academics, journalists, and trial attorneys — of shooting direct questions at protagonists and witnesses is unlikely to yield insights. The story of rescue is too private a garden that is easily profaned by a casual or over-eager visitor. The gate is locked most of the time; to crash it with a tape recorder or a video camera slung over the shoulder feels like an intrusion, even an ambush.

On the other hand, a pilgrim's reverential stance can also make a perceived idol wince. Should rescuers who have given some explanations of themselves be called banal?

To my mind, their words echo the complexity of biblical simplicity that helped set our standards for memorable character. When confronted with the insistent, inevitable question, "Why did you do it?", rescuers give a version of what many students consider an annoyingly stiff answer — "I did what I thought needed to be done" — which is something of the opposite of Cain's sly response to God's inquiry into Abel's disappearance: "Am I my brother's keeper?" In the Bible, as in our world, the most satisfactory explanations come from the entirety of a life story, which can yield a truth as close to the Anglo-Saxon "truth and nothing but the truth" as our multicultural sensitivity can muster.

Neither the killers nor the angels were banal. They were driven by the root passions of their souls. Or to switch metaphors, each was drinking to the bottom of his glass the strongest liquor of his life. Each was forced to act out what lay hidden in the core of the self.

It was stone-faced, blind fate — the most inventive dramaturgist of them all — which dispatched to Budapest *Obersturmbannführer* Eichmann and Second Secretary Wallenberg who confronted each other in the last months of history's most destructive war. They battled over the fate of hundreds of thousands of souls, the last large Jewish community still alive and functioning in Hitler's Europe.

At his trial in Jerusalem seventeen years later, Eichmann said that in no country did ordinary local citizens offer the Nazis as much help in rounding up Jews as they did in Hungary. That assessment is invariably quoted by those Hungarian Jews who regard that surge of assistance to Eichmann as the unspeakable collective act of a nation that they say they can never forgive.

On the other hand, Hungary also provided the right stage for Wallenberg at least partly because even some of its opportunists bowed to the romantic hero — the fair prince from far away — many Hungarians instantly recognized in him, and because some of the killers reflexively obeyed the mirage of a distant authority such as the Swedish crown. And, just as important, his magnetic personality inspired a large supporting cast of helpers and sympathizers.

In his study of the Holocaust in Hungary, historian Braham finds that the Christian neighbors with whom Hungarian Jews "had shared a common destiny for over a thousand years remained basically passive." In his opinion, the anti-Nazi resistance movement was "weak," and he condemns "the leftist-progressive effort" on behalf of Jews as "an impotent shell."

Randolph Braham is an eyewitness as well as a careful scholar of documents. But his judgments are uniformly stern. His approach to those who defied the Nazis tends to be dismissive because he measures their achievements while thinking of the great majority of Jews who received no help. More rescuers should have come to the fore, he seems to suggest, and anti-Nazi resistance should have been far more organized and effective. He is right, of course, but he also implies that rescuers and their sympathizers barely deserve to be mentioned because they failed to change Nazi policy and they could save no more than a small fraction of Hungarian Jewry.

True, Gentiles who helped Jews operated mostly in Budapest, and even in Budapest the majority of Jews were trapped by the regulations enforced by the police, the gendarmerie, and, in the end, by the armed gangs of the Arrow Cross. Moreover, it is the historian's traditional assignment to study institutions and their policies rather than to examine individual lives. With the notable exceptions of Second Secretary Wallenberg, and Pastor Sztehlo, the rescuers were private individuals acting on their own and using their personal resources, and they made a difference only to small numbers of people.

The five individuals this book focuses on formed a significant minority. There were others like them — several are mentioned in various chapters — and not all of them are included in the list of Righteous Gentiles certified by Yad Vashem in Jerusalem. (A recent study by Gabor Kadar and Zoltan Vagi, two Hungarian Jewish historians in their twenties, documents more than one hundred rescuers in Hungary.) None of them altered the course of history — the kind of grand history defined by the rise and fall of nations, the victories and defeats of armies marching across national boundaries, and the collisions of ideologies — but they did save many thousands of souls, including their own. To my mind, that is also history, albeit on a grassroots rather than the over-the-treetop level, as the stories chronicle the shifting fortunes of private lives carrying the burden of great events that lay beyond their ability to affect.

The number of souls that rescuers saved in Hungary does not come up to more than one percent of the Jews the Nazis killed in Europe. But there is more to history than bottom lines. We should not be so overwhelmed by judgments deduced from a computation of large numbers — horror multiplied by horror — that we ignore the small number of exceptions: those who dodged the crematoria and the firing squads. The Holocaust has burned into our century's consciousness the elegiac wisdom of the talmudic maxim: if someone saves just one life, it is as if that person saved the whole world.

The undeniable truth is that the great majority of the victims did not encounter people who helped them. I cannot forget the laconic words of my cousin Kati Krausz, originally of Huszt, Hungary and now of Migdal Haemek, Israel: "When we had to leave our homes to board the trains to

Auschwitz, nobody offered us help, and nobody said a comforting word to us. There was nobody on our side. Nobody. Not a single soul."

Berenbaum, a rabbi and an educator, is right in raising his voice against mystifying the rescuer "because we require that mystification" as a counterweight to "an unrelenting story of evil." He uses the example of Denmark's King Christian who was unquestionably sympathetic to Jews, but who did not wear the Star of David as some writers have erroneously stated and lecturers on the Holocaust keep stating. Berenbaum reminds us that we ought to face the truth rather than comfort ourselves with the kind of fiction which allows us "to confront the despair and remain as whole as one can remain in a journey into the abyss."

The five rescuers portrayed in this book were spurred by a diversity of motives. The threat of an inhuman action kindled a smoldering rage in a foreign patrician as well as in a member of the Budapest lumpenproletariat. Others were driven by compassion for the victim that accompanied a lonely, unfulfilled life, or by a devout Christian's need to demonstrate God's loving-kindness, or by a code of honor. Finding ways to dodge and to defy a criminal power elite, the rescuers proved that the litany of the majority, "nothing can be done," was an excuse, even a lie.

While killers and opportunists were alike in their conformism, each angel pursued a path that was his or hers. The rescuers made up a motley crew, and none of them could have been identified beforehand as a candidate for a rescue mission: a member of a prominent family in a country uninvolved in the war, a janitor who liked to pick fights in the tavern, a lifelong victim in affairs of the heart, a village pastor committed to deepening the Lutheran faith of his parishioners, and an anti-Nazi journalist who felt guilty for not doing something concrete against the Nazis. They surprised themselves by choosing new roles that also astonished people who thought they knew them well. They invented and refined their devices, and while engaged in rescue work, they found that they could rely on powers and skills they had not known they had.

CHAPTER TWO

The Prince from Far Away:
Raoul Wallenberg

Who, when I cry, will hear my call among the angelic orders?

Rainer Maria Rilke: *The Duino Elegies*

In a cabinet built into bookshelves lining a Budapest apartment, passports, cash, and important letters press against a flat flashlight, two inches wide and three inches long, known as "made-for-the-pocket." Its black lacquer is flaking. The tiny bulb disappeared some time ago; the slot where the battery used to be now collects powdery rust.

The original owner of the flashlight, Istvan Radnoti, died in 1964. His widow followed him in the early 1990s, and the flashlight now belongs to their son, a philosopher, and his daughter Anna, a journalist. When Anna was about ten years old, her grandmother told her how such a cheap little industrial product became a family relic.

The time was a fall afternoon in 1944, and the place Budapest's cavernous, vault-like Western Railroad Station, shrouded in soot, and dimly lit so as not to attract the attention of American and British pilots then bombing strategic targets. Along with many hundreds of other Jews, Istvan Radnoti, then forty years of age, was being herded into cattle cars bound for the so-called labor camps in Germany. Hungarian police and heavily armed Arrow Cross men swarmed all around. Screaming, they cursed the Jews for thinking that they were "out for a promenade" and

33

threatened to "let loose some bullets" if they didn't board the wagons faster.

Suddenly, the crowd parted to let through a tall, dapper civilian wearing a homburg, unmistakably a foreigner, who told a policeman in strangely accented but fluent German that he must speak to the officer in command. As the people all around fell silent, Istvan Radnoti heard the man identify himself to the Hungarian commander as the representative of the Swedish Legation and warned him to release forthwith a number of people under the protection of the Kingdom of Sweden who had been mistakenly rounded up for deportation.

In halting German, the Hungarian attempted to answer, but the foreigner barked in the imperious manner of Nazi officers that the mistake must be corrected immediately and that he, as the competent diplomatic representative of Sweden, is under orders to take his proteges with him.

Without waiting for a response, the foreigner drew a sheet of paper from his pocket: the list. But it had gotten too dark to make out the names. He called out: "Does someone here have a flashlight?"

Istvan Radnoti stepped out of the crowd, walked over to the foreigner, and focused his flashlight on the paper. As the foreigner read the names aloud, scores of people lined up behind him. When he was done, he thanked the flashlight's owner for his help and asked him: "But aren't you on my list?" Istvan Radnoti said that unfortunately he was not. "Now you are," the foreigner said, and took him by the arm as they strode out into the night, followed by the others who had responded to the roll call — the lucky minority wrenched from the maw of the Nazi killing machine, and safe, at least for the moment.

"I will always treasure Grandfather's flashlight," said Anna Radnoti in 1995. "It is our life."

Was there really such a foreigner? Did a Swedish diplomat by the name of Raoul Wallenberg walk this earth? How could the Nazis, Hungarian and German, be so gullible as to fall for his gall and the make-believe authority of the Kingdom of Sweden to protect Budapest Jews?

Talking about Wallenberg to my children, I had a hard time persuading them that he was not a fantasy invented by J.R.R. Tolkien or a Jew daydreaming about a miracle. Yes, I told them, Raoul Wallenberg did exist. His slender silhouette in a well-tailored greatcoat is remembered by people even if they caught a glimpse of him only once. "A noble man," Jews whispered in awe when he walked past them, "an angel." Those clinging to the cadences of their faith added: "May the Almighty bless him with a long life."

During his six months' stay in Budapest, wartime censorship made it unthinkable for a newspaper to publish a sentence concerning his rescue work. No radio broadcast, foreign or domestic, mentioned him. The U.S. intelligence documents that mentioned his name and mission began to be declassified in the 1970s and some of them are still secret. The Wallenberg legend spread the way legends have always spread, by word of mouth, gaining in strength each time yet another eyewitness passed it on and attested to its truth. Among the people he was sent to help and their sympathizers, the name Wallenberg became a password of hope.

That he rescued more Jews than any other person in Nazi-occupied Europe is a statistical fact. Whether that number was 20,000, or twice, or five times that many depends on how we apportion his share of responsibility for the survival of different groups with different documents, some issued by his office and others forged. But the numbers tell only part of his saga which turned into a bedtime fable as it happened, a rare soul-soothing Holocaust story, and a piece of folklore as particular to Hungarian Jews as their belief that the Almighty is most likely to listen to a heartfelt prayer on the eve of Shavuos, the Feast of Tabernacles commemorating the day Moses received the Ten Commandments, when, devout Hungarian Jews say, "the dome of heaven opens up to pleas from the earth below." In this case, a prince from a faraway kingdom arrived with a last-minute escape plan for Jews about to be sent to their death. Relying on his native sang-froid and a patent of protection granted by his good-hearted king, he browbeat the guards and freed intended victims.

I first heard the name Wallenberg from my father Aladar. He was proud to tell me after the war's end that Ibolya, his daughter from his first marriage and then in her early twenties, had worked as a courier for

Wallenberg. She thought the Swedish diplomat was the most admirable person she had ever met.

"Beautiful and vivacious, Ibolya had a great deal of presence," Father said. "She was an amateur actress. In high school she once played Hamlet, and she was very good. She enjoyed acting, and it was not hard for her to pass off as a Gentile."

But in the end — at the very end — the Arrow Cross caught her carrying a packet of Swedish passports, and they shot her a few days before the Russians conquered Pest in January 1945. Father never told me how he found out. He would not explain how he could be so confident about what he presented as facts. I did overhear members of my mother's family, who had been fond of Ibolya, criticizing him for not searching harder. I do not know if he did or did not; what I remember is his solemn, tight-lipped certainty that the Arrow-Cross had shot his daughter.

To this day we do not know where Ibolya's body may be — thrown into the Danube or buried in one of the mass graves. All that is left of her is a terse inscription — "She died a martyr's death and rests in an unknown location" — carved in a book opened in the middle, carved out of white marble. The book rests on the grave of her husband, Miklos Klein, a rabbi who told us upon his return from a camp in Germany that he did not wish to live any more. He died a few months later, alone in a small rented room. The cause of his death was unknown to my parents — or my parents did not wish to know.

A Hero Foretold

Whether Jewish or Gentile, many Hungarians half-expected the appearance of a hero as improbable as Wallenberg. "If we survived this long into this terrible war, we'll get through it by one means or another because someone will turn events in our favor," Father used to say in early 1944, before he had to report for duty in a labor battalion. Along with other savvy, big-city Jews, he weighed the odds from day to day like a bookmaker. He anticipated a *deus ex machina* — a surprise outside intervention — and, like other educated Hungarians, he relished repeating that phrase in the original Latin, which lent it an air of irrefutable authority.

Father was betting on "the ultimate decency of individual Germans," a people he knew and liked from his student days in Berlin and from the 1920s when he crisscrossed Germany and Austria as a traveling salesman. Thanks to his Viennese mother, he spoke German like a native; moreover, he picked up several of its dialects, and he liked to entertain friends and clients by mimicking them. "If a German talks to me," he used to say, "I can respond in the dialect of his region, and he won't think of harming me." He thought it was "only reasonable to believe" that Germans would "respect and honor" the fact that like him, many Hungarian Jews admired Germany's *Kultur* and *Volk* as "of the highest quality," which was his favorite praise, a salesman's mantra pronounced with appropriate *gravitas*.

Other Jews felt more like my mother Anna, born in a small village and raised by devout Orthodox parents for whom only faith could loosen the grip of misfortune. Worrying and crying, she kept saying, "What have we done to deserve to be treated this way? Why do the Nazis hate us so much?" When fearing that there was no way out, and the Nazis were closing in, she said: "It cannot go on like this. God is bound to send someone to help us." To me that unknown person resembled the Angel of Good Deeds who also figured in the fairy tales I heard from her, her mother, and other family members.

Wallenberg seemed to have stepped out from a story Hungarians first read as children, in books they could not put down but went on reading with the help of a flashlight under the blanket. These were novels such as the Baroness Orczy's *Scarlet Pimpernel* and Alexandre Dumas' *Count of Monte-Cristo*, which led a child through implausible plots in which ordinary men constructed new, commanding personalities for themselves and defeated seemingly overwhelming forces. As eyelids began to quiver and droop despite the suspense contrived by the writer, a lucky child could, through the gauze of a dream, slip into the dungeons and palaces of faraway lands. In the morning, the flashlight battery might have gone dead, and the impressionable reader could not be sure at which place in the narrative the novel ended and the dream took over. That blurring of boundaries and the freedom of action it conferred felt like liberation from the shackles of the physical world.

The roster of heroes who kept Hungarian children under their spell was headed by Don Quixote and Cyrano de Bergerac, each a champion of decency and justice, truth and eloquence; each an architect of an alternative time superior to the corrupt, banal present. Yet another enchanted land to enter was King Arthur's Camelot. His knights of the Round Table, engaged in quests to rescue those in distress, beckoned to many young Hungarians looking for meaning and purpose in life. It made good political sense for the ruling elite between the two world wars to promote the adjective "chivalrous" to sum up the nation's character.

Summoning all the grand themes of West European romance and adding a few of his own was the most popular Hungarian writer of all time, Moric Jokai, who created in the nineteenth century a series of battles fought by heroes and villains. His generation and those that followed devoured his tales — more than one hundred volumes of novels and short stories — and modeled themselves after his protagonists who invariably vanquished evil, miraculously, at the very last moment.

In the twentieth century, every Hungarian adolescent in the habit of reading books mourned for "little Nemecsek," the lowest-ranking and the most looked-down-upon member of a teenage street gang in Budapest — or "club" in the parlance of the time — who sacrificed his life for his friends in Ferenc Molnar's 1907 novel, *The Paul Street Boys*. Tactfully, Molnar did not identify Nemecsek by ethnic origin. But the name had a foreign ring, suggesting that he belonged to some minority or another. The submissive, scrawny boy, son of a poor, bedraggled tailor, amounted to nothing among his peers. "Like the number one in arithmetic, he neither multiplied nor divided other numbers," Molnar wrote. Yet Nemecsek turned into a hero. He was the linchpin of victory over a far more powerful rival group given to such outrageous actions as expropriating marbles by shouting "the ugly Teutonic word" *Einstand,* which in those days defined "a terse and unmistakable way of proclaiming a state of siege, the right of force, of the fist, of brigandage." For generations of youthful readers, Nemecsek's tragic passing away — from pneumonia contracted while slipping into enemy territory — spurred compassion for the underdog and the victim, and contempt for the perpetrators of *Einstand*.

In 1944, devout Jews living in another realm of inspiration whispered among themselves that the Messiah was certain to arrive soon and bring the war to an end. This legend originated with saintly, secretive rabbis who made their calculations on the basis of holy books they studied day after day and long into the night. They thought that the mysterious man from the distant, little known north, Wallenberg, might just be the Messiah's surprise emissary.

In war-weary, grim Budapest waiting for the Germans to flee westward but also fearing the Russians in pursuit of them, Wallenberg seemed "something like a Martian," Geza Paikert recalled in an article years later. Paikert was an anti-Nazi Gentile who worked with Wallenberg. He and other Hungarians found the Swede inexplicably optimistic and strangely unafraid of challenging the all-powerful Germans and their crazed Hungarian stooges, members of the extreme-right Arrow Cross movement.

But neither Paikert nor his friends could explain Wallenberg's passionate engagement in saving the lives of strangers, a people not his own, whose culture and history he knew only slightly.

"Most of us thought that Wallenberg was Jewish, but he wasn't," wrote Paikert, later a history professor at Le Moyne College in Syracuse, New York. "He certainly was not the stereotypical blond-haired, blue-eyed Swede." Paikert described Wallenberg as "very good-looking, alert [and] close to six feet, with dark hair and fine features." He had an "air of authority."

Jeno Thassy, a Hungarian army officer decorated by Yad Vashem of Jerusalem as a rescuer of Jews, remembered Wallenberg as "unmistakably superior in every way": with the manners of a European patrician, in control of his facts and funds, and admirably fluent in English, French, and German, which Thassy had to mix — much too clumsily, he thinks — to make himself understood.

Thassy went to see Wallenberg to ask for Swedish safe passes for Jewish friends he was hiding. But Thassy soon realized he should have been equipped with a recommendation, a referral. Declining the request, Wallenberg probably took Thassy for an agent provocateur, a Gestapo plant. "He was cool and logical," Thassy told me in the late 1990s. "He made me feel small and insignificant — as well as the son of a small and insignificant nation. In a way he was right on both counts. I was regrettably inept in my attempts to rescue Jews. I should have been far more prepared in presenting my appeal to him. Our meeting was my failure — not his."

Wallenberg's ability to project authority proved all-important in a tradition-bound, semi-feudal society where upper class manners and a proud bearing often counted for more than actual status, and the mere appearance of authority could substitute for real power.

Wallenberg's position at the Swedish Legation did give him some leverage. Hungarian foreign ministry officials and members of the police force, SS officers, and even Arrow Cross functionaries were wary of what a diplomat from a neutral nation would say about them as an observer and as a potential future witness in a postwar reckoning. In private conversations, some of them tried to impress him with their humanitarian ideals, and Wallenberg knew how to exploit such an opening like no one else among neutral diplomats stationed in Hungary.

With their country allied to Germany, by then seen by Hungarians as the war's likely loser, most Hungarians wished that they too, like Sweden, were neutral. They envied Sweden as a prosperous nation on the continent's northern extremity, able to stay out of the wars of Europe much the same way a count ensconced in his mountaintop castle could ignore brawls in the village tavern. It only enhanced Wallenberg's aura of mystery that Hungarians could not understand why he, a scion of a wealthy family, would give up the comforts of peace and risk his life for others in a place that was hell and getting worse.

Wallenberg was only thirty-one years of age when he arrived in Budapest in July 1944; after the Soviet conquerors kidnapped him in January 1945, he probably lived for many years in the gulag. In the

1990s journalist Victoria Pope of *U.S. News & World Report* tracked down and interviewed several trustworthy witnesses who had met with Wallenberg in the 1950s. Like others who followed Wallenberg's trail, Pope believes that hidden somewhere in the depths of the Soviet nether-world of prisons, labor camps, psychiatric institutions, and ex-prisoners' colonies, he might have been alive as late as the mid-1960s. Some of the researchers ask: why couldn't he have survived into the 1970s, as some ex-prisoners testify he did, and possibly even beyond that?

The belief in Wallenberg's survival many years past his official Soviet (and now Russian) death date is widespread among his one-time pro-tégés, as well as some of those who have studied the testimony offered by witnesses. Those he rescued and others who admire him cry out: the man who saved so many lives *cannot* be dead. At a 1996 Holocaust com-memoration in New York, many in the audience shouted "yes" when they heard Ambassador Per Anger, once Wallenberg's colleague in Buda-pest, declare in his slow, deliberate, imperturbable Swedish manner: "I think Raoul may be alive."

The applause was intense and went on and on, and it seemed as if it would not end, but when it did, a sudden hush followed, broken by the arrhythmic tremors of men and women sobbing.

The Assignment of a Lifetime

In her biography titled *Wallenberg: Missing Hero*, Kati Marton begins the Wallenberg saga with a casual elevator chat between two strangers who worked in the same eight-story building in downtown Stockholm. One, Kalman Lauer, was short, squat, and impulsive, the owner of a small export-import firm which marketed goose liver pate and other Hungarian delicacies; the other, Iver Olsen, tall, lean, and deliberate, whose overt job at the U.S. Legation was that of a financial officer. When Olsen learned that Lauer was a Hungarian Jew, he wasted no time in ask-ing his help to find a Swede "with good nerves" willing to go to Nazi-occupied Budapest to rescue Jews. Lauer promptly recommended his employee Raoul Wallenberg who happened to be on National Guard duty just then.

The job interview took place within a few days, and the three men traveled on a warm June night to Saltsjobaden, the elegant summer resort built some fifty years earlier by Gustaf Oscar Wallenberg, Raoul's beloved grandfather. Raoul Wallenberg was on a twenty-four-hour furlough from the National Guard, arranged by the influential Olsen who knew by the middle of dinner that he found the right man: strong-willed, resourceful, multilingual, afraid of nobody, and eager to make his mark. Wallenberg had a B.A. in architecture from the University of Michigan, and he lined up valuable contacts in Washington where, some American officials believe, he was introduced to President Franklin Roosevelt. Wallenberg had visited Hungary on several occasions and made a few friends. Most important, he detested the Nazis and was raring to join the Americans in defeating them.

Wallenberg's youth and lack of experience in diplomacy and covert operations did not discourage Olsen. As Lars Berg, another young attaché at the Swedish Legation in Budapest, later wrote, Wallenberg at that time "was nothing but a blank page"; he had no contacts among "the ruling Germans and Hungarians in Budapest," and no familiarity with the Hungarian language.

Nor did Olsen worry that his candidate came from a family, usually described as "the Swedish Rockefellers," whose many companies helped supply the German war machine with ball bearings and other strategic materials. The Office of Strategic Services (OSS) — the precursor to the postwar Central Intelligence Agency — kept a file on the head of the family, Jacob Wallenberg, it described as "the principal financial figure in Scandinavia" and "largely responsible" for negotiating the Swedish-German trade agreement that upset Washington. OSS documents say that Jacob Wallenberg openly sympathized with German nationalism, though not necessarily the Hitler brand. The well-informed Olsen might have also known that Jacob had recently turned down cousin Raoul's request for a job in any one of the extensive Wallenberg network of business firms and that Raoul felt slighted.

Olsen's boss, the rotund, jovial Herschel Johnson, approved of Raoul Wallenberg after dining with him. The young Swede was so eager to persuade the American minister about his suitability for the assignment that he somehow left the impression that his late father had been Jewish, a misunderstanding subsequently enshrined in U.S. government files, including a recently declassified CIA study from 1981. Researchers have since identified his nearest Jewish ancestor: his mother's great-grandfather, which qualified him as an Aryan even by the strictest Nazi laws of racial purity.

As Lars Berg described it, upon hearing about the choice of Wallenberg, President Roosevelt himself gave "the necessary instructions to the State Department." Within hours, Johnson met with the Swedish foreign minister. "The Swedes did not raise any objections," Berg wrote. "Raoul Wallenberg was appointed second secretary of the Swedish Legation in Budapest." Unbeknownst to the rest of the world, he would be disbursing American funds to save Jews. The money came from the U.S. War Refugee Board (WRB), which Roosevelt set up in January 1944 in response to repeated requests from the American Jewish community. The WRB's mandate was "to rescue endangered refugees." It was also engaged in gathering intelligence.

The Swedish government agreed to this unusual arrangement to help relieve mounting U.S. pressure to stop their trade with Germany. "Sweden was no longer truly neutral after it became clear that the Allies would win the war," recalls Donald Jameson, a veteran American intelligence officer. He believes that had the Wallenberg project been proposed earlier in the war, the skittish Swedes, who in the early part of the war permitted German troops to pass through their territory to conquer neighboring Norway, would have balked. It was only in December 1944 that the chief of the Scandinavian Section of OSS advised Washington that Sweden "is ready to assume the role of a belligerent neutral." It was also about that time that Swedish firms refused to extend credit to Germany to buy ball bearings, an action which may be interpreted as the recognition by the exceedingly cautious Swedes that Germany was about to lose the war.

For Raoul Wallenberg, the assignment was the chance of a lifetime, an opportunity to live up to the great expectations that had been instilled in him as a child. Olsen cabled the War Refugee Board in Washington that Wallenberg was so eager to get started that he "left in a hell of a hurry with no instructions and no funds." He flew to Berlin where he declined the offer of his sister, the wife of a Swedish diplomat, to spend the night in their house. Instead, he caught the next train to Budapest.

When his train stopped at the Hungarian border, he saw cattle cars packed with Jews bound for what the Germans called "labor camps" but which Allied and neutral governments knew were extermination camps. Allied intelligence also knew that the liquidation of Hungarian Jewry, Nazi-occupied Europe's last remaining large Jewish community, had begun two-and-a-half months earlier, with trains carrying 12,000 people a day to Auschwitz. The countryside had been cleared of Jews, more than 460,000 of them, and the Germans now targeted the capital Budapest, then the home of more than 300,000 Jews, including those who had been baptized but whom the Nazis still considered Jewish because of their racial origins.

On July 9, 1944 Wallenberg presented himself at the Swedish Legation in Budapest, equipped oddly for a diplomat. This is how colleague Per Anger remembered the event in his book *With Raoul Wallenberg in Budapest*: "He was carrying two knapsacks, a sleeping bag, a windbreaker, and a revolver." In what Anger called Wallenberg's "typical joking style," he explained that the purpose of the revolver was "to give me courage. I hope I'll never have to use it."

Two days before Wallenberg's arrival, Regent Miklos Horthy, Hungary's head of state, ordered a stop to the deportations. Horthy's uncharacteristic decisiveness was prompted by a series of protest messages he received from the deeply perturbed Swedish King Gustaf V and the concerned Pope Pius XII, as well as from the outspoken President Roosevelt. FDR threatened that Hungary's following a Nazi model in its treatment of Jews would dim the country's prospects in a postwar settlement. In Per Anger's opinion, Horthy, who thought of himself as an old-fashioned European gentleman, was not impressed with Roosevelt, whom he regarded as a posturing New York politician. But Horthy was troubled by the Swedish king's disapproval, and the stern words shocked him. They both belonged to Old Europe — pre-Nazi, pre-First World War — and Horthy, a descendant of petty nobility, reflexively deferred to royalty.

However, Hungary's head of state had to assert his authority against that of Lieutenant Colonel Adolf Eichmann of the SS, the foremost German expert on the "Final Solution" of the Jewish problem. Eichmann had arrived in Budapest on March 21, two days after Germany invaded Hungary, its nominal ally whose government had been resisting Hitler's demand to eliminate what the Nazis called "the Jewish island in Central Europe."

First Secretary Per Anger explained to Wallenberg in their first meeting at the Swedish Legation that the Germans will not go along with "sparing the Jews of the capital for good" and that the fate of Jews depended on what the German occupiers had in mind for them.

Anger showed his new colleague documents the legation had been issuing to a few hundred Jews who qualified for residence in Sweden by having had some connection with that country, however tenuous. The documents were "provisional passports" for those awaiting emigration, "visa certificates" for prospective travelers to Sweden, and "protection letters" endorsed by the Red Cross that had less value than the first two papers. Promptly, Wallenberg suggested a new, far more impressive document: "a protective passport." It was a fancy identification paper carrying Sweden's national colors of blue and yellow, and its emblem of three crowns. To the uninitiated, it seemed a passport. Wallenberg was convinced that it was important that the document look official and expensive — or, in a word that both Hungarians and Germans respected, "serious."

In the months to come Wallenberg persuaded Hungarian and German officials to accept his contention that a Hungarian Jew equipped with such a Swedish protective passport, called *Schutz-Pass* in German, was virtually a Swedish citizen, waiting to emigrate to Sweden as soon as transportation became available — and that in the meantime he or she and the immediate family were under the protection of the Swedish crown. These were absurd claims without legal precedent which could work only in a time of absurdity — and when promoted boldly by a person as strong-minded as Wallenberg. Concerned about public opinion in Sweden and elsewhere, the Hungarian government promised that those who hold such "passports" would not be deported to Germany and that they would be allowed to live unmolested in buildings on the Pest side of the city, on the east bank of the Danube river, in the so-called Swedish houses Wallenberg purchased or rented. The blue-and-yellow Swedish flag fluttered over them; signs at the main entrance declared them Swedish state property.

The number of such Swedish protégés had to be very small, the Hungarians insisted. Wallenberg flatly rejected figures in the hundreds, and in the end the agreement specified 4,500 as the upper limit and restricted applicants to those who could prove some connection with Sweden.

But the Hungarians could not control the number. Worried about depreciating the value of the protective passports, Wallenberg's office initially issued only a few thousand over the agreed-upon number. But soon, the number of documents handed out rose above 10,000, and, eventually, to more than 20,000, which is the low figure used by scholars trying to determine how many people Wallenberg saved.

The *Schutz-Pass* numbers jumped again after the German-engineered Arrow Cross putsch on October 15, 1944 and the removal of Regent Horthy who failed in his attempt to cancel Hungary's Axis membership. The deportations promptly resumed under the new regime, which was totally subservient to Germany and determined to liquidate all remaining Jews. Wallenberg responded by organizing other neutral diplomats such as Switzerland's in setting up "an international ghetto," which soon sheltered 33,000 Jews, 7,000 of them with Swedish papers by then known locally as "Wallenberg passports." With gallows' humor, Jews referred to him as "Budapest's number one landlord."

Wallenberg became increasingly reckless as Arrow Cross units combed the city, even entering his "Swedish houses," to round up Jews whom they either shot or crowded into cattle cars bound for concentration camps. Wallenberg had himself driven to train stations, brickyards, the ghetto, and other collection points, each time ordering the officer in charge of the transport to release the people whose names he had on his list as recipients of Swedish protective passports. At the beginning, the list had some relationship to the one maintained by the legation. But soon Wallenberg developed the routine of making up bogus lists which quick wits grasped, and they reacted as if their names had been called. The ruse was amazingly successful though the list was almost as fictitious as the protective authority backing it.

On one occasion, having missed an Auschwitz-bound transport in a Budapest railway station, Wallenberg took off in his car, raced the train for more than a hundred miles, and caught up with it at the old Austrian border. He walked up to the Hungarian commanding officer, made his usual demand to take custody of his protégés, and returned to the capital accompanied by a few hundred people riding on rented trucks.

As the Red Army moved in on Budapest, the Nazis were running out of time to make the city *judenrein*. With public order breaking down, Wallenberg no longer felt constrained by the agreements he had negotiated with the Hungarian government. He shrugged when Hungarian officials complained that Jews forged thousands of copies of his protective passports. Most of the day he had his car driven from one location to another, handing out more documents and claiming that others were on the list of receiving them. His relentless energy matched that of the Nazis. On occasion, the Nazis had moved quicker, and they told him, mockingly, that the Jews he was looking for were already "fish swimming in the Danube." Wallenberg knew that the phrase meant that they had been shot at the river's edge. He turned around and left without saying a word.

"Wallenberg was never intimidated and didn't betray any sign of nervousness," Paikert recalled later. "Instead, he acted very much like a man in firm control." As an employee of the Swedish Red Cross, Paikert remembered driving with Wallenberg to the train station at Kelenfold, on the western outskirts of Budapest. "We were going there to distribute the Swedish protective documents because we knew that was a spot where the Nazis were rounding up Jews for deportation," Paikert wrote. Wallenberg showed the Hungarian policemen his Swedish credentials that "impressed them very much." Briskly, he told them that he had "emigration documents for several people." Then he plunged into the crowd, "waving documents and shouting, 'You — Mr. Katz! Mr. Berger!

We have your papers!' The names didn't really matter, of course. Most of them were just made up."

Then Wallenberg handed out documents to those who stood nearby. Others were asked if they had any documents. Once they flashed a driver's license or a ration card, Wallenberg would say, "Come with us." Paikert wrote: "In the confusion, even people who had nothing were able to slip away."

Paikert noted that when passersby saw Jews rounded up on the street, "most people turned their heads and didn't want to know what was going to happen to them. They wanted to believe that yes, the Jews would be transported to labor camps, but, oh no, they wouldn't be killed." While not wanting to have the Jews killed, they did want to "make an end to the Jewish power." Paikert's reporting neither apologized for, nor denied the sad truth: "After having been incited by Nazi propaganda, many people enthusiastically applauded the anti-Jewish persecution, saying things like 'Finally!' or 'It's about time!' and 'We needed Germany to do this for us.'"

Wallenberg's personal example — perhaps even more than his persistent lobbying — inspired others in neutral embassies, such as Switzerland, Spain, Portugal, El Salvador, and the Vatican, to issue hundreds of papers of protection of their own. But they were traditional diplomats trained to avoid creating a public spectacle, and reluctant to offend the host government, or to act counter to its laws. None of them dared to go as far as Wallenberg — in issuing as many documents as he did, in showing up at collection points for the transports to the death camps, and in fearlessly confronting the Nazis and the police. And of course nobody else had Wallenberg's audacity of using bogus lists.

When the Soviet forces surrounded the Hungarian capital and trains could no longer get through to Germany, Hungarian Nazis ordered thousands of Jews of all ages to march westward on foot, guarded by Arrow Cross thugs. "Those who could not keep on walking any farther were shot to death or quite simply left to their fate if they were not considered even worth a bullet," Lars Berg reported. "The long road to Vienna was soon lined with unburied decaying corpses."

Wallenberg raced after the Jews who were marched off, and he hastily procured trucks to bring them back to Budapest. Berg noted: "Uncountable were those Jews who during their death march toward Vienna already had given up all hope then suddenly received from one of Wallenberg's 'flying squadrons' a Swedish protection document."

Berg, who was previously stationed in Berlin, explained the method Wallenberg used in dealing with German officers: "You could order even high-ranking Germans around by raising your voice just a little and giving it the right firmness. The Germans were used to obedience." This was especially true if the person wore civilian clothes. When the Germans could not read the rank on someone's shoulder, "they preferred to obey orders. They could never know if the person in front of them happened to be one of Hitler's or Himmler's special delegates."

While intimidating some Nazis, Wallenberg bribed others, and he cultivated those who indicated a spark of sympathy for the Jews. Within a few months, he built a network of agents who, according to a CIA study, numbered more than four hundred. "If the Ministry for Interior Affairs had planned a new action against the Jews, Raoul would know about it in advance and could take countermoves," Lars Berg wrote. "If the experts in the Ministry of Justice were working on a new law against the Jews, one of the jurists would be paid by Wallenberg to insert necessary loopholes in the text. If a police officer was ordered to raid a certain house, his cousin would already be an employee of Wallenberg's, and the *razzia* would be made with 'closed eyes.' For Wallenberg nothing was impossible."

Could Wallenberg, or someone like him, have found a similarly receptive environment with strategically placed co-conspirators in, say, Romania or Poland or the Baltic area? Or Germany? Not very likely. The tragic fact is that President Roosevelt's War Refugee Board, finally launching its projects in March 1944 with the drum-roll of high hopes, came much too late for most of European Jewry. The Board tried hard and had some successes in Romania and Bulgaria. But, for instance, it could not convince Jews in the Baltic countries that they were being offered passages to Sweden. They feared that the project was a trap intended to deliver them to Germany.

The War Refugee Board and other organizations failed to organize another rescue mission comparable to Wallenberg's. Nor could they find another Wallenberg.

Actor, Negotiator, Humanitarian

Could something as simple and unsophisticated as a belief in goodness and a desire to foil evil explain Wallenberg's motives? The answer is yes, but he seemed to have had the time of his life doing what he saw as morally right.

In her biography of Wallenberg, Elenore Lester called him "a practical man who cared about decency. His soul was forged in two centuries of enlightenment, in the ideals of humanism, fraternity and progress. It was his passion for those values that trapped him into the new age of darkness."

Another biographer, Harvey Rosenfeld, drew upon a quotation from Winston Churchill in offering a characterization: "There are no great men, only ordinary men facing a great challenge."

The writer whose judgment is most subtly shaded is Kati Marton. She found that Wallenberg's qualities of "courage, steadfastness, unselfishness" we seldom associate with "real, living people" because they are "the stuff of epic poems, novels and films." Marton thought that "an excess of hubris" might have been Wallenberg's only fault. "He had observed his own miracles and perhaps he had begun to believe them," she wrote. "He had lost a sense of his own mortality."

What impressed Prague-born Professor Yehuda Bauer of Hebrew University in Jerusalem and a prominent historian of the Holocaust is that Wallenberg's rescue operation "was so very public" and that he was not afraid to challenge commanding officers in the presence of their subordinates. "Yet," Bauer noted to me, "he was not a braggart but a very modest man."

Lars Berg argued in his book that the most remarkable element in Wallenberg's actions was that "they were not based on any legal rights whatsoever. . . Neither he nor the Swedish Legation had any right at all to interfere with the way that the Hungarian authorities chose to handle their internal problems — in this particular case, the Jews. . . Neither weapons nor soldiers gave weight to his words. His only source of power was his unfaltering faith in himself and the righteousness of his mission."

Per Anger pointed out that Wallenberg was "an inventive negotiator" who knew "how to squeeze out the best deal," and "a smart business-man" who had a way with money. "Raoul always enjoyed the process of negotiations," Anger said to me in a conversation in 1996, with a broad grin settling on his deeply lined face. "It was the practical results that pleased him — not the agreement itself and certainly not the profit. And he loved the challenge of outsmarting others."

In his youth Wallenberg impressed his friends in Sweden with his imi-tations of Adolf Hitler. "He was a very good actor," Anger said. "He made us laugh a lot." Anger perceived a parallel between those imitations and his confrontations with Nazi officers in Budapest. "When walking up to the Nazis, the soft-spoken intellectual Raoul turned into an aggres-sive, brutal man," recalled Anger who had known Wallenberg from childhood and in military service, years before their meeting as col-leagues in Budapest. "He became another person. But I knew that inside he was laughing — at the Nazis and at himself. He loved the playacting. He was a man who knew that life is a big theater and that most of us can be our natural selves only as babies. For the rest of our life, we have to play the parts assigned to us. But the difference is that Raoul *chose* his part."

Anger said he looked up to Wallenberg as a man who found a way to make use of his talents and who fought the Nazis with gusto. "Raoul had a zest for life," he said. "He was a warm human being. He was also a nat-ural humanitarian — he was born that way. He always took the side of the weak and the persecuted. I had to learn from him."

In early 1944 Anger had been issuing Swedish passes before Wallenberg upgraded them and greatly increased their number. Anger explained that helping people in need did not come naturally to him because he was always taught to live by rules and regulations. "It was hard for me to do what I did," he confessed. He said he needed the inspi-ration of his friend Raoul's "free spirit" and "instinctive sympathy for the victim. I had to train to become a humanitarian. Raoul needed no train-ing. He knew exactly what to do."

With a melancholy smile, Anger recalled a frequent Wallenberg remark in Budapest: "I am such a coward." But was Wallenberg playacting in that instance too? Anger thought about the question for a few seconds and then announced that he could not be sure.

Berg emphatically denied that Wallenberg was a brave man by nature. "During the air raids, he was always the first one to seek shelter, and he was badly affected when the bombs sometimes fell a little too close to us," Berg wrote. "But when it was a question of saving the lives of his protégés, then he never hesitated a second. He then acted with a challenging boldness and bravery, though his life mostly was much more in danger then than during the air raids."

From his letters and comments it appears that Wallenberg exulted in the freedom of action he had in Budapest. He could operate outside the narrowly defined laws and conventions of any one country or community. He reveled in the universalism of his mission: as a neutral Swede, he was sent by the Americans to fight their German enemies in Hungary. A Lutheran, he was saving Jews. Though posted as a diplomat, he ignored the restrictions of that code-bound profession. He himself would determine what was right — not the Foreign Ministry in Stockholm, nor the U.S. War Refugee Board, nor the Office of Strategic Services in Washington. In a war in which the rules were set by the Germans who themselves had no scruples, he joyfully placed himself above the law.

In no time at all he learned to manipulate Hungarians who were normally afraid to do anything to upset the Germans, but who at the same time were often wary of what would happen to them after the war. Both Hungarians and Germans worried about the legendary brutality of the approaching "Russian hordes." Wallenberg feared no one. He was an independent agent accountable only to his conscience.

But during air raids, he was like everyone else. He could do nothing to stop the bombers, so he cowered.

Surrogate Fathers, Silent Partners

Like Dumas's Count of Monte-Cristo, Wallenberg was blessed with a surrogate father devoted to him, though usually from a distance: his paternal grandfather Gustaf Oscar Wallenberg, who served as Sweden's ambassador in capitals such as Tokyo and Ankara. Gustaf Oscar himself was the powerful son of a powerful father, Andre Oscar, who had founded a bank and turned it into an industrial empire, Scandinavia's largest. Among Andre Oscar's twenty children (from two wives) and their numerous descendants were financiers, bishops, and diplomats (whose ranks included a foreign minister) — people who were often invited to eat at the king's table. Swedish historians say that the Wallenbergs have contributed more than any other family to transforming Sweden from an agrarian society to a modern industrialized country. They were intrepid travelers and bold entrepreneurs, like the Vikings of distant centuries. Worshipping the founding fathers of his family and his nation, the child Raoul called them "Big Men."

In the words of his cousins, Gustaf Soderlund and Gitte Wallenberg, Raoul's grandfather Gustaf Oscar was "a great individualist and completely uninhibited about speaking his mind." They characterized his openness as a "very un-Swedish trait" and "doubtless the source of irritation to many who would tolerate the Wallenbergs' power and influence as long as it was accompanied by personal modesty." Almost as an afterthought, the cousins added: "Wallenbergs were brought up to believe that whatever they touched would turn into gold."

Gustaf Oscar kept a watchful eye on his grandson after his only son, Raoul's father, himself a man of altruistic character and great promise, died of cancer at age twenty-three, shortly before Raoul's birth. Their correspondence, published in 1995, is dominated by the affectionate grandfather who went to great lengths to explain his many firmly-held views. He also made it clear that he fully expected his grandson to share those views. For instance, Gustaf Oscar condemned the narrowness and provinciality of Swedish education that taught students "to march to a regular beat and always keep in step" and failed to train them to acquire "the indomitable will to succeed." He wanted Raoul to study in a university in America, "to get direction in life," to learn self-reliance, and to become "a well-organized fighter." He also warned his grandson that conformists who fall in love with some pretty girl, get married before age thirty, and then raise a family soon realize that everything they had done was wrong. He delighted his grandson when he first wrote that he was

Portrait of Raoul Wallenberg in his office at the Swedish Legation in Budapest in late 1944. Photo credit: Thomas Veres.

On November 1, 1944, at the Jozsefvaros train station in Budapest. Jews stand on the platform, about to be deported. Raoul Wallenberg (on the right with his hands clasped). He is flanked by a Hungarian gendarmerie officer named Lullay and a Jew holding up a Swedish protective passport. Photo credit: Thomas Veres.

thinking of retiring from diplomacy and forming "a world bank" in partnership with Raoul. As a teenager, Raoul thought that nothing in the world could be more grand than forming a profitable new family venture and serving as "a banker to the whole world."

Following his grandfather's advice, Raoul traveled alone across Europe and all the way to Istanbul at age twelve, went to America to earn a college degree, and toured dangerous places such as rural Mexico. He also worked in banks in South Africa and Palestine to learn about banking. His letters to his grandfather paint a touching picture of childish eagerness to satisfy his mentor and role model. Nowhere is there a hint of youthful rebellion, a note of irony; nor an attempt to bend the old man's iron will. Raoul developed second thoughts only on one issue. After his apprenticeship in two banks, he decided that banking, which reminded him of a pawnshop, was not for him, and he declined Grandfather's offer of a partnership. However, in every other respect, Grandfather's word was law.

In wartime Budapest, Raoul was no longer a student of life training for extraordinary success. He did not need to worry about living up to Grandfather's standards by carrying out such character-building exercises as cramming for exams, learning languages, living frugally, soaking up the entrepreneurial spirit, and braving civil unrest. In Budapest, he could apply what he had learned and he proved what he was made of.

What made Raoul Wallenberg different?

He declined to revel in the comforts of his class. He decided that the Wallenberg family motto, "To Be — Not To Be Seen" was insufficient. He did not court the most influential members of the Wallenberg clan, such as head of the family Jacob, which could have earned him a chance plump with material and social promise. Instead, he turned to his grandfather, a prickly individualist who did not rate high in the inner councils of the Wallenberg financial empire.

When confronting high-ranking German officers and their Hungarian cohorts in 1944, Raoul Wallenberg acted alone and followed his instincts. But his grandfather, who had died seven years earlier, remained a silent partner whose admonitions made it easier for him to disregard the cautionary advice of the Swedish foreign office and the moderating voice of his colleagues at the legation. He was by no means marching "to a regular beat," nor "keeping in step." He found a "direction in life" that went far beyond Grandfather's expectations. He was not after founding yet another Wallenberg fortune. He volunteered for a unique, dangerous international mission that not even his worldly-wise grandfather could have foreseen. He was applying his willpower, which became indomitable as he faced adversity and danger, to saving lives.

Challenging the Nazis to let go of their Jewish prisoners was an objective commensurate with Raoul Wallenberg's ambitions. He found his calling as a latter-day knight errant rescuing the helpless innocent and as an altruistic Viking risking his life for a people not his own. He was to be the greatest of all Wallenbergs.

At one time Gustaf Oscar sternly warned his grandson: Wallenbergs do not allow for failure. Fortunately, Raoul's mother, Maj Wising, was gentle and compassionate, and she tempered those indomitable tycoon genes.

His maternal legacy infused Raoul's conquering drive with warmth. For instance, Pal Szalai, a former Arrow Cross believer, knew he found his guiding star when his offer of cooperation in rescuing Jews — which he had initially feared would be seen as a ruse or a trap — prompted Wallenberg not only to shake hands on the deal but to embrace him as well. Now contemptuous of the Nazis' ideology but uncertain of how he might be received on the other side of the battle, Szalai needed the extra reassurance given by the impulsiveness and the body contact of a hug, which helped to form a bond stronger than any signature along a dotted line. The mutual trust between Wallenberg and Szalai became a critical factor in the last days of the Nazi rule over Budapest, when the fate of the ghetto's inhabitants hung in balance.

Similarly, Jews who were afraid at first that Wallenberg might be a stereotypical "cold and distant Scandinavian" soon discovered that he lived for saving the lives of the strangers whom he chose to call "my people."

No phrase could have had a stronger effect on Hungarian Jews. Hearing such words pronounced by a complete outsider, or even hearing them attributed to one, was enough to bring forth tears. To members of a minority cast out from the nation, who felt they had been reduced to "hunted animals," and who were devastated because of "abandonment by lifelong friends," Wallenberg's heartfelt identification, summed up in the simple yet magically inclusive words "my people," signaled the hope of survival and held out the possibility of what they wistfully called in those days "a better world."

Dinner with Eichmann

Wallenberg was not afraid to meet with Eichmann; to the contrary, he was eager for a confrontation. "Wallenberg was probably the first person who had ever dared to baffle and oppose [Eichmann's orders]," wrote Lars Berg in his memoirs. "Until then he had met little or no resistance against his massacres and plunderings throughout various 'liberated' countries."

Berg recalled how on meeting Eichmann by chance, Wallenberg graciously invited Eichmann and his deputy to dinner in his apartment, hoping that "an abundance of good food and precious wines" might help in bringing "a difficult transaction to a successful end." What the diplomat Berg seemed to hint at was that Wallenberg planned to bribe the SS leaders to halt the deportations.

However, strangely enough, Berg added, "the overworked Raoul" forgot that he had invited the two SS men. "He came home late as usual from his office and found two rather irritated and thirsty guests waiting for him," Berg reported. "It was an awkward situation to have invited two of the most important Germans in Budapest to an empty house, especially on the cook's day off."

Characteristically, Wallenberg did not lose his cool. First he mixed drinks for his guests, then telephoned Berg for assistance. Ever helpful, Berg invited the three men over to his house. Wallenberg returned to his guests and announced, with what Berg described as "perfect ease": dinner was to be served in the home of another Swedish diplomat. "Thanks to our excellent cook, the dinner was a great success," Berg wrote, "and I am sure that Eichmann never even suspected that Wallenberg had forgotten about him."

What Berg did not say was that to a fastidious German bureaucrat — which Eichmann was — forgetting about an invitation extended would have been an unforgivable affront, aggravated by the awareness of a class difference. A vacuum salesman prior to his SS career, Eichmann was ill at ease with people above his social station. Though he traveled widely as an SS officer organizing the slaughter of Jews, he could not match the sophistication of the aristocratic man-of-the-world Wallenberg, and Eichmann must have been uncomfortably conscious of that.

The conversation after dinner, as chronicled by Berg, was only a moral victory for Wallenberg, though Berg characterized it as "one of Eichmann's many defeats against Wallenberg." Berg believed that "in fearless, clear, and logical terms Raoul tore the Nazi doctrine into pieces and predicted the Nazis' speedy and complete destruction." True, for a Swedish diplomat, expected to be meticulously cautious and neutral — and at the mercy of the Germans in a German-occupied city — the words were reckless. Berg's explanation in his book was cautious: "But Wallenberg always followed his own course."

As for Eichmann's response, Berg dismissed the "well-learned propaganda phrases" that sounded "empty." To Berg it was clear that Eichmann lost the battle of wits; Wallenberg's "intelligent argumentation" was superior.

Wallenberg's analysis also included "an earnest exhortation to Eichmann to stop the senseless deportation and likewise unnecessary killing of Hungarian Jews." But on this critical issue — the objective of the dinner party — Eichmann yielded no ground to Wallenberg. The humanitarian might have won the argument, but the Nazi did not learn the lesson intended.

In Berg's recollection written a year or so after the event, Eichmann conceded that Wallenberg's analysis was right and volunteered the surprising statement that he "never believed in Nazism as such but it has given me power and wealth." However, in 1957, when interviewed in his hiding place in Argentina by a trusted Dutch Nazi journalist, Willem Sassen, Eichmann claimed to have been an idealist killer of Jews, rather than one who simply followed orders. "Had we killed all of them, the

10.3 million, I would be happy and say, 'All right' we managed to destroy an enemy," he declared in a tape-recorded interview intended for publication after his death.

According to an SS colleague, in his last address toward the end of the war, Eichmann told his men: "I will leap into my grave laughing, because the feeling that I have the deaths of five million people on my conscience will be for me a source of extraordinary satisfaction."

Berg's account of Eichmann's words, related after being wined and dined by the two Swedes, reflected a different mood. "I know that this pleasant life will soon be over," Berg quoted Eichmann telling Wallenberg. "My planes will no longer bring me women and wines from Paris nor any delicacies from the Orient. My horses, my dogs, my palace here in Budapest will soon be taken over by the Russians, and I myself, being an SS officer, will be shot down on the spot. But for me there is no rescue anymore."

Perhaps for the benefit of the patrician, above-it-all Wallenberg, the *Obersturmbannfuhrer* exaggerated both the luxuries available to him as well the odds for his future capture by the Russians. In fact, he did not stay to fight the Russians in Hungary, as some of his comrades did. He escaped to Austria and was eventually arrested by the Americans. With his identity concealed, he fled to Buenos Aires where he lived under the name of Ricardo Klement until Israeli agents caught him in 1960 and flew him to Tel Aviv. His trial in Jerusalem ended in his conviction, and he was hanged in 1962.

In Berg's house in Budapest, Eichmann did not respond positively to the deal, the terms of which Berg left unspecified, offered by Wallenberg. Instead, Eichmann pledged that he would go on exercising his power "ruthlessly" and prolong his "days of grace" in liquidating Budapest Jews. Moreover, he warned that he would do his utmost to defeat Wallenberg's rescue efforts and that Wallenberg's diplomatic passport would not help if he decided that it was "necessary to do away with you. Even a neutral diplomat might meet with accidents."

Having rebuffed Wallenberg, Eichmann and his deputy got up and left. "He did not seem at all angry," Berg observed. "With the unfailing politeness of a well-brought-up German officer, he said good-bye, thanking us for a charming evening."

Ever a diplomat, Berg suggested that "maybe Raoul did not gain much by his frank argumentation. But sometimes it could be quite a relief for a Swede to be able to give his straightforward opinion to a German SS officer." Berg's consolation was that Eichmann "left the house very much impressed by Raoul's fearless and strong personality."

However, the tragic fact is that Wallenberg failed in his objective to talk his antagonist into any sort of collaboration. The enemy proved unyielding. The methods used with lesser Nazis did not work with the man whom his boss *Reichsführer* Heinrich Himmler called "the master himself." Aiming his words at the commander whose order could stop the killing, Wallenberg missed.

The Battle over the Ghetto

The expert in the "Final Solution," who had presided over the liquidation of Jews in France, Poland, Slovakia, and Greece, had one last project before the Nazi retreat into Germany. With the Red Army only a few city blocks away from Budapest's central ghetto, Eichmann ordered his SS men and some Arrow Cross personnel to kill everyone there — up to 70,000 Jews, most of them very young or very old.

Wallenberg learned about the order from Pal Szalai, the disenchanted Arrow Cross official who had been a key ally while serving in the strategic position as the liaison officer between the Arrow Cross Party and the Budapest police. According to Szalai's postwar testimony, which the prominent Budapest journalist Maria Ember accepts as truthful, Wallenberg said he would go immediately to talk to August Schmidthuber, the SS general and the highest ranking German officer in Budapest, and issue the threat that he, Wallenberg, would personally make sure that the war crimes court will hang Schmidthuber if he did not stop the massacre.

Szalai countered that it would be better if *he* went to Schmidthuber and delivered such a message. If *you* go to see Schmidthuber, Szalai warned Wallenberg, he could have you shot to eliminate the witness who would accuse him. Wallenberg accepted the ex-Arrow Cross man's advice.

Szalai rushed to Schmidthuber to deliver Wallenberg's message. The general swallowed hard and decided that it would be wiser to forego the killing and save his own life as well. In Szalai's presence, he phoned his subordinate, calling off the SS and the Arrow Cross men, just as they were about to leave for the ghetto.

By that time Eichmann probably reached Vienna, having flown out of the Hungarian capital encircled by the Red Army. He did not know until much later that he failed to bring about his last massacre and that the man who foiled his plan was the Swedish diplomat whose assassination he had neglected to arrange.

When it came to Wallenberg, Eichmann failed to live up to his standards of ruthless efficiency. After one unsuccessful assassination attempt — an SS bomb blew up Wallenberg's car without him in it — Eichmann did not issue another liquidation order. Or if he did and was responsible for a truck ramming Wallenberg's car from the rear and causing minor injuries, posterity does not know about additional attempts. But with many hundreds of SS under his command, not to mention the trigger-happy minions of the Arrow Cross, Eichmann could have easily arranged for what he so subtly described to Wallenberg as "an accident." The strange fact is that he did not.

A possible explanation has to do with Eichmann's arrogance. As a senior representative of the elite SS in Budapest, he might have decided that he was so superior that he could afford to ignore a diplomat from an insignificant country who stood in his way. The Swede was a meddlesome outsider, a mere annoyance. Perhaps Eichmann did not think of Wallenberg as a challenger of equal power who must be dealt with accordingly.

Wallenberg could have also been summarily shot by any of the Hungarian officers he challenged at train stations and elsewhere. Or he could have been laughed at, treated as a kind of Don Quixote, a dreamer out of sync with reality.

From the vantage point of the present, it is hard to understand the reasons some lieutenant in charge of an Auschwitz-bound transport — a mere cog in the machine — did not put an end to Wallenberg's interventions. The Germans and their Hungarian partners did not hesitate to shoot other defiant individuals, for instance a Lutheran village pastor in northern Hungary who refused to bless the arms to be used in the war, or Gentiles who were found to be hiding Jews.

Nor did Eichmann do something else that would seem obvious: issue an order to his subordinates, or to the Hungarians, that the Swede must be bodily removed from a train station. Short of such an order, the officers were uncertain. Glorifying unquestioning obedience, the German and Hungarian military codes did not prepare a junior officer in command of a unit guarding a train station or a brickyard on how to cope with a civilian from a neutral country, seemingly in authority, who was neither a subordinate nor a superior, neither an ally nor an enemy. Just exactly what was an officer to do? Wallenberg was wise enough not to give the officer time to think.

Wallenberg's intervention was so quick, out-of-the-blue, and unheard-of, so surrealistically brazen, and delivered with such unblinking arrogance that he stunned the officers he confronted. He did more than trigger their fear of making a blunder. Somehow, he temporarily incapacitated their rational judgment. It was as if he had hypnotized them.

For Wallenberg, the recognition of his power over the prisoners' guards gave a heady sensation. They listened to him! He could not stop. He was as invincible as the heroes of old. Or so it seemed. It was left to the Soviet Union, that sibling empire of twentieth century evil, to wreak revenge on Wallenberg and to put out the fire in his soul.

Our Man in Budapest

For nearly six decades, U.S. intelligence officials kept mum about Wallenberg lest they confirm the Soviet charge that he had been an American spy in Budapest. The silence might have served a purpose as long as there was hope that the Soviet Union could be somehow pressured or shamed into releasing him. But the USSR melted down, its political prisoners were liberated, and a new candor emerged in the U.S.-Soviet relationship. Does Washington still have a reason to keep up the pretense that Wallenberg's American connection consisted solely of disbursing U.S. War Refugee Board (WRB) funds to bribe German and Hungarian officials to spare Jewish lives and to buy buildings where the Swedish crown would protect them?

Recently declassified documents and interviews with veterans of U.S. espionage operations in the 1940s suggest that saving Jewish lives was not the only assignment Wallenberg pursued. The CIA formally acknowledged to this writer that he was a valued American intelligence asset in Budapest at a time when there were few such persons. Indeed, between the German invasion in March and the Soviet capture of the capital city in January, he was the one man who could transmit information — via radio, cable, and the diplomatic pouch — to the Office of Strategic Services (OSS) about events in Hungary. He kept in touch with resistance leaders and reported on the progress of the Red Army.

His funds came from the WRB, which American intelligence veterans now identify as an espionage operation disguised as a relief organization. OSS officials gave the WRB the attractive codename "Garbo." The codename was not accidental. Far from frowning on the Board as "just another one of some half a dozen busybody clandestine agencies set up by the president and answerable only to him," in the words of intelligence veteran James McCargar, the OSS extended to the WRB its enthusiastic endorsement, which was important because both the State Department and the Pentagon were opposed to setting up the WRB. As recorded in a memorandum of a meeting on March 7, 1944, Irving Sherman of OSS told WRB director John Pehle that "refugee work offered substantial avenues for OSS intelligence and that OSS contacts would be of the utmost importance to the success of any refugee program."

The choice of Wallenberg, a businessman, and the WRB's focus on refugees combined OSS Director William Donovan's two principal beliefs about intelligence, says a CIA officer, a student of the OSS. He notes: "Donovan believed that a businessman was the best kind of intelligence officer and that refugees provided the best sources of intelligence."

According to a recently declassified document, on the same day that Pehle of the WRB and Sherman of the OSS reached agreement on their future cooperation, OSS headquarters in Washington cabled its Stockholm station chief, OSS officer #155, to make sure that his subordinate dealing with Eastern Europe, #799, knew that not only was the OSS "in complete accord" with the WRB project to rescue Jews but that the project "represents the initial exploratory action in plan for cooperation between the 2 agencies which may reach out to additional theaters."

Ten days later, another OSS cable from headquarters reassured #155 in Stockholm that the WRB "desires you to employ your own discretion in every procedural question, including that of conferring with the minister." Thus when it came to rescue projects in Eastern Europe, #155 did not need to comply with State Department rules and check with his overt superior at the legation. Then the cable pointed out yet another reason for OSS participation in the project: "to offer rapid and efficient communication, for which we believe we will gain important benefits in return."

"Communications is the key here," says John Taylor, a World War II specialist at the U.S. National Archives. "If the OSS was in charge of communications, it knew what went on and could thus have a handle on policy and operations. Besides, offering to get a confidential message hand-delivered in another country was an OSS specialty. This is how the OSS made friends and recruited people."

An indication of the intimate relationship between the two organizations was that the Norwegian-born and Swedish-speaking Olsen, who had been working in Stockholm under cover for the OSS as its #799 since 1943, was asked to represent the WRB as well.

"Olsen went to Stockholm to crunch numbers for the OSS," said Meredith Hindley, an historian specializing in the WRB and the OSS. "When he was in charge of OSS currency exchange operations, he realized that buying currency from refugees also helped him to pick up intelligence from them. He accepted the WRB's assignment and ran with it, making good use of it for the OSS. He also recognized the value of

Wallenberg's zeal. I'd be surprised if Wallenberg was *not* involved in activities other than rescuing Jews." Hindley's research has also revealed OSS-Board "partnership" in two other projects. The first was to supply Norway's anti-Nazi underground with food, money, and arms; the second to rescue 1,200 civilians by boat from the Baltic states. The Soviets were wary of the Baltic rescue, which ended when the Red Army overran the area. But it proved to them that OSS and the Board worked hand in glove.

On June 9, 1944, exactly a month before Wallenberg's arrival in Budapest, WRB Director Pehle received a message from Olsen of the OSS and the WRB: Operations authorized by the WRB in Bulgaria, the Baltic states, and Hungary are under way. "In all three matters the facilities of the OSS have been and are being used and it is expected that the OSS will reap some advantage from all three operations." The officer who sent the message was Lieutenant Richard Helms of the OSS, then posted in Stockholm and later director of the CIA.

Yehuda Bauer of Hebrew University, a leading historian of the Holocaust, told me: "You can't differentiate between the OSS and the War Refugee Board. They were closely related parts of the U.S. war effort, and Wallenberg saw no contradiction between the two. He promised to report for both. There is no doubt on my mind that Wallenberg was involved in OSS operations."

One 1954 memo in the CIA's Wallenberg file that says it straight out is from a CIA informant whose name the declassifiers inked out. The informant refers to an influential Hungarian in Stockholm, Kalman Geiger, who "assisted informant in inserting Roul [sic] Wallenberg into Hungary during WW II as an agent of OSS."

While Wallenberg focused on securing the cooperation of working-level officials — for instance the Hungarian ex-Arrow Cross man Szalai and a certain Gestapo colonel — who had the power of life and death over groups of Jews, he also sought out dozens of Hungarian politicians and other public figures who were actual or potential members of the anti-Nazi underground. His objective was in line with OSS Director Donovan's instructions to his people dealing with East Central Europe: "the first step" was to set up contacts with influential members of the ruling class not in sympathy with the Nazis. The goal: "to immobilize and isolate the 18 German divisions in the Balkans."

Arrogant with the enemy, Wallenberg was congenial with the men he hoped to talk into organizing an effective anti-Nazi resistance, similar to the ones the Yugoslavs, the French, and the Norwegians had created. According to a report cited in a declassified article in the CIA's house organ, Wallenberg even "rounded up weapons for the small band of Jewish resistance fighters in Budapest."

Among the politicians Wallenberg met with was Regent Horthy who after the Allied landing in Normandy looked for ways to free his country from its alliance with Germany. A stickler for protocol, Hungary's head of state would not have consented to grant an audience to the most junior diplomat from the Swedish Legation — unless that Second Secretary had another, hidden role. One declassified American cable specified that though Wallenberg was not authorized to speak for the WRB, he could offer to transmit messages back and forth.

One brief message, declassified in 1994, is from the SI — which stands for Secret Intelligence — section of the OSS stationed in Bari, Italy, to OSS Mediterranean area headquarters in Caserta, Italy. The communication is from November 7, 1944, which was a critical time between the German-engineered local Nazi takeover of the Hungarian government on October 15 and a projected military uprising in late November by a British-connected anti-Nazi resistance group. Through most of 1944, a second, American-connected Hungarian resistance group tried to broker a separate peace with the Allies and even succeeded in flying out a delegation to meet with the OSS in Italy in early October. (Another delegation flew to Moscow.) Queried about the leader of the second group that visited the OSS in Italy, Geza Soos, Hungary specialist Earl Fuller of the Secret Intelligence branch of the OSS informed his boss that he did not know the man's current address but that Soos "may be contacted only" through the Swedish legation in Budapest. "Raoul Wallenberg of the same legation will know if he is not in Budapest," Fuller's message specified.

The document makes it clear that Wallenberg was in touch with Soos, a key resistance leader who had gone underground a few months earlier. (Frequent meetings with Soos were also noted in Wallenberg's diary, which the Russians returned to his next of kin in 1989.) Soos slept in a different apartment every night. For Wallenberg to know the tightly held secret of where Soos stayed indicates a close working relationship. Moreover, according to the same declassified cable, "Soos had Swedish signal plan," which another cable defines as "radio intelligence communications." He sent his messages via the Swedish diplomatic pouch, and the Swedish Foreign Ministry promptly forwarded them to Olsen who in turn sent them on to Washington. (In the files of OSS cable traffic between Washington and Stockholm, there are references to "the Budapest pouch.")

Clearly, the OSS could rely on Wallenberg to pass on messages. One wonders whether the OSS might have wanted to contact Soos in connection with the planned military uprising of the British-connected group, which the Gestapo uncovered a few days before it was scheduled to take place. According to files declassified in 2000, from August to December 1944 the OSS was ready to land a sizeable team in Budapest and set up a base in coordination with an anti-Nazi Hungarian military unit.

The need for American intelligence officers to penetrate Hungary is a recurrent theme of great urgency in the now declassified OSS files on the Balkans, which fill dozens of gray five-inch-thick boxes crammed with folders. "One of the most difficult intelligence problems of this war has been the actual penetration of Germany, Austria and Hungary," Fuller wrote in June 1944 to his superiors at the Caserta OSS headquarters. He recommended establishing "an intelligence chain" with help from Marshal Josip Broz-Tito, leader of Yugoslavia's communist resistance. OSS officers dispatched to link up with Tito's *partizani* were repeatedly instructed to press that request. Tito has "a few tenuous lines into Hungary," said one message to Washington in late July 1944. "However, Tito has shown little interest." Whether on Moscow's orders or for his own reasons, Tito was unhelpful.

"Despite a lot of effort, OSS did not have an active penetration team in Hungary at the end of the war," says James McCargar, an intelligence specialist who joined the U.S. Embassy in Budapest in 1946. But with the Red Army conquering Hungary in the latter part of 1944, American projects to dispatch a covert OSS team were replaced with a plan to send in an overt OSS mission, with the approval of the Soviets, the country's new masters. The surprising recommendation was that of all the capitals soon to be liberated, Budapest should have the largest OSS "city team" — a staff of fifty-one officers. Vienna, historically a far more strategic city than Budapest, was to have only thirty-three OSS officers; and Prague, more of an industrial and commercial center than Budapest, twenty-two. Belgrade, then — and later — the focus of American policy in the area, merited twelve. Nothing in the declassified files explains what could have made the Hungarian capital so important as to rate such a large intelligence team.

On December 28, 1944, with the Red Army already in control of parts of Budapest, the Joint Chiefs of Staff in Washington ordered the OSS in Caserta to dispatch to Hungary, "at the earliest practicable date," an OSS unit. On January 13, the same day Wallenberg made his first contact with Russian soldiers, a roster of fifty-six OSS officers to be stationed in Budapest — five more than earlier indicated — was sent to the American general heading the Allied Control Commission in Moscow. But a month later, with Wallenberg already in Lubyanka, OSS headquarters was informed: "It appears that the Budapest team will be drastically curtailed." On May 1, 1945 OSS Director Donovan received a cable: OSS Budapest city team is disbanded.

Could it be that the early OSS focus on Budapest had to do with a plan to build on Wallenberg's extraordinary success in setting up a rescue network? That is the suspicion of U.S. intelligence specialists. The 1981 CIA study of Wallenberg says that some four hundred people worked for him, and they were a dedicated, effective corps tested in fire. Then, thinking ahead, did the OSS plan to link up with Wallenberg's ambitious project for an American-assisted reconstruction of the war-ravaged country? During the siege of the city and in the midst of attempts to stop Auschwitz-bound transports, Wallenberg was said to have often discussed his idea for something like a Marshall Plan, which he envisioned as American-funded.

Unfortunately, the files at the National Archives give not a clue, and for six weeks after the Soviet capture of Wallenberg, nothing is declassified from the chronological file. What we are left with is the cryptic remark, written in 1982, by the chief of the document declassifying team — name blacked out — explaining why so many documents remain classified in the OSS file: "Classification is being maintained on the documents because of the possible adverse effect their release could have on the Wallenburg [sic] affair.]"

Over the years, American officials have publicly maintained that Wallenberg was not a spy and that he worked *with* the War Refugee Board, not *for* the American intelligence agency. Nevertheless, Wallenberg's name appears on the roster of those individuals, Americans and foreigners, who "worked for OSS in one capacity or another," as one archivist in charge of wartime records explains. The roster is a two-volume computer printout of some 2,000 names, kept in the U.S. National Archives in College Park, Maryland. Another archivist cautions that a name on the computer printout "does not absolutely mean that the person worked for OSS [though] the great majority of the roughly 2,000 people listed were OSS officers, agents and assets. The printout is the closest thing to an OSS roster."

"Wallenberg was not on the OSS payroll," says one former OSS officer familiar with the classified files. He was spending War Refugee Board money to rescue Jews, the officer argues, but as a Swedish diplomat and an independently wealthy man, he did not accept a U.S. salary. So, technically, he was not an OSS agent on contract, the officer concludes.

Asked if the OSS knew what Wallenberg was doing, the OSS veteran said, "Of course, yes. OSS had to know what Wallenberg was doing. And we knew."

Wallenberg was not the type of individual the OSS would have recruited for a monthly salary and have him sign a contract, says a veteran U.S. intelligence officer who recruited many agents and assets. "It would have been a bad mistake to offer money to the kind of person he was, an idealist and from a wealthy family," the officer says. "Thank God, Olsen didn't do that."

William Colby, the CIA director who began his career as an OSS operative in wartime Norway, told me a few months before his death in 1996, "Raoul Wallenberg was the kind of person we were interested in."

Whether Wallenberg was an agent in today's technical sense — contractually engaged and remunerated by the OSS — mattered little to the Americans at the time and even less to the Soviets. "The OSS people and others who fought that war on the intelligence front were not bureaucrats," CIA's Jameson said. "They were members of the same club. They knew and trusted one another. They would have laughed at our efforts nowadays to distinguish between an agent who got paid and someone who simply helped us out, inspired by his beliefs." Having examined the declassified OSS documents about Wallenberg, Jameson says he has no doubt that the Swede was "an important American intelligence asset, rare in that part of the world in those days."

The CIA does not feel the need to clarify its precursor's relationship to Wallenberg. But after discussing the declassified files used in this study, CIA historian Kevin Ruffner was authorized to say in 1995 that on the basis of those documents, "it is a reasonable conclusion that Raoul Wallenberg was of benefit to American intelligence."

Jameson, a former senior CIA official, interpreted the CIA statement as "a virtual admission that Wallenberg was used by us. It is a minimum statement the CIA can make and still be plausible." Jameson believes that in this case "the usual CIA supercaution" is enhanced by "considerations for the Wallenberg family and what the Zhirinovskys in Russia might do with a CIA statement."

Doomed from the Beginning

In his dealings in Budapest, Wallenberg did not reveal his American connection. Instead, he stressed that he worked for the Swedish crown, in line with his legation's emphasis that King Gustaf had a special humanitarian interest in the fate of Hungary's Jews.

For all his precautions, though, Wallenberg was a marked man from the moment he accepted the assignment. The Soviets were already planning their conquest of Hungary and wanted no Western heroes in their way. "The Soviets had one of their best espionage teams in Stockholm during the war, and they watched the U.S. embassy very closely," said James McCargar, who served at the time as a U.S. diplomat in Vladivostok. "They doubtless knew Olsen's OSS affiliation, and they must have known of Olsen's meetings with Wallenberg. Whether Wallenberg worked for OSS or the War Refugee Board, and whatever he did to save Jews, the Soviets had him pegged as an American agent before he left Stockholm."

A CIA officer who once headed the Hungarian desk added: "Wallenberg was a doomed man from the beginning. The fact that he was a heroic rescuer of Jews only strengthened the Soviet determination to get him. They hated heroes. I could just see how they laughed when Raoul told them that he saved Jews because he believed in humanity. As far as the Soviets were concerned, he was not a Swedish diplomat but an American imperialist agent — and that sealed his fate."

Moreover, Olsen had contacts with emissaries of SS Chief Heinrich Himmler offering the United States a separate peace — which was the deal the Soviets feared throughout the war. To Soviet intelligence officers trained in Stalinist paranoia, it was clear that Olsen was connected to Jacob Wallenberg who promoted such a separate peace, which in turn explained Olsen's decision to send Jacob's cousin Raoul to Budapest as part of a team working toward that separate peace.

Another puzzle in the Wallenberg story concerns his insistence on getting in touch with the highest Soviet authorities as soon as the first soldiers of the Red Army burst into the cellar where he took shelter during the siege of Budapest. Reluctantly, the soldiers agreed to escort him to headquarters where he spent the night. It is not known what transpired, beyond what Wallenberg told his Hungarian Jewish friends: he told the officer he met with that he wanted to go to Debrecen, the provincial city some 130 miles to the east then serving as the regional headquarters of the Red Army. He said he wanted to speak with the commanding officer and ask for food and medicine for the ghetto. It is probable that the Soviet officer in Budapest did not respond to his request but sent a report to Debrecen and perhaps Moscow, and waited for instructions.

Why was Wallenberg so eager to get in touch with the Soviets? The Swedish Legation did not ask him to. His superiors at the legation did not cross the river to Pest to take up contact with the Russians but waited on the Buda side. Colleague Lars Berg recalled that he had tried to convince Wallenberg that it was safer to stay in the legation building in Buda. After all, with Pest already cleared of German troops and Arrow Cross thugs, his rescue mission was completed. "But he refused," Berg wrote. "His place was with the Jewish people he was protecting in Pest."

His own personal safety was never one of Wallenberg's prime considerations. Was he anxious to get the new masters of Hungary to make sure they realized the urgent needs of "his" ghetto? Or did he also want to give his American friends a first-hand report about the Russian army?

During the siege of the city he had a map, complete with colored pins that he kept moving, which showed the Red Army's progress in and around Budapest. On one occasion during the fighting, he insisted on being driven to the top of Castle Hill, and he asked the local photographer he hired, Thomas Veres, to accompany him. Braving the constant heavy shelling, he checked out the Russian gun positions and asked Veres to photograph them. The adventure sounds like the collection of field intelligence.

On January 14, 1945 the Russians allowed Wallenberg to return to the cellar where he had stayed to pick up his belongings. But three Soviet soldiers on a motorcycle equipped with a sidecar followed his Studebaker.

Wallenberg told the Russians that before leaving for Debrecen, he wanted to visit the so-called international ghetto he had set up, and they raised no objections. Wallenberg had a chance to witness a few of his protégés, still wearing yellow stars, cautiously venturing outside.

Walking through the ghetto, Wallenberg ran into Laszlo Peto, the childhood friend from a summer camp in Switzerland who had greeted him shortly after his arrival six months earlier in Budapest. He told Peto about his Soviet escort and about his plan to go to Debrecen.

"He was supremely confident," Peto remembered in 1995, at age eighty-one, speaking on the telephone from his home in Sao Paulo,

Brazil. "He quipped about not being sure if he was a guest or a prisoner of the Russians. But it was a joke, an example of his wry humor. He could have escaped easily. His Russian escorts stood by their motorcycle, unconcerned that he spent more than half an hour walking around the ghetto."

Peto talked to the Russians and found them relaxed. "They didn't act like a prisoner's guards," Peto said. "It didn't occur to me to suggest to Wallenberg that he ought to cut loose from the Russians. But even if I had suggested that, I could not have persuaded him. He was not a person who could be swayed."

Nothing is known about what happened in Debrecen between Wallenberg and the Soviets. Perhaps Wallenberg did not meet anyone in authority in Debrecen. He might not have even reached Debrecen. But fellow prisoners have testified that by the end of January 1945 he was in Moscow's infamous Lubyanka Prison.

In 1948 the Budapest Jewish community commissioned a bronze statue of Wallenberg, and the city gave the memorial a prominent location. But the statue vanished the night before it was to be dedicated. If it had not been for the resourceful photographer Wallenberg had once hired, Thomas Veres, taking a picture of the statue as soon as it was put in place, people could doubt that it ever existed.

A Red Army unit was seen putting the statue on a truck, and it later turned up in Debrecen where the image of a nameless man slaying a snake stood for years in front of a medicine factory, and a tablet identified the meaning as "science defeating sickness." With their macabre sense of humor, perhaps Soviet officials selected Debrecen as the site for the statue because it was there that Wallenberg formally became their prisoner.

During the communist rule, one tablet in a shabby Budapest street was allowed to mention Wallenberg's name, and the carefully censored text identified him as a man who "saved tens of thousands of people" and "disappeared during the siege of Budapest." But until perestroika ended Hungary's status as a satellite, no book could be published about him in the People's Republic.

Hungarian Jews, rescued from deportation by Raoul Wallenberg at the Jozsefvaros railroad station on November 28, 1944 walk back to the International Ghetto of Budapest. The photo was taken by Thomas Veres from Wallenberg's car as they drove past the group. Photo credit: Thomas Veres.

Ambassador Per Anger of Sweden in his office, in front of the portrait of his friend and colleague, Raoul Wallenberg. Photo credit: courtesy of the U.S. Holocaust Memorial Museum Photo Archives.

Missed Opportunities

Sweden did not press hard for Wallenberg's return. When in 1946 the Swedish minister in Moscow, Staffan Soderblom, was given the rare privilege of an audience with Stalin, he inquired meekly about Wallenberg, but quickly volunteered that he himself believed that the Nazis had probably killed his fellow Swede. Stalin must have interpreted that remark as lack of Swedish interest in the matter. After all, the minister did not even ask him to acknowledge Soviet custody of Wallenberg. Never missing a chance to score a point, a few months later Deputy Foreign Minister Andrei Vishinsky sent a note to Soderblom to inform him that Wallenberg was not in the Soviet Union and he was "completely unknown to Soviet authorities." Soderblom's explanation was that he did not want to offend the Soviets. But posterity's judgment is that his offer of an excuse to the dictator helped seal Wallenberg's fate.

At various times, Soviet diplomats expressed their private view — as if there had been such a thing in the Soviet Union — that it was the Hungarian Nazis who killed him, or that he died in 1947 while under investigation in Lubyanka.

The statement that shocked Sweden was by Professor Alexander Myasnikov, chairman of the Soviet Academy of Medical Science and personal physician to Nikita Khrushchev, the party's leader at the time. In 1961 Myasnikov told Dr. Nanna Svartz, a professor of medicine at Stockholm's Karolinska Hospital, that Wallenberg was in poor health, a resident in a mental hospital in Moscow following a long hunger strike. Svartz asked that she be taken to see him immediately, but her visa ran out and could not be extended.

Upon her return to Sweden, she immediately alerted the prime minister who wrote to Khrushchev, requesting permission for a Swedish doctor to visit Wallenberg and to bring him home.

Khrushchev summoned Myasnikov who proceeded to deny his earlier statement to Svartz. Myasnikov claimed that he had been speaking German with Svartz, and she misunderstood him. As both professors were fluent in German, his denial does not seem to reflect anything other than the pressures that the Soviets must have put on him. Four years later, Myasnikov was dead, the victim of a heart attack, a favorite KGB method to do away with an unwanted person.

In 1978 Jan Kaplan, a Russian Jew whose application to emigrate to Israel was rejected, wrote a letter reassuring his daughter, already in Israel, that former political prisoners such as himself live long lives. As an example, he mentioned that in 1975 he had met a Swede in Butyrka Prison, a prisoner for more than thirty years yet in good health. Kaplan's revelation was published in newspapers across the world. As Wallenberg was the only Swede missing in the Soviet Union, it was assumed that Kaplan referred to him. Within days, Kaplan was arrested again. A year or so later he was released but died soon afterwards — of a heart attack.

According to a declassified State Department file, as late as 1979, during a visit to Stockholm, a Soviet deputy foreign minister by the name of Zemskov, used blunt language to warn the Swedish government to stop "irritating" Moscow with "gossip" and "forgeries" involving Russian Jews who claim to know something about Wallenberg's whereabouts. His Swedish opposite number replied that because the Soviets misled Sweden about Wallenberg up to 1957, the possibility cannot be excluded that "misunderstanding" or "confusion" about him still exists in the Soviet Union.

Zemskov interjected that it was not so remarkable that the Red Army took Wallenberg prisoner in Budapest, as there were strong indications that "Raoul Wallenberg was an American spy."

While arresting Wallenberg in violation of the convention on diplomatic immunity they signed many years earlier, the Soviets could reasonably believe that they captured an American intelligence asset. For the Soviets, all that mattered was that someone had worked for the Americans — or had lived in the West. McCargar remembers tracking the results of Stalin's order, issued shortly after the end of the war, summoning all his intelligence agents. "All those who returned were arrested," McCargar said. "Very few people survived from the Soviets' famous Red Orchestra that helped them win the war." In comparison with the number of people thus liquidated and in terms of their contribution to winning the war, Wallenberg's imprisonment was a small matter from a Soviet point of view, and, consequently, McCargar explains, the United States did not pay much attention to Wallenberg either. In Moscow and Budapest, McCargar recalls searching for plenty of Americans. "But Wallenberg was a Swede," he said. "I didn't know he had worked for us."

The consensus of people concerned with Raoul Wallenberg's fate is that Jacob Wallenberg, head of the family, made a mistake in turning down President Harry Truman's offer to ask the Soviets to release Raoul Wallenberg. "We Swedes will take care of him," is said to have been Jacob Wallenberg's reply to Truman, adding that Raoul was probably no longer alive anyway. The Swedish tycoon also explained to Truman that Swedes have to be very careful what they and anyone on their behalf tell the Russians because little Sweden does a lot of business with its mighty neighbor.

It made no difference to the Soviets whether it was the OSS or the similarly clandestine War Refugee Board that funded Wallenberg's mission and received his reports. From their point of view, he was a spy, pure and simple, and he worked for the American imperialists. The routine attempt to turn him into a Soviet agent failed, which is hinted at in the foreign ministry papers that post-communist Russia released to his next of kin. What might well have clinched his fate was his belonging to the fabulously wealthy Wallenberg clan. "Had his name been other than Wallenberg, the Soviets would have let him come home a long time ago," said one Swede, a member of the Stockholm committee organized to lobby for Wallenberg's release.

For years, U.S. intelligence believed that the Soviets were certain that Raoul had been acting on orders from cousin Jacob Wallenberg who endorsed German nationalism and who argued that Anglo-American insistence on Germany's unconditional surrender was a huge mistake. The OSS file on Jacob Wallenberg and his numerous German Nazi connections outlined his banking-commercial-industrial empire that pocketed vast profits doing business with the Germans.

But the OSS was not blind-sighted by the Soviets' crude Marxist determinism that maintained that class and financial interests define consciousness and character, including Raoul Wallenberg's. Olsen and the OSS recognized what the Soviets could not or would not: Raoul Wallenberg was a rebel in his family and an intrepid innovator in confronting a totalitarian system. ("In Sweden and within his family, Raoul was an odd man out," a Swedish diplomat who spent years studying the case once told me.) Choosing him, an untried, rash, and unabashedly ambitious youth, for an assignment as impossible as rescuing Jews in Nazi-occupied Hungary was perhaps the most inspired hire of a gifted outsider since the British dispatch of T.E. Lawrence to stir up the Arab revolt against the Ottoman empire during the First World War.

The two governments that could have felt obliged to swap Wallenberg for a captured Soviet spy — a well-established cold war practice favored by the Soviets because of its implication of moral equivalence — decided against it. "Sweden doesn't do such things," Foreign Minister Osten Unden primly declared in 1959. A senior CIA official recalls hearing "some talk" in the late 1950s and early 1960s about swapping Wallenberg, but the idea was rejected and did not reach the status of a recommendation by the spy agency. The fear was that such an offer would have implied a vindication of Moscow's contention that Wallenberg had been an American spy. The official explained, "We did not offer a swap in cases where we felt we had sufficient grounds to contend that the person was not engaged in spying for us."

Each of the two governments that should have moved to rescue Wallenberg had its own strong reasons not to come clean about his wartime role. Worried about denting its shield of neutrality, Sweden would not want to acknowledge that it had allowed U.S. intelligence to use a Swedish diplomat working out of a Swedish legation. Fighting the Cold War's propaganda battle, the United States was loath to let Moscow score a point that the West's humanitarian hero had been a U.S. intelligence asset. Convinced of the truth of their charge, the Soviets thought Washington's demurral a sanctimonious lie, another annoying instance of America's claim to moral superiority.

Sighted in the Gulag

Over the years, dozens of people claimed to have seen Wallenberg as a gulag prisoner, or heard about him from others who claimed to have seen him. Some appear to be genuine sightings. For instance, Victoria Pope's research identified a number of credible witnesses who testified that they had met Wallenberg in the notorious Vladimir Prison, some 150 miles east of Moscow, in the 1950s, and others, such as three Polish prisoners, who remembered him from a Siberian camp.

But many, perhaps even most of the sightings, are hearsay and conjecture, or reflect wishful thinking. Since the 1970s Wallenberg has been recognized throughout the world as a hero of the Second World War, and human nature being what it is, people want to have something to do with him as a way of identifying with his tragedy or pointing to their own sufferings in the gulag, or both. Many sightings by former prisoners are based on misunderstandings or are fabrications, in the hope of fame or contacts or even pecuniary gain, or for the purpose of telling a story. Spending time in the gulag is not necessarily conducive to a great respect for truth.

Some of the sightings originate with Russian officialdom that has not given up the Stalinist love of melodrama. For instance, one recently declassified CIA report reveals that in March 1983, at three o'clock in the morning in Geneva, a Soviet diplomat by the name of Sasha Pavlov banged at the door of an acquaintance of his, a wealthy Norwegian. Pavlov woke up the Norwegian to relate to him what he had just heard from a source he described as reliable: Wallenberg died a few days earlier somewhere near Moscow where he had been under house arrest.

Was the passing on of the information a rare case of early glasnost — a scrap of privileged news finding its way out of the Soviet Union? Was Pavlov, widely suspected to be working for the KGB, trying to prove his bona fides to a Western contact, or at least his helpfulness? Or was the purpose a diversionary maneuver to create commotion and confusion among Westerners interested in Wallenberg who only two years earlier had been given honorary American citizenship? Or was the KGB's idea behind the predawn call an attempt to give the final burial to a man who should not have lived in the first place?

There are no clear answers to these questions. Mystery also shrouds the reasons for Khrushchev's decision to stop denying that Wallenberg had been imprisoned in the USSR and to allow the issuance of his death certificate that later the Russians would acknowledge was a forgery. But why didn't that great denouncer of Stalinist terror release its victim, and why did he silence his own personal physician, Professor Myasnikov, who had given away to a Swedish colleague the state secret of Wallenberg's confinement in a mental hospital?

Hungarian historians do not believe the official Russian claim that his files have disappeared, either burned by people responsible for his incarceration or lost in that vast filing system that tracked millions of prisoners in the seventy years of the Soviet empire. "The Soviet system of accounting for political prisoners was incredibly meticulous," says Karoly Kapronczay, who in the early 1990s headed a special commission, appointed by Hungary's first non-communist government in four decades, to find Hungarians missing in the gulag. "Every interrogation, every document showing a transfer from one prison to another, and every medical examination however cursory — every piece of paper about an important prisoner — exists at least in triplicate, stored in three different archives: in the prison's, the KGB's, and the Interior Ministry's. We found traces of almost everyone the Russians judged important, and even some people we hadn't known about. The system was obsessed with documenting all of its enemies, and administrators were afraid to throw out a single scrap of official paper."

Kapronczay and his investigators even found the voluminous files complete with the record of the interrogations, a death certificate, and the precise location of the ashes of a Hungarian prime minister in the 1920s, Count Istvan Bethlen. Kidnapped by the NKVD in 1945 in Budapest, even his presence in the Soviet Union was flatly denied prior to the historians' study.

Within two years, Hungarian investigators were able to locate the files of dozens of their compatriots who had been army officers, government officials, and influential citizens before ending up in the gulag. But they had to have been judged important to be documented. The files do not account for the 20,000 soldiers fighting alongside the Germans who disappeared during the war, and some 10,000 civilians the Soviets kidnapped after they occupied Hungary and whose names and burial places the Soviets did not think needed to be recorded.

The Hungarians did not ask about Wallenberg. "That is the job for the Swedes," explained one top official in Budapest. "He was one of their citizens, not ours." Nor could the Hungarian commission find out anything about Vilmos Langfelder, a Budapest Jew who served as Wallenberg's chauffeur and was arrested with him. "When we mentioned Langfelder's name," says Kapronczay, "the Russians said they had no documents mentioning him, and they made it very clear that they don't want to talk about him at all. We could not find out anything. They simply froze at the mere mention of Wallenberg's name — or his chauffeur's."

Something in the Wallenberg story made the Soviet state clam up and cover the tracks, far more so than in the cases of its other prominent victims. The attitude persists among Soviet loyalists today. After all, following his initial denial echoing his predecessors, Mikhail Gorbachev acknowledged the truth about the Soviets massacring tens of thousands of Polish officers in the Katyn forest — a far more damaging admission because of its impact on Russia's relations with its Polish neighbor. However, to date not one page of the transcript of what Wallenberg told his interrogators has been released, not a single medical report, not one piece of paper revealing how his captors evaluated his case. Not one official who dealt with him, or supervised others who dealt with him, has come forth with a testimony or offered some recollection of his behavior as a prisoner.

The KGB's tight hold on Wallenberg might have had something to do with the fact that a number of top Soviet leaders happened to be personally involved in Wallenberg's arrest. In 1945, Leonid Brezhnev held a high position in the Red Army unit responsible for security operations in Hungary. Another reason for what the Germans call *nicht anruhen* —

not to touch — the Wallenberg case was that the marshal who commanded the Red Army in Hungary at the time was Kliment Voroshilov,
later head of state. Nikolai Bulganin, Khrushchev's first partner in the
post-Stalin experiment in collective leadership, signed off on the order
for the kidnapping, as he was deputy defense minister at the time.

As for the Nazis, the archives they left behind barely mention
Wallenberg's name. Why should they? He was an anomaly: an enemy
they did not kill even though it was within their power to do so. So he
managed to hold back a few thousand Jews from the gas chambers. But
why report on what he did? He was an insignificant obstacle in Nazi
Germany's struggle to wipe out the Jewish race.

A Murder Trial Scripted in Budapest

The most bizarre attempt to declare Wallenberg dead took place in
the People's Republic of Hungary. As described by Maria Ember in her
book published in Budapest in 1992, with a title that translates *They
Tried to Blame Us*, the KGB had first wanted a trial to prove that the
Arrow Cross had killed Wallenberg. Ember, a prominent Hungarian
journalist, found the documents that made use of confessions by convicted Arrow Cross murderers prior to their executions. But the winds
shifted. The year before his death in 1953, Stalin decided to stage a show
trial to move against the Jews, and he or someone else developed the idea
of involving Wallenberg.

In the late summer of 1952 the Hungarian secret police arrested Pal
Szalai, the disillusioned Arrow Cross official and Wallenberg's most valuable recruit. The interrogation began with a Soviet officer telling Szalai
in the folksy style favored by senior KGB types, that a brick fell on his
head, dropping from very high up, and that the impact usually kills.
Only a doctor intervening quickly could save his life.

It took some time for Szalai to understand the meaning of the parable: the government decided that he was to serve as a star witness in a
show trial and that only his full confession could save his life. After torture and mind-altering drugs administered over several months, he
learned about his role. As he explained in 1989 to Ember, he was scripted

to testify that in the last days of the Russian siege of Budapest he witnessed two Jewish leaders standing over Wallenberg's body, their revolvers still smoking after they shot him dead. The stage chosen for the murder was the cellar of the American Embassy in downtown Budapest.

A few months later, in January 1953, the Hungarian secret police arrested two Jewish leaders it selected as Wallenberg's murderers. The arrests followed the TASS report on the disclosure in Moscow of "terrorist doctors" plotting with "the Jewish bourgeois-nationalist" Joint Distribution Committee, then as now a respected Jewish charity headquartered in New York. A third Hungarian Jewish leader was arrested in April, a month after Stalin's death.

But the communist authorities could not decide, Ember discovered, how large to make "the monster trial." At one point, Jozsef Cardinal Mindszenty was to be involved, as well as some former high-ranking secret police officers of Jewish origin, including the chief of the secret police, accused of being a Zionist spy. The Hungarian plan was to produce a local version of the Soviet "doctors' plot" which was designed to prove that the doctors were trying to kill Stalin as part of a vast, worldwide Zionist-imperialist conspiracy.

The Budapest trial was to show that Jews had killed their best friend, Wallenberg, and thus the Soviets were innocent of arresting him. It was an unbelievable construct, worthy of the Soviet leader who shortly before World War II eliminated the most talented men on his general staff as German spies and who in the course of his long life only trusted one man, Hitler, whom he expected to live up to his pledge not to attack the Soviet Union.

Confessions were soon extracted from two of the Jewish leaders. The third, severely tortured because he refused to confess, died, probably due to injuries from torture. He was a much-decorated army captain in the First World War who insisted on wearing his uniform during the Second World War even though as a Jew he was expressly forbidden to do so.

A large number of Jews, some active in communal life and others in the communist party, were also to be involved in the trial that was supposed to start in late 1953. Though preparations for a show trial in

Budapest proceeded even after Stalin's death in March, eventually his heirs canceled plans to extend to Hungary the doctors' plot, which Khrushchev cited in his secret speech in February 1956 as an example of Stalin's paranoia and "an excess of the cult of personality."

No Heroes Allowed

The failure of Soviet investigators to identify an ulterior motive they would accept must have infuriated them. "The Russians could not accept that a Swede would risk his life for Jewish people," Ambassador Anger said. "Such a thing just wasn't in their dictionary."

Marxism-Leninism concedes no possibility of bourgeois selflessness or classlessness, and Stalin's own brand of folk wisdom relied on the corruptibility of man. Had Wallenberg acknowledged having sought Jewish money or engaged in spying for the United States — or even for Germany — the Soviets would have understood and might have eventually released him. His refusal to spy for the Soviet Union galled them. But what might have sealed his fate was his insistence on the purity of his motive. Stalin hated heroes, as did his brainchild, the secret police. Gulag survivors say that prisoners the KGB derisively called "heroes" were always in for the harshest of punishments.

When in the early 1980s I discussed the Wallenberg case with a senior Soviet diplomat (and reputed KGB colonel) in Washington, Boris Davydov, he acknowledged that the Swede had been a heroic rescuer of Jews, but insisted on his having been an American spy as well. When reminded that the United States and the Soviet Union were allies at that time, he lost his temper. Raising his voice, he charged that the Wallenberg affair was "blown all out of proportion" to serve as ammunition for anti-Soviet propaganda. In the heat of the argument, he allowed himself the liberty of straying from the Party line. He conceded that Wallenberg might not have died in 1947 and suggested that the Swede might well have been killed later, in prison or a labor camp, "as so many other people were killed in those days." But he was an American spy, wasn't he, Davydov returned to his original point, so why is the U.S. government so self-righteous that it does not acknowledge that fact?

The Soviet diplomat had other grievances as well. "Isn't it indecently disproportionate," he asked, "to insist on talking about one man while millions perished? Isn't it unjust to the memory of the millions of martyrs to raise above them a single individual and manufacture a hero out of him? Don't people do that in this case because there is an opportunity to beat up on the Soviets who themselves sacrificed so much to defeat Nazism? Isn't such a public relations exercise also a gross distortion of what happened in World War II, weighting history in favor of just one individual?"

What the Soviet diplomat and the system he represented always rejected was that it is precisely the individual who mattered and will always matter, and that defying the might of a totalitarian government comes down ultimately to the decision of one person. In Wallenberg's case, it was his private, sovereign folly of acting on his own — regardless of the governments he opposed and represented — that saved tens of thousands of lives and exempted them from what Marxists call "the objective forces of history."

"We Could Have Had Him Back"

Among Swedish government officials charged with keeping track of the Wallenberg case, the long-time unofficial consensus has been that he died in July 1947 or so. (Officially, the line was that "we do not know.") That was the date originally communicated to the Swedish government in 1957 in a diplomatic note signed by Andrey Gromyko, the grim Stalinist stalwart then deputy foreign minister, who claimed that the cause of death was a heart attack. For more than four decades, the Gromyko note constituted what the Russians called "the final and definitive answer." Then on November 27, 2000, a spokesman for President Vladimir Putin's Kremlin made front page news in the Western world by announcing that the Soviet secret police shot Wallenberg in Lubyanka prison on July 17, 1947. The spokesman, probably chosen because of his credibility in the West, was Aleksandr Yakovlev, a highly regarded liberal, once a key aide to Mikhail Gorbachev in the heyday of glasnost and the director under Putin of the government commission on exonerating vic-

tims of the Stalin era. Yakovlev used the word "murder" and characterized his statement "the absolute truth." His sources, he said, were top
former KGB officers "who knew everything."

Yakovlev preempted the publication of a long-awaited report by a
Swedish-Russian research commission scheduled for January 2001. After
nine years of work by more than a dozen scholars, two reports were published, reflecting the failure of the two teams — and their governments
— to agree on fundamental facts. The Swedish side declined to endorse
the Russians' key conclusion about Wallenberg's murder and expressed
its hope that one day the Russians will come up with documentary evidence concerning Wallenberg's fate. Others called Yakovlev's assertion
yet another lie, designed to stop further research on Wallenberg's life in
the gulag past 1947. Bluntly put, in 2000 the Russians said that, yes, we
killed Wallenberg, but then we killed the man who ordered the execution, Viktor Abakumov of the NKVD, and now we admitted everything
— now isn't that enough to put the matter to rest?

The Russians voiced anger that the Swedes — and other Western students of the Wallenberg case — would not accept their word at its face
value. Apparently, the Russians had hoped that their dramatic confession, which high-ranking Swedish sources believe was approved and perhaps even initiated by Putin, would put an end to the probe that dragged
on and continued to mar Russia's image in the Western world.

The Swedish members of the commission tried to interview everyone
who might have known about Wallenberg's fate but they did not push
hard in gaining access to them — or in getting the story out of those they
did interview. "It would have been undiplomatic and un-Swedish to do
so," a Swedish commission member told me. For instance, the Swedish
team accepted the Russian demand that its interviews with Russian witnesses be conducted in the presence of Russian government officials,
including a representative from the secret police now called FSB. "The
Swedish inquiry has been perfunctory and bureaucratic," said one American scholar who observed Swedish diplomats in action. "They were
tired of the case."

But three independent researchers attached to the Swedish team —

Marvin Makinen, Susan Mesinai, and Susanne Berger — broke new ground. Their findings strongly suggest that Wallenberg survived well beyond 1947. Berger greatly upset the Swedish Foreign Ministry by finding evidence in Swedish archives of repeated Russian overtures to swap Wallenberg for Soviet spies. On the basis of archival records, she charged that the Swedish government was hesitant, if not unwilling, to advocate fully the cause of Wallenberg's rescue from Soviet captivity. Her research reveals that the Soviets first approached the Swedes about an exchange in 1946 and then again initiated a two-year series of informal discussions on the subject that the Swedish side chose to break off in 1957. The most recent Soviet initiative uncovered by Berger involved Otto Danielsson, a senior official in the Security Police — the Swedish equivalent of the FBI — who participated in secret negotiations with the Soviets seeking the release of Stig Wennerstroem, a Swedish air force colonel arrested in 1963 and convicted as a Soviet spy. In 1966, the Swedes refused to pursue the matter of a swap and insisted on treating the two cases separately. (In a private conversation with me in 2000 Berger added that Wennerstroem received a pardon in the 1970s and lives as a free man in Sweden.)

Berger seems to explain the facts behind Per Anger's anguished words: "Raoul's imprisonment is the fault of the Swedish government. We did not fight for him the way we should have. *We could have had him back.*"

Says Tom Lantos, the Hungarian-born U.S. Congressman from California whose wife Annette was saved by Wallenberg and who spearheaded the campaign to make him an honorary citizen of the United States in 1981: "The Swedes have been spineless."

The truth of the Wallenberg case eludes us. We are stranded in between the extreme caution exercised by Sweden's Foreign Ministry and the deceptions spun by the Russian "special services." Both Swedish and Russian officials sound pleased when they say at the end of every discussion that key facts remain unknown. "It may be that we'll never find out the truth," more than one Swedish diplomat confided to me, without a trace of regret. When pressed, Russian officials say that the documents have been burned or were lost, and the people who would remember

Wallenberg are all dead, or their memories can no longer be trusted. Both Swedes and Russians suggest that the world ought to drop the case, and they ask essentially the same questions: Why waste time trying to ascertain whether he died in 1947 or later? What difference does it make? Why do we want to know? Why do we have an obsessive interest in finding out how Wallenberg lived the latter part of his life?

The belief in Wallenberg's survival has been as hard to give up as the article of the common faith that claims that sooner or later good people must be rewarded for their good deeds. Yet after the anniversary of his kidnapping passed the half-century mark in 1995, the odds for his survival seem increasingly implausible. The hope that he may be alive was quietly abandoned in Western political circles in the early 1990s, a year or two after the collapse of the Soviet Union and after a number of approaches to the Kremlin's post-Soviet rulers led nowhere.

Ambassador Anger protested as late as 1995. Over the years he had no doubt that his old friend was still alive, hidden somewhere in Russia. He was confirmed in that feeling in 1989 when he accompanied to Moscow Wallenberg's next of kin, invited by the new Russian government. Anger's evidence: a number of sightings he considered credible and the absence of a valid death certificate, which is as much of a must in Russia as a birth certificate.

Anger's theory was that in 1957, or a little earlier, the Soviet government decided that it would be best to write off Wallenberg as a victim of Stalinist terror, so the KGB was ordered to provide him with a new name, a new identity, and they stashed him away in a remote location. The post-Stalin leadership was wary of having him killed; instead, they decided that "Wallenberg" was dead.

A thoughtful diplomat with many connections, Anger would not say how much of his theory was his own hypothesis and how much was based on privileged information from sources he would not divulge. What he suggested was a tragic reverse of the romance of the Count of Monte-Cristo, the fugitive who rebuilt his life and gave himself a new identity after his miraculous escape from an island prison.

Retired from diplomatic service in 1979 — his last post was in Canada — in 1989 private citizen Anger persuaded his old friend

German Chancellor Helmut Kohl to telephone Mikhail Gorbachev, then the Soviet president. Anger was invited to listen on an extension phone how the savvy German made his appeal through an interpreter: "Why do you keep Wallenberg? Let that old man go."

Gorbachev did not answer the question, Anger said. (Nor did Leonid Brezhnev before him, Anger added, after Jimmy Carter raised the issue with him during their summit meeting in Vienna, the first American president to do so.) When Anger went to see Gorbachev in the Kremlin and presented the same appeal, Gorbachev showed "no interest in Wallenberg." Analyzing the Soviet leader's words and body language, the veteran Swedish diplomat concluded: Gorbachev implied that he had no power over the KGB; he intimated that he could not force the KGB to deliver Wallenberg. But, Anger stressed, Gorbachev did *not* say — and it seemed to the Swedish diplomat that he carefully avoided saying — that Wallenberg was dead.

Boris Yeltsin's presidency opened new possibilities to investigate Wallenberg's fate. That chance existed in the first two years of the new Russia, Anger said, but then the KGB closed ranks, restored its control, and "the window closed." Anger perceived the KGB as far more tightly knit than the Mafia, with its officers protecting one another as if bound by an oath; it is an organization above the law and beyond the president's control, and it can still keep Wallenberg as its prisoner despite what the big boss says in Moscow, especially when the boss is not as awe-inspiring as some of his predecessors.

"We don't know where he is now or what his mental state is," Anger said in 1995. "But the Raoul I knew was strong. He could be alive today." Born in 1913, a year later than Wallenberg, Anger made it his business to visit gulag survivors of about the same age, and he found many of them "surprisingly resilient," and in some cases stronger than their contemporaries who were never imprisoned.

If Wallenberg's capture was prompted by Stalin's paranoia, why didn't his heirs who denounced his legacy let Wallenberg go? Why do they still refuse to release whatever is left of him? While the Berlin Wall tumbled and the Kremlin owned up to Stalin's responsibility for the massacre of tens of thousands of Polish officers in the Katyn forest, it is still a deep state secret what Wallenberg said to his interrogators, and what the jails, camps, and psychiatric institutes where he was held recorded about his behavior. Could the KGB, obsessive about keeping records and sending copies to central filing systems, be telling the truth when saying that all documents having to do with Wallenberg have been destroyed? "Never!" thundered the normally low-key Anger, "Impossible!"

In 2002 Anger died, carrying some weighty secrets to his grave. Several of us who spent time interviewing him and even received some confidences from him are convinced that he knew far more about Wallenberg's fate than he let us in on. He gave hints and he offered hypotheses that he insisted were personal, but he would not suspend his code of silence as a Swedish diplomat. The U.S. government may one day declassify all the OSS files that will reveal the full story of the assignments Wallenberg volunteered for in addition to his rescue mission. Similarly, the Russians may eventually divulge their reason for arresting him — whether they expected his powerful family to ransom him or if they considered him a master spy they might eventually "turn" to work for them. One day we may also learn if the Russians had an overwhelming reason to keep him captive — or, equally possible, if there was no such reason, and he was the victim of bureaucratic indecision and delay, the routine everyday brutality of an inhuman system.

A Prisoner's Tale

Alive or dead, says folk wisdom, there is no third way. The Second World War proved otherwise. In the spring of 1945, as survivors began to return to what had been their homes in Hungary, my family received a message from a childhood friend of my mother's favorite brother Anti that he would visit us on a certain day but that he was a bearer of sad news. He arrived with tears in his eyes and wasted no time to tell us his story.

With my parents and some dozen relatives gathered around him, he explained how he and Anti had found themselves in the same labor battalion, digging tank traps in northern Hungary from dawn to darkness, day after day. In late 1944, a group of them decided to escape. Hearing the sounds of artillery exchanges all day, they suspected that the Russians could not be too far. The plan was to disappear in the woods and reach the Russian army or the Slovak guerrillas in the Carpathian mountains, and join them to fight the Germans.

One moonless night ten Jews made their break. But they were spotted when still within shouting distance from the camp, and their Hungarian military guards ran after them, shooting. But then firing began from another direction, probably from the Russians, and the Hungarian soldiers retreated. As silence eventually descended, the fugitives huddled. Two men were missing, and one man was dead. "I focused my flashlight on his face, and it was Anti," the childhood friend said, with tears streaming down his face, and everyone in the room wept.

The friend said he quickly dug a shallow grave, buried Anti, and said Kaddish, the prayer for the dead. Then the seven of them speedily made their way north. Soon, they ran into Russian troops who threatened to shoot them. One of the fugitives who knew some Russian explained that they were Jews and wanted to fight the Nazis. The Russians laughed at them derisively. They were all taken prisoner, forced to dig trenches. After a few months they were told that the Red Army liberated Hungary and they could go home.

There was no reason to doubt the friend's account. A quiet, unassuming man, he had been a schoolmate of Anti's, known to most everyone in the family since his childhood.

My mother Anna kept asking him: "Are you sure that the man you buried was Anti? Are you sure?"

He said he wished he were less sure.

But miracles do happen. Two years later, a postcard came from an unspecified location in the Soviet Union. A rubber stamp stated that it was sent from a labor camp, and the signature was Anti's. We could not believe what we read. (Officially, the Soviets had repatriated all Hungarian prisoners of war, but everyone in the country knew that it was just another Soviet lie.) The handwriting was a little shaky, but the names of family members he greeted — starting with his mother, followed by his wife, his three sisters, two brothers, and three in-laws —

proved beyond doubt that the writer was Anti. He was alive! My mother wept uncontrollably, this time from joy. She said she felt — she somehow *knew* — that Anti's friend must have buried another man.

A few more postcards came, and the text was almost identical: after greeting family members, he assured us that he was in excellent health and that he was well taken care of. Finally, in 1948, we received an official notice, specifying the time of Anti's arrival in Budapest.

At least twenty of us from the family went to welcome him at the Eastern Railroad Station that we found surrounded by hundreds of policemen. We were told to wait outside. We arrived more than an hour early, but hundreds of others had come even earlier, and we spoke to families that had been waiting for days, with relatives taking turns. Soon there were thousands of people. We found out that regardless what the official notice said, the time of a POW's return was uncertain, and there was no one to ask for a list of those on any particular train.

The crowd formed two parallel lines in a serpentine path in the broad, square-like space that extended from the station's exit doors to the streetcar station. After a train finally arrived and the POWs came out, they passed in between the two lines, so relatives, who kept shouting the names of the people they looked for, could scrutinize each of them.

Recognition was not easy. The returnees were emaciated, even though, as we later found out, they had been fed plenty of potatoes and bacon the preceding week or two. Their cheeks were sunken, heads shaved, and eyes listless. Most of the tattered clothes they wore had once been military uniforms that were invariably much too large for them. Only some returnees had the strength to shout the names of their family members or announce their own names. Most of them trudged through the serpentine path silently, with their heads down, exhausted, and weighed down by their backpacks or bundles. They looked as if they had been ordered to go to their own funerals. When relatives identified one of them, the same words rang out, again and again: "Is it really you?" and then the POW's name was repeated many times, for reassurance.

Hours passed, and another train came, unloading hundreds of men. We screamed Anti's name, and we searched the faces which after a while seemed to merge into one expressionless, anonymous composite. We feared that we would not be able to identify Anti or that his train might come on another day.

Suddenly my father Aladar jumped out of the queue, and hugged and kissed someone who to the rest of us did not at all look like Anti. He was a bent old man, not the young blade in his mid-thirties we had known, the best dancer in the family who had performed on stage as a song-and-dance comedian. His face did not suggest the clownish character we remembered, and he did not seem to recognize any of us. But my father insisted that it was Anti, and each of us shouted "Anti!" as we hugged him and kissed him. He looked at us sadly. At last he spoke. He asked, "Where is my mother?"

We recognized his voice that had the lilt of our accent, a singsong peculiar to our region in northeastern Hungary. He was, thank God, our Anti. But he still did not seem to know our names, which made my mother cry.

He clutched his battered little bundle and would not let us carry it for him. With growing despair, we repeated our names to him as we walked together to the streetcar. It took a long time, several hours, after we reached our apartment and my mother served him his favorite caraway soup — and reminded him that it was warm, not hot, just the way he always liked it — before he gradually began to remember us, repeating our names one by one.

Huddling around him and talking to him about pleasant memories from before the war, the family patiently waited for him to put together a sentence, other than his question about his mother's whereabouts, which he repeated a few times, getting evasive replies. A day or maybe several days, passed before he realized where he was. It was after the family decided that "he was coming back to normal," someone, probably his eldest brother, was chosen to tell him that his mother was no more, reduced to a puff of smoke over a place called Auschwitz.

Siberian Fantasy

In 1944 Laszlo Peto, whose father served as vice president of the wartime Jewish Council in Budapest, had the assignment of keeping in touch with Eichmann's office every day. He could never recover from the trauma of his powerlessness in working with the Germans and the charges of collaboration that followed. The Jewish Council or *Judenrat*, set up because Eichmann insisted on dealing with one group, was excoriated by some Jews after the war because of its alleged "subservience" to the Nazis. Council members countered that they satisfied some of the Nazis' demands in the hope that they could avert or at least postpone the catastrophe of deportation, and they pointed to their partial successes.

Living in Sao Paulo, Brazil, attorney Peto published a novel in Hungarian in 1982, with a title that translates as *The Endless March* and with the subtitle *Requiem*. "I poured my memories of the war into a novel," he told me in 1995. "But only the format and some of the stories are novelistic." He said he had hoped that by writing such a book he would "get rid of the oppressive dreams about the past," even though as "an amateur psychiatrist" he knew he could never get rid of them completely. "I believe that the schizophrenic mass murders of our terrible century cannot be analyzed rationally, with a sane mind," he said, explaining his protagonist's madness. "They can only be approached on yet another level of schizophrenia."

Much of *The Endless March* is undisguised autobiography, and its protagonist is unmistakably Peto, placed by his brother — which in the language of the psyche equals himself — in an insane asylum in Brazil where he landed after the war. But he thinks he is in prison, and he attempts to answer what he thinks must be the charges against him. Each chapter is a letter to an all-powerful committee that he believes is investigating his case. He will reveal all he knows, he promises. But first the committee must satisfy his three requests, each requiring communication with the dead: to call witnesses who, he is certain, will exonerate him of any wrongdoing while working for the Jewish Council, to arrange a response to his letters addressed to his long-dead, beloved wife, and last and most critical to find a way to discover what happened to his childhood friend and wartime ally Wallenberg.

The protagonist testifies how his Jewish Council tried to save Jews. He admits errors of judgment; he weeps for the people whose deportation he was unable to stop. Then in a chiaroscuro dream which he finds far more vivid than the brilliantly colored tropical reality that surrounds him in Brazil, the protagonist ends up in an underground Siberian sanatorium where the KGB kept its most important secret prisoners, most of them old Bolsheviks purged by Stalin and believed to have been executed long ago. One of them is Nikolai Bukharin, once a rival to Stalin, who is still committed to the triumph of the great Bolshevik experiment. "Neither the tactical mistakes of the leaders, nor their various intrigues to gain power or to keep it matter much," Bukharin hectors his visitor, as if addressing a Party forum. "What matters is that the future is ours, in line with the laws of history's progress."

The protagonist counters that history has no laws because "it is a series of unique events that cannot be foreseen and will not repeat themselves." Every great ideology from Marx to Spengler and Toynbee is "a myth dressed up as science" — as myth is humankind's response to questions it cannot answer. "We cannot tolerate the vacuum of doubt," he tells Bukharin, "we produce multicolored, reassuring myths that exempt us from the need to think."

The finale of the fantasy is a visit with Wallenberg whom the protagonist finds crouching, with face to the wall, in the corner of a white-tiled room where he lives by himself. He is silent and barely moves all day long, the doctor explains. Only his hand caressing a scrap of black velvet seems to be alive.

Wallenberg shows no interest in his visitor and does not recognize his old friend whom he first met when they were both in their teens. He does not react to words recalling their days together in Switzerland and Hungary. He shows no sign of understanding, no indication of intelligence. He is one of the living dead.

"Bandits, heartless, degenerate murderers — what have you done with him?" the protagonist cries out, and he breaks down and cannot stop sobbing.

There is a whimper from Wallenberg, "whose narrow shoulders and skeletal back trembles" and who seems to "thrust his head into the concrete wall, as if looking for a place to hide."

"Do you want to change someone's fate?" asks the Russian doctor softly, her hands on the protagonist's shoulders. "Leave him in his own world, about which we know nothing. Don't try to jerk him back into the hopeless present."

A Camp of Silence?

Peto's terrifying vision springs from his conviction that Wallenberg not only survived many years after the date the Soviets claimed he died, but that like other victims of the Soviet system, he spent many years in so-called psychiatric institutions, isolated from other inmates, and administered mind-altering drugs. Peto turned into fiction his recurrent nightmare that echoed his insistent, intolerable, innermost certainty about what he thinks must have happened to his friend.

The substance of his conjecture does not issue from some "multi-colored ideology" that the old Bolshevik Bukharin or an equally inventive anti-Bolshevik might have devised. Peto's vision is grounded instead in the monochromatic, routine brutality of everyday Soviet practice and in his generation's experience of fearing the worst forms of inhumanity by totalitarian systems, only to discover later, as my Uncle Anti used to say, that "the truth is invariably several degrees worse than could be imagined by an ordinary, rational person."

To accept as a likely fact that Wallenberg's captors destroyed his mind before they destroyed his body amounts to conceding that the world belongs to the Hitlers and the Stalins, just as they always claimed it does. Though such an acknowledgement is a "normal" adjustment to an insane world, by non-totalitarian standards it is a form of madness similar to the one that afflicts Peto's protagonist. Such madness is an impeccably rational reaction to the genocide that the Nazis nearly completed, as well as to the fate of the unforgettable outsider who foiled their genocidal plan in a way no one else did.

In a world dominated by Hitler and Stalin, a defiant soul like Wallenberg could not be allowed to live for long. Heirs such as Nikita Khrushchev and Leonid Brezhnev, eager to win Western approval for the Soviet system, feared that his release would cause too much negative publicity. As for Gorbachev and Yeltsin, they were apparently never told that Wallenberg's fate was the kind of Western priority that would have justified a stern direct order to the KGB to find that Swede — or else. One thoughtful American diplomat in the position to know confessed to me: "We never 'educated' the Russians to believe that 'coming clean' on the Wallenberg case could be to their benefit."

"For many years, Raoul has been in a 'camp of silence,' the kind of super-secret camp where the inmates are treated humanely but no one is ever released or even transferred to another camp," one well-connected European activist engaged in a search for Wallenberg for many years told me. Citing a confidential source from one of the Baltic states, the activist contended that at least up until the late 1980s, Wallenberg lived in such a sanatorium-like institution, along with other aging foreigners, mostly Polish officers who were spared in Stalin's Katyn massacre, as well as a few Germans, Italians, and Hungarians, all of whom were allowed to live out their natural lives.

Sober, skeptical, and unburdened by gratitude to a man who should be their national hero, Swedish diplomats raise their eyebrows and curl their lips when hearing such reports. They say they have no confirmation that there is, or ever was, such a camp of silence. Of course, they cannot check out that sort of information, they add, they do not have the means. In short, the Swedish government can do nothing, which does not seem to upset its representatives; to the contrary, powerlessness vindicates decades of Swedish passivity. The government's job is "to cope with the real world," as one Swedish diplomat explained to me, "and a camp of silence is a phantom camp, just as Wallenberg himself is a phantom." Tracking down either is not high on a Swedish diplomat's list of priorities, though all, or nearly all, Swedish diplomats have taken part at one time or another, usually early on in their careers, in investigating Wallenberg sightings. It is an obligatory part of their training. The Swedish government also feels obligated to deal with inquiries from meddlesome foreigners concerning a phantom that does not have the decency to go away.

U.S. spy satellites are said to have tried but failed to pinpoint a camp of silence at one suspected location, one hundred and seventy kilometers northwest of Moscow. In the 1970s, U.S. intelligence put together an atlas of the gulag, complete with information about the type of camp and the level of security maintained. But can such an atlas be complete if current American intelligence suspicions (and Peto's nightmares) are right about the Soviets (and Stalin's North Korean disciples) having for long used underground facilities for their most secret projects?

Toward the end of his life, Andrey Sakharov, the grand old man of the anti-communist opposition, is said to have driven around one area in the vicinity of Leningrad, in search of a suspected site for a camp of silence. Though by that time he was a member of parliament, the KGB stopped his car and warned him to stay away. Wallenberg might have been imprisoned in such an institution, probably under another name and possibly no longer aware who he was and who he had once been.

The question is unanswered: if Wallenberg is dead, why have the Russians not identified his grave nor produced his death certificate and thus at long last put an end to the mystery which they find politically embarrassing?

As a young man, Raoul Wallenberg was sturdy in body and spirit. Born in 1912, he would be in his nineties as these lines are written. But why cite statistics in the manner of a life insurance salesman whose business is to discount with each passing year a person's life expectancy? Wallenberg was an extraordinary being, not a statistic. It breaks the heart to talk about him in the past tense.

The obdurate refusal of Russian officials to tell the truth about Wallenberg's fate is unconscionable, suggesting that the Soviet "special services" are still above the law and their network still shields those who once handled the enemies of the communist system. In his case, the Bolshevik slogan, "No information, no problem," is still operative. Nevertheless, those who owe their lives to Wallenberg and others who see him as a hero of the century cannot and will not give up demanding a truthful account of his years in the USSR — and if he is dead, the location of his grave. Unless the demand is met, the Russian Federation is still a Soviet union.

CHAPTER THREE

The Rages of a Dark Angel: Mr. Kanalas

"Every angel is terrifying."

Rainer Maria Rilke: *The Duino Elegies*

The chick was a ball of brown and gold down, with a vivid yellow beak and matching legs. She was always on the move. I named her Koverke — "chubby" in Hungarian — and the first home I found for her was a cardboard box which my father had discarded as no longer sturdy enough for carrying the merchandise he sold, grinding stones. I trained Koverke to eat breadcrumbs and chopped-up potato peels out of the palm of my hand.

I was six years old, and my parents had just rented a two-story apartment building on the outskirts of Budapest where the noisy big city softened into a quiet small town, still part village, called Zuglo. To the east lay the Great Plain, Hungary's flat heartland; to the west, the Danube, the country's proverbial main artery, some forty-five minutes by streetcar. I asked the janitor, whose word was law, if I could keep Koverke in a cage in a corner of the building's small back yard. When he said yes, I jumped up and down shouting "thank you." He also permitted me to plant a few pole beans; the vines soon clambered over the wire fence that surrounded the property.

When my parents first heard about my projects, they both had the same strained expression on their faces; they could not decide whether to smile or to cry. The year was 1944. Our fellow Jews in other European countries had already been shipped to German "labor camps," a term that was as imprecise as it was ominous. Eavesdropping on adult conversation and listening to the radio, I knew that we, Hungarian Jews, were next on Adolf Hitler's list "to be rubbed out" — *ausradieren* — which was one of the threats in his flood of words I understood very well. In the German-language kindergarten I attended, the teacher used the same word when telling us to erase a misshapen letter or a wayward line in a drawing. I suspected what my parents did not want to say in front of me: they were not sure if we would be around by the time the chick would start laying eggs or the beans would be ready for picking. But busy in the here and now, I did not spend much time thinking about threats that came from another country and lurked in that far-off time grownups call the future.

My parents too had reasons to be pleased with the immediate present. Strangely enough, business picked up for Father who for years had been making a precarious living selling the grinding stones he designed and took great pride in, calling them "the very best there is in the world." He collected certain kinds of rocks in the hills around Buda and in the mountains that ringed Hungary, and he carried them home in a large, leather-reinforced, and many-pocketed canvas backpack so wide that a hip belt had to secure it around the waist. Khaki in color, it was his prized possession from the days before the First World War in Berlin where he had studied engineering. He lugged the rocks to a dingy cellar workshop where a worker so caked with dust that he looked like a statue pulverized them, added water and cement, and poured them into different molds. The particular blend in each grinding stone was Father's trade secret. When someone asked him about the ingredients, he explained courteously that the blend depends on whether the stone sharpens blades cutting wood or metal, or works on lead crystal. But he would not reveal a single ingredient.

For Father, the grinding stone stood for civilization and progress as it banished nature's chaos — haphazard, stagnant, and useless. He admired the efficiency of wheels driving wheels and the achievement of chiseled, polished surfaces subordinate to a higher order defined by symmetry and grace.

Fortune smiled on Mother too. A wizard with needle and yarn — as well as with flour and sugar and eggs — she found three clothing stores, including one of the most expensive in the old, fashionable Inner City by the Danube, which agreed to buy the sweaters she knitted. They were known as "Norwegian" because of their designs featuring reindeer, an arctic animal unknown in Hungary. In the original version, two reindeer, frozen in solemn symmetry, faced each other. The bramble-like antlers received much artistic attention, and their tips reached as far as the opening for the neck.

In Mother's dynamic redesign, a single reindeer bounded across the chest of the sweater, and the sleeves and the back had pine trees strewn on them. Upon receiving such a sweater as a birthday present, her brother-in-law Levente praised her, only half in jest, for expressing "the joy in freedom of movement" and making him, a slow walker on account of his weak lungs, "feel like the swiftest of all reindeer."

Thanks to sales of stones and sweaters, my parents could at long last afford a rented apartment, however modest, consisting of two small rooms, a tiny kitchen, and a miniature bathroom. For the first time in my life, we were not staying with relatives or subletting a single room in someone else's apartment. The neighborhood was strictly low-income, for hardworking people such as shoemakers, streetcar conductors, and watch repairmen who liked to call the boxy buildings such as ours "modern." In fact, they were all plain, without any of the stucco vines and leaves, and the concrete arches and curlicues customary in the capital city proud of its high style.

The Wolf's Song of Winter

I do not remember suffering from poverty or the lack of a permanent parental home though, mostly because my parents used to send me off, for several months at a time, to live with cousins in the small town of Huszt, on the northeastern rim of the Carpathian mountains, now called

Chust and part of Ukraine. Getting there took a day on a slow train, and my eyes fastened on the scenery as it shifted from the plains that suggested a sandbox to rolling hills that seemed perfect for sledding, and finally to waves upon waves of steep, tree-mantled mountains, the home of lots of wild animals such as bear and boar, fox and wolf and deer. "Somewhere in those woods are the beautiful, mysterious, and seldom-sighted lynx," each relative who accompanied me added, though uncertain whether I needed the reassurance that a lynx is just an overgrown housecat or the thrill that it is the local kin of the cheetah and the tiger.

With their own two children in their twenties, my cousins were delighted to have me run around in their house that seemed like a castle to me. I admired the spacious attic, a forest of beams and rafters, made of the local pine that the family-owned lumber mill sawed and planed. The father, Yeno Krausz, was related to my father Aladar and the mother, Marishka, to my mother Anna, and I called them "uncle" and "aunt," which is how children were expected to address all adult relatives. Uncle Yeno was big, jolly, and noisy, and Aunt Marishka small, subdued, and quiet, but I loved them equally, and I loved being part of their extended family of more than fifty relatives busy visiting one another, arguing and complaining, shouting and whispering, wagging fingers and jabbing stomachs, trading jokes and outdoing one another in laughing and eating. Every dinner seemed like a Passover Seder, and as a cousin on both my maternal and paternal lineages, I was a welcome guest in each of the Krausz households. They loved the idea that I was "a relative twice over," an excess they wholly approved of.

The Krausz were a clan. On one occasion, when Mother's younger sister Mara visited them, they took her to a fancy ball that was to elect a beauty queen, the town's own Miss Huszt. The Krausz men bought up most of the tickets that also served as ballots, and they put Mara's name on every one of them. She was attractive and personable, but what decided the contest in her favor was the Krausz vote. When in the 1970s her son Levente and I mischievously confronted her with what I learned from Cousin Kati Krausz, Mara was at first embarrassed, trying to convince us that it was not really a beauty contest and the Krausz men did not cheat. But in the end, Mara confessed that our indiscreet Cousin Kati, several years younger than Mara and perhaps a bit jealous of all the attention showered on her, was in fact right.

I had my own room that I shared with a huge, good-natured St. Bernard named Harry by Uncle Yeno who admired the English. Harry followed me everywhere. Unbelievable as it seemed to me, Harry listened to my commands to come, sit, or roll over. From my window, I saw mountains bristling with pine trees, and during winter nights I could hear the wolves howl, sometimes dozens of them, stretching out their "ooooo" for minutes, with the pitch rising and falling. "You are very lucky to hear them sing their song of winter," Uncle Yeno told me. "In other seasons, they don't sing so beautifully. Let's listen carefully to their song and let's try to figure out what they are saying."

Hearing the wolves, Harry would at first run to the window, put his front paws up on the sill, and respond with a sustained growl. But the wise old dog that he was, Harry soon decided that the wolves were no threat to the household he guarded, and he crawled back to his usual spot, under my oversize, old-fashioned bed that resembled the horse-drawn sleigh Uncle Yeno used for going up into the mountains. Clearly, there was no reason to be afraid.

During my last stay in Huszt, in early 1944, I noticed that my relatives engaged in a lot of intense discussions out of my earshot, but I was not sensitive enough to notice how worried they were. On previous visits, they kept postponing my departure, and eventually Uncle Yeno sent a train ticket to Mother to come and collect me, and then he and Aunt Marishka talked her into staying for a few weeks, to which Mother gladly agreed as she and Aunt Marishka were first cousins and the closest of friends since childhood. But that last time in Huszt I was suddenly told that Uncle Yeno and Aunt Marishka unexpectedly had to go out of town for several weeks and that one of the young Krausz relatives would take me back to Budapest. (Years later I learned that Uncle Yeno wanted me to return home right away because a friend of his in the local government warned him that all the Jews in Huszt would soon be herded into a ghetto as the first stage to their deportation to Germany. He thought it would be safer for me to be in Budapest. I do not know why he and the rest of the Krausz clan did not go to Budapest.)

But I did notice that the parting was more sad than usual, and many more members of the family than on previous occasions accompanied me to the train station. Both Aunt Marishka and Uncle Yeno had tears in their eyes when kissing me goodbye. This time Uncle Yeno did not make his joke about my next visit when he would absolutely and definitely teach me how to use a gun so he could take me along on a hunt for wild boar, which called for a daylong hike into far-off, high mountains. Nor did Aunt Marishka have a chance to complain about her husband "making all that fuss about an animal we won't eat" or to make faces while he tried to "corrupt" me, a recurrent accusation.

Back in Budapest, I eavesdropped on my parents' conversations and listened to the radio. I became aware of the restrictions placed on Jews, the most visible of which was the decree issued by the new, pro-Nazi cabinet on March 29, 1944: outside their homes, all Jews above the age of six must wear a six-pointed star of a conspicuous, canary yellow color, ten centimeters by ten centimeters, on the breast, on the left side of the outermost garment.

For once, Father, ordinarily an indifferent Jew, displayed pride in being Jewish. Furious, he declared that if the Nazis were to try to set us apart as "pariahs," and the symbol they forced us to wear was to be a star of shame, at least our stars would be the proud stars of King David. He told Mother to buy the finest fabric in the most brilliant hue of golden yellow. He put on his best dark suit, which was almost black and made the yellow star stand out. He told me to wear my one jacket, at least a size too large for me, and reserved for special occasions.

After praising Mother for the expert job she did in stitching the stars made of cut velvet, Father insisted on going out for a walk on the main street of our neighborhood. Mother, who hated "making a public spectacle of one's self" and always worried about "what the neighbors will say," refused, and stuck by her refusal. She also did not want me to go, but Father was adamant.

I remember feeling pleased with Father's defiant stance; I was proud of his pride. "Straighten up and walk like a soldier," he kept telling me as I tended to slouch. Several times we paraded up and down the main street of our neighborhood. Father had a most solemn expression on his face — as if he had been awarded a medal for bravery. There were plenty of people on the street, some of whom we knew, and many of them averted their eyes when they saw us. I do not remember any hostility. But no one greeted us or signaled any sympathy. After we got home, my parents barely spoke to each other for days.

Nearly every week that followed brought new government decrees such as shutting down Jewish-owned stores, limiting the hours Jews could spend outside their homes, forbidding Jews to travel on trains, and banning social contacts between Jews and Gentiles. By the spring of 1944 the new laws forbade Father to travel inside the country, let alone to Germany, Slovakia, Croatia, or parts of Serbia. He could not hunt for the rocks he needed, nor visit his clients. In fact, the latest decrees did not allow him to conduct any business.

One day an old associate of his, a quiet, soft-spoken Gentile whom Mother used to look down on as "mousy" knocked on our door. He and my father quickly struck a deal, and he became Father's front man, selling grinding stones from the boxes Father kept in the apartment. While the partnership violated the new laws, which meant some serious risks for the Gentile, Father told Mother that the profit-sharing formula they agreed on was "fair and equitable," which was his highest praise for a business transaction.

Nevertheless, the Nazi hunt was closing in on us. In late spring or perhaps early summer, Father, then fifty-two years old, had to report for duty in a labor battalion which, he somehow found out, would be digging anti-tank ditches but on Hungarian soil — thank God, everyone in the family said. When saying goodbye he told us that "the illogical war" would be over shortly, that Mother and I will come out of it just fine, and he'd be back soon. He took me aside and assured me that Mother would take good care of me. At a daybreak as gray as lead, he walked out of our apartment building with a self-confident salesman's stride, with his trusty German backpack bulging and arms swinging high. "We'll win the war," he had told us. "We" meant our family.

Mother said nothing to contradict him, but I sensed that she did not like Father's new sales pitch. Shortly after Father's departure rumors reached us about sealed trains carrying to Germany entire communities from towns in eastern Hungary where most of our relatives lived. We received no word from our cousins in Huszt, and I knew from Mother's evasive answers to my questions that she suspected the worst, which at the time meant doing forced labor. I also overheard a remark by Uncle Levente, a journalist whose judgment and sources of information everyone in the family respected, that the Germans were killing most of those deported, and only the strongest among them were selected to work in munitions factories. Mother could not bring herself to believe that, nor could her sister Mara, Levente's wife. The two sisters told him that such things simply could not happen and that he should not be talking like that.

In Budapest — home to more than 300,000 Jews, including tens of thousand who converted to Christianity but the new law considered Jewish nevertheless — every few weeks food rations available to Jews were cut back, as were the hours they could spend outside their homes. In June we were ordered to move into the ghetto downtown or into one of the apartment buildings, scattered throughout the city, marked with six-pointed yellow stars. We did neither. Soon, gangs of Hungarian Nazis began going from house to house, rounding up Jews who, like us, disobeyed the law.

The Many Faces of Mr. Kanalas

Adding to our uncertainty about the future was the janitor, who, my parents decided soon after our moving into the building, was a foul-mouthed drunkard. (We also heard from neighbors that he was an instigator of brawls in the tavern.) He walked around with a three-day growth of beard, often muttering curses. He kept quarrelling with his wife who was nearly twice his size. They had no children, and he blamed her, on the top of his voice, for being barren. From time to time, the concrete stairwell of the apartment building served as an echo chamber for a duet of his basso fulminations and her soprano cries. Mother was sure that he beat her.

He insisted that the tenants call him Mr. Kanalas, a respectful appel-

lation which none denied him, primarily out of fear. In Hungary the janitor traditionally has a clandestine, quasi-official governmental function
of keeping an eye on tenants, and it is assumed that they are police
informers, paid each time in cash — not a very large amount but enough
to make a difference in their monthly budgets. For most of the twentieth century in Hungary, when a tenant fell under suspicion of wrongdoing, the janitor was among the first to be contacted by the police, or
the secret police. If the janitor did not cooperate, he could lose his job
that came with a small, one- or two-bedroom apartment that was rent-
free, often below ground level but in most cases with a window that also
enabled him to keep an eye on the traffic through the building's front
door, his special responsibility.

Besides collecting the garbage, the janitor's daily duties included
keeping the entrance and the stairway clean. He was dependent on the
tenants' tips to supplement the meager salary paid by the building's
owner. The bulk of the tips, known as "gate-money," came from tenants
who rang the bell when the front door was locked, usually between
eleven in the evening and five in the morning, and the janitor or his wife
had to get out of bed each time to let them in. In the building's social
hierarchy, he was at the bottom rung, with no chance of moving up.

Parents warned us children to avoid Mr. Kanalas, which was not easy
because he liked to talk with us, and he was always friendly. As he swept
the stairs or changed a light bulb, he sang, usually operatic arias, and he
had a beautiful voice. (Mother was most impressed, and she wondered
aloud "how such a fine big voice could come out of such a scrawny little fellow.") He and I talked as I watered my bean plants that festooned
the rusty fence, and I fed and played with Koverke. She grew into a
respectable gold-and-black hen about to start laying eggs yet she did not
mind sitting on my lap. She also followed me like a dog when I took her
for a walk on the street. When we passed by him, Mr. Kanalas clapped
and sang a marching song from an opera. "Greet the janitor politely,"
was Mother's standard instruction. "Listen to his talk only if you must.
But do not stay for a conversation. Tell him that you are expected at
home."

On one occasion when Mother and I were returning home, Mr.

Kanalas was sitting on the ground in front of the building and barely managed to grunt a greeting. Mother dragged me past him in a great hurry, saying in a loud voice that she had left something cooking on the stove. (That was her favorite excuse whenever she wanted to make a quick exit, perhaps because she would never forget about a pot on the stove.) I first thought Mother was upset because my greeting had been a bit too elaborate and cheery: "A very fine good evening to you, dear Mr. Kanalas." While Mother did think that I was overly polite, she explained that she wanted to get out of the janitor's sight as fast as possible because he was drunk, very drunk. I understood, as she had often warned me to stay out of the way of people who smelled of alcohol.

As two Jewish families lived in the apartment building, the new law required that the janitor affix a six-pointed yellow star on the front door or above it. But Mr. Kanalas did not. "Don't worry about the star," he told both families casually. He let it be known what he thought: the crazy Nazis and their stupid laws will not last for long.

Nevertheless, his reaction astonished us one night when three or perhaps four or five men banged on the building's locked front door. We woke up to the shouting. They said they were from the Arrow Cross — Hungary's own Nazis — and they demanded to be let in to search the apartments for Jews they knew were hiding there.

A wiry little man in his fifties, Mr. Kanalas replied by threatening to step outside, break every bone in their bodies, and chop up their vital organs unless they left the premises immediately. After the thugs repeated their demands, Mr. Kanalas raised his voice. He warned them that he would beat their flesh into a pulp and strain it through the front door's keyhole to make sausages that he would eat for breakfast. He possessed a voice so powerful — a resonant, rich bass — and he kept up a nonstop volley of threats, curses, and expletives so menacing that the thugs beat a retreat, without catching a glimpse of their challenger.

Mr. Kanalas had a different reaction a week or so later, when a similar gang on the same assignment appeared and several men barked the order "Open up, we came for your Jews!" Again invisible behind the locked front door, he roared that it was a nasty, unbelievable, and unforgivable insult to imply that he, as a law-abiding, honest janitor, and a true Hungarian patriot all his life, would agree to be employed by Jews, the worst criminals on the face of the earth. If he as much as laid eyes on a Jew, he would personally take charge of torture and execution.

Again, the words burst out of Mr. Kanalas in a terrifying, nonstop, rapid flow. His description of what he would do to a Jew he caught was so detailed and so graphic — full of blood and gore and severed body parts — that it turned my stomach. But the demands to open the front door stopped after a while, and the Nazis left without entering the building. Apparently, they believed that our janitor must be one of them.

Though Mr. Kanalas twice chased away the Nazis, Mother did not think that in the long run we could rely on him. She was particularly disturbed that when she attempted to express her gratitude, Mr. Kanalas walked away. He acted as if she had not been present, Mother said, deeply offended. Clearly, he did not wish to talk about the incidents.

"He could have easily handed us over to those thugs," Mother told her sister Mara who came to visit us. Aunt Mara said Mr. Kanalas would do no such a thing. She declared that she found "something surprisingly noble" about him.

"But what do we have in common with him?" Mother countered. "He is not a friend of ours, and he'll never be one." She was especially concerned that one day he might switch sides, as alcohol does strange things to people. "And why not?" she asked. "After all, as a crude, uneducated person, isn't he like so many of the Nazis?" By the close of the conversation the two sisters came to an agreement, as usual, with Aunt Mara ending up slightly more skeptical than Mother about our protector's motives. It also became clear to me that with Father away, Mother was physically afraid of Mr. Kanalas.

As summer turned to fall, the Nazi fury extended to Gentiles who helped Jews. Posters printed by Hungarian Nazis were plastered all over town, with a huge screaming red headline declaring, "We will tear to pieces" any person giving aid and comfort to the Jewish enemy. The verb they used — "*felkoncoljuk*" — drifted down from Hungary's distant pagan past, and it meant live, ritualistic, piece-by-piece dismemberment. Their symbol, the so-called arrow cross, was a violent variation of a pre-Christian cross, with all four tips ending in arrowheads.

In late summer I started picking beans — the first harvest in my life — but I do not remember feeling festive. Then one day, following an air raid probably targeting a munitions factory a mile from us, I found Koverke lying on her side, motionless, with her scaly feet, much like a dragon's, up in the air. There was no sign of blood, so she was not hit by a shrapnel. "Koverke must have died of fright," Mother suggested, sharing my sadness. "Chickens cannot tolerate big noises like the sound of an explosion. Their little hearts break." Mr. Kanalas volunteered to take care of Koverke's remains.

One cold, rainy November day Mother and I left the building without saying goodbye to anyone — and without wearing the six-pointed star on our coats. She hoped to find a safer place to hide, and she did. But that is another story.

The war ended in Hungary in April 1945, when a massive Russian offensive swept out the last German units stationed in the country. A week or two later, Father knocked on his brother-in-law Levente's door — the one permanent address in Budapest that all our relatives went to first and where Mother and I had been living since early March. It was close to midnight, with everyone asleep, and Aunt Mara who opened the door did not recognize him at first. Dressed in rags, filthy, and emaciated, my dapper father looked like a beggar. Only his oversize khaki backpack, now empty, looked familiar. Everyone was greatly relieved to see him alive, and I tried to stay awake to listen to his story he must have finished telling close to dawn.

In his methodical way, Father began talking about the work his labor battalion was engaged in from dawn to dusk: digging ditches and hammering granite boulders into gravel. Then he moved on to the subject of punishments ordered by the armed Gentile guards often without any justification. During winter they made their victims stand barefoot for hours in a bucket of water which soon turned to ice in the subzero weather.

I dozed off but woke up toward the end of his tale, when he described how the Russian troops moved in from the east and the Hungarian Nazis ordered everyone to march to the west, supposedly to reach labor camps in Germany. Somewhere on the road not far from the border with

Austria, Father collapsed. The guards shoved him into the drainage ditch to the side of the road, fired at his head, and left him for dead.

But the bullet only grazed his neck. After the last of the marchers disappeared from sight, he got up and started walking in the opposite direction, toward Budapest, a distance of some one hundred and fifty miles. Whenever he heard the rumble of tanks, he ran for cover behind hedgerows or trees. At first the tanks were marked with the black swastika, but soon he noted a differently shaped tank, bearing the five-pointed red star.

He begged villagers for food and water but was afraid to ask for shelter. He feared he would be reported to the authorities. He slept in the fields. Though famously good at keeping track of time and remembering numbers, he lost count how many days it took him to reach Budapest.

Mother happened to have a high fever, so it was her sister Mara who cooked Father some beans, which was the only food in the house. He insisted on washing and shaving first, then he ate voraciously. Next morning he borrowed a suit several sizes too big from brother-in-law Levente and ventured out, looking for a job and an apartment. Much to everyone's surprise, the post-Nazi municipal government hired him to obtain the materials needed for repairing the famous baths of Buda, badly damaged in the war.

Next, Father achieved the impossible by getting the municipal government to assign us an apartment. It was half of the upstairs of a partly bombed-out villa, now divided into apartments for four families. Built when the century was young and playful, the structure was an eclectically romantic fantasy, a stage set. Its narrow, Venetian-style "bridge of sighs" connected the flat, "Mediterranean" roof to the verdant hillside; a spacious "Moorish" balcony, adjacent to a "medieval" round tower, gave us a great view of the river Danube, a most desirable feature in the capital city. The living room had stained-glass windows like a Gothic church.

We all loved the location, Rose Hill, one of the many hills of Buda, once the favorite haunt of the Turks who had ruled the city for a century and a half. It reminded me of Huszt. But the person most pleased was Mother who had always missed having a proper home. Born in a spa-

The author's parents, Anna Schwarcz and Aladar Fenyvesi, in front of her mother Roza's house in Debrecen in the late 1930s.

The author's cousins, Marishka and Yeno Krausz with their son Imre, dressed for a masquerade in Huszt in the 1930s.

In the foreground is the author's cousin Kati and the second to her right is her father Yeno Krausz, standing on logs in the Carpathian mountains in the mid-1930s.

The Budapest apartment building today on Kerekgyarto utca 13 where the janitor Mr. Kanalas defended two Jewish families from Nazi thugs in 1944.

cious village house that had a floor of pine planks mopped every Friday afternoon, she longed for a city apartment with a few hundred square feet of parquet she would make shine. In contrast, Father, who enjoyed being on the go as a traveling salesman, did not really mind moving from one rented room to another.

It took us a day or two to clear the rubble from the rooms, mostly shattered windowpanes and chunks of plaster gouged out by bullets. Work was invigorating, it was as if we had swept the war out of our lives. While Father was taping translucent wax paper on the windows and the French doors — a sheet of glass was a black-market item that only gold or dollars could buy — the buzzer sounded. I opened the door and then shouted on top of my voice, "It's Kati!"

Daughter of Marishka and Yeno Krausz, Cousin Kati was skin-and-bones and her complexion ashen — most unlike the pretty, stylish woman in her early twenties we remembered. She nearly fell over when she lifted me in her arms.

"Are you alone?" I asked, my tears flowing, my hands draped around her neck, and with my parents joining in one big hug.

"Yes," she said, and then added slowly, as if carving an inscription on a tombstone, "I am *completely* alone."

We understood, and then all four of us wept, with no one being able to say anything for a long, long time, as we tried to learn to live with the knowledge that her parents, her brother, and his wife and their baby had all been killed. No one could say a word, and the silence — a reflection of the Krausz relatives silenced — was unbearable. So we cried and cried like a rain unable to stop.

In a few weeks we found out that except for another young woman and her daughter, Kati was the only member of the Krausz clan, once numbering more than fifty, who survived. Kati said she had no desire whatsoever to go back to Huszt, not even for a visit, because she had "nobody and nothing to go back to." Of course she stayed with us. Two years later, she crossed the Austrian border illegally and went on to settle in Israel.

A Wealth of Crystals

Before the war, Father took great pride in his collection of crystal ware which he bartered for his stones used in cutting, grinding, and polishing the crystals in factories and workshops throughout Hungary, Austria, Yugoslavia, Czechoslovakia, and Romania, set up in the waning days of the Habsburg empire and later encouraged by the new nationalist regimes. Father rhapsodized about the crystals' "exquisite, jewel-like, baroque facets so cleverly copied from other ornaments of a bygone world." Admiring the precision craftsmanship that went into their production, he explained that each piece came ballooning out of the long pipe of a glassblower who manipulated the molten glass mixed with lead oxide. The glassblower needed the talents of both a singer controlling the intake and the outflow of his breath and of a pastry cook building up layers and patterns.

But the fluid mass of glass must be at the same very high temperature. If there is a difference of more than a few degrees between the core and the edges, the fusion is imperfect, and months, sometimes years later, the piece will suddenly split in two.

Father also liked our crystal ware because they were showy luxury items, far more expensive than our modest economic status would have justified. They were the only precious things we owned. But Mother thought them perilously fragile and much too fancy for us.

I loved looking at the crystals refracting sunlight. Whether lustrous black, dark ruby, or deep purple, they sparkled in many tints of the rainbow. Their crenelated lips and chiseled designs such as oak leaves, sheaves of wheat, and blooms of ox-eye daisy conjured up castles and crowns, fields and forests. But I resented that my parents, worried that I might carelessly drop and break a crystal, would not permit me to pick up one except under adult supervision.

The night before Father left to join his labor battalion, he meticulously wrapped each crystal in newspapers I was in charge of crumpling up and handing over to him. He packed all of them in a large wicker trunk, purchased for the occasion, to which he tied cardboard signs which declared in Hungarian, German, and Russian: "CAREFUL! DELI-CATE GLASSWARE! EXTREMELY FRAGILE!" In each version, Father underlined the word "fragile" three times.

Soon after we cleaned up the new apartment and the streetcars of Budapest started rolling again, my parents went to the old house in Zuglo in the hope of recovering whatever might have been left of our possessions. They came home with one item: the wicker trunk filled with crystal ware. Though our apartment was broken into and plundered after we left it, the wicker trunk remained untouched. Even its lock was intact, and the reason dawned on my parents as they unpacked the treasures in the new apartment: in wartime, with bombs and bullets flying and roofs and brick walls collapsing, no one in his right mind would steal something breakable. What must have stopped the looters was the sign on the trunk warning that its contents were fragile.

Father was as proud of retrieving the crystals as a general whose bold ruse translated into a battlefield victory. He also canceled the ban on my touching them. At the age of seven and a half, I was judged responsible enough to hand over the pieces to him, one by one, as he chose their new locations. (Mother opted for a strategic withdrawal to the kitchen.) Displayed on top of bullet-pocked wardrobes and rickety tables, the collection of goblets, vases, fruit bowls, and ashtrays looked as incongruously grand as tails and white tie worn with a pair of shorts.

But looking at the crystals reassured Father that soon he would be able to resume his prewar business, travel to neighboring countries, and track down his old clients. Within a few months he would be digging up rocks, carrying them home, and having them pulverized and molded according to his carefully calibrated specifications. He was confident that the wheels of European industry would start turning once more, cutting and shaping raw materials, and making them as smooth and polished and fragile as civilization itself, and he could earn a living eventually matching the level of our crystal ware collection.

Before entering the old apartment, my parents first rang Mr. Kanalas' doorbell, eager to express their gratitude. The stranger who opened the door introduced himself as the new janitor. He kept saying that he had never met Mr. Kanalas who, he gathered, had been fired because of his habit of picking fights — and of course his drunkenness.

Neither the new janitor nor any of the tenants offered a clue where Mr. Kanalas might have gone. Nobody wanted to talk about him. (Could he have vanished in all the fighting, Mother asked, misty-eyed.) The other Jewish family in the building also disappeared, and neighbors did not seem to know whether the Nazis had taken them away or they had found another place to hide.

A few weeks later, on a bright early summer day the buzzer sounded in our new apartment. Mother opened the narrow slit of a security window in the upper part of the front door that allows a peek at a caller. She was taken aback by the unshaven, dirty, disheveled stranger who greeted her in a loud but shaky voice. Mother took one whiff and knew that the man had been drinking.

She asked what he wanted. When the man identified himself as Mr. Kanalas, Mother said, "Wait just a minute," closed the little window and hurried to the kitchen. She took all the cash she kept in an envelope stashed behind the flour bin, rushed back to the front door, opened the little window, and handed the bundle to Mr. Kanalas.

"I don't want any of your damned money," Mr. Kanalas began shouting on top of his voice, that strong voice we remembered so well. Neighbors could hear every word. He flung back the banknotes through the window, cursed my mother, and staggered down the steps shouting terrible things about us, and cursing, cursing, cursing. He went on nonstop about filthy money and the even filthier people who had plenty of it and thought they could buy with it everybody and everything. He would teach such people a lesson, the lesson of their life.

Mother broke into tears and told me to run after Mr. Kanalas, asking him to come back, please, we'd like him to sit down in the living room and speak with us.

I did as told. But Mr. Kanalas paid no attention to me. I told him that I was raising a white chick called Maxie who turned into a rooster and was just as tame a pet as Koverke had been. I invited him to take a look at the rooster.

He did not answer me. He kept walking unsteadily while cursing on top of his voice, in a rage and unmistakably drunk. After successfully negotiating a long, steep flight of steps, he was making his way downhill toward the street with amazing speed.

His voice was the same powerful, resonant operatic bass he had used against the Arrow Cross thugs. But this time we were the targets of his torrential fury, a recitative of wrath delivering humiliation, shame, and guilt. It was a whirlwind that could not be stopped.

Mother shouted from our terrace overlooking the serpentine road below that I must come home right away, and I did. She decided that she must face Mr. Kanalas herself. She mopped up her tears with a white handkerchief she clutched in her hand — it flared like the white flag soldiers use to signal their surrender — as she hurried after Mr. Kanalas.

After about half an hour, she returned, looking somber. "I could not find him," she said. She thought he must have reached the crowded street at the bottom of Rose Hill, and there was no way of telling which direction he might have taken.

In tears, Mother blamed herself, explaining then and for years to come that she had been afraid of drunks ever since her childhood in her native village of Gyulaj. She told the story how after an unusually bountiful wheat harvest on her father's fields, the ordinarily non-drinking foreman of the harvesters was persuaded by his team of men to celebrate in the tavern. After only one glass of wine, the foreman got roaring drunk, started shoving and pushing his men, and kept demanding more wine. When the tavern owner refused to serve him, the foreman got up and killed the owner with a single blow.

Because of that memory, Mother said, she could not drink a sip of wine even on festive occasions. She kept saying that she was terrified of Mr. Kanalas and could not think of letting him inside the apartment with only the two of us at home. On the other hand she would never forgive herself for shutting out Mr. Kanalas and failing to find a way to express her gratitude for saving our lives, not once but twice.

After Father came home and listened to her story, he assured her that she did the one sensible thing in keeping an intoxicated man out of our home and offering him money. Storming out was Mr. Kanalas' choice and not her responsibility, Father declared. It was an ill-advised, impetuous act revealing the basic instability of his personality. Despite his undeniable merits, "the former janitor" was "a sordid character" we should not be associated with, Father said. As for his alcoholism, everyone knows that it is the curse of the working class — a regrettable example of its members' lack of self-restraint and a principal reason for their failure to get ahead in life. Father recalled that when in the course of his work with grinding stones he dealt with the proletariat, a monetary value was attached to every transaction. "Cash is the right currency of discourse with members of the working class." he said.

"I don't disagree with you," Mother said, "but I don't like your argument."

Father was not troubled, and he could not understand all the anguish caused by Mr. Kanalas.

"Life is about respect and integrity," Father intoned.

"Love and hope," Mother countered.

A Central European burgher, Father upheld the high standards of his class, namely moderation, rationality, and predictability. Nevertheless, he could not get over Mr. Kanalas' inexplicable ability to find us. My parents had left no forwarding address in the apartment building in Zuglo, and Budapest is of course a large city.

Father dismissed the Nazi period as a brief, temporary rupture in the contract among the classes and as a freakish relapse into chaos. He expected a quick return to normalcy and to the rule of law, and he argued that as soon as possible all of us in the family should forget "the absurd war" and focus on what lay ahead of us. "The Nazi madness is over," he said, "and so is the Kanalas episode. The account is closed."

We never saw Mr. Kanalas again.

Did Mr. Kanalas shield us and the other Jewish family in the apartment building because he imagined that as the janitor, tenants were under his authority, even his protection? But what made him take such a high risk? He had to be aware that the Nazi thugs he defied could have shattered the lock with a single bullet or simply forced the door open, as they did in other buildings. He must have also known that once the thugs found a single Jewish tenant, he would have been considered "a stooge of the Jews" and an accomplice who could have been shot, or at the very least taken to prison and beaten up, then possibly sent to a concentration camp.

Was Mr. Kanalas the kind of person who impulsively rises to the challenge of a physical threat, unmindful of the consequences? Or could it be that as a facile talker he enjoyed a good argument, secure in the knowledge that his repartee would be superior? Did he relish such confrontations and thrive on the risks that his fast tongue got him into?

Answers to these questions come from the tavern, the parliament of the drinking class, and the one neighborhood forum for a diversity of opinions and personalities. In most every tavern where the language spoken is Hungarian and the alcohol of choice is the famously potent eau de vie distilled from plums or apricots or cherries, there is a customer known as the Champion of Justice, or, simply, The Champion. He will come alive whenever the turn of conversation gives him a chance to rail against the unjust and inhuman ways practiced by the powers that run the world. The fault is fundamental, he thinks, and could even be irreparable, perhaps concealed in the very nature of things, if not coeval with Creation. But wherever the fault is, a decent human being must stand up for justice and humanity; there is no other way.

Not given to small talk, The Champion may feel that it is inconsistent with his intellectual dignity to join others in complaining about such mundane matters as, say, lightning-like aches in his lower back, or an ornery daughter who doesn't want to get married. But he will jump at every chance to defend a victim of injustice and curse out those targeting such a person. He will protest a violation of his high standards even if the neighborhood informer is present and the following day he is taken to the police station for "a little conversation" which almost always includes a beating, often a severe one.

Another tavern regular is The Actor. He will walk over to a woman of easy virtue, address her as Your Grace, and inquire if she has purchased her winter wardrobe, or whether she will spend the upcoming winter in the South of France or perhaps on a Greek island. If told to go away and mind his own damned business — or even if his reception is friendly — The Actor will soon exit from the scene he created. He will make his way over to the bartender, make a deep bow, call him Your Majesty, and assure him that his subjects in the Kingdom of the Tavern are still as happy under the sway of his scepter as they were on the day of his coronation.

Sometimes the act does not last longer than a few minutes, sometimes it goes on and on, and bit players join in. The Actor is paid in broad smiles — a rare commodity in the tavern — and an occasional shout of "well done, pal," which is even more rare. His performance is a transfiguration almost as welcome as the one that turns rotting plums or apricots or cherries into a crystal-clear alcoholic beverage but lets the aroma of the fruit linger on the palate most pleasingly. After a few glasses of the potion, the mind is no longer confined to the smoke-filled tavern but can float over islands of tranquility as blessed as the leafy orchard that yielded the fruit.

But once The Actor tires of romantic theater — or does he switch to another play in another genre? — he reenters reality by reminding the woman of easy virtue that for every new wrinkle she acquires she must charge less for her services. She strikes back by saying she will never have anything to do with him for all the money in the world. The Actor ambles over to the bartender and calls him a cheat who dispenses the cheapest liquor in town yet charges more for it than the competition two blocks away. The bartender tells him to go and take his act somewhere else, and The Actor vows that he will leave instantly and never again put his foot in the tavern. Never!

Of course he stays, and he is back the following day, ready for another performance.

Mr. Kanalas was both a champion of justice and an actor. He freed himself from the many constraints of his lowly station by espousing a worthy cause, and he stepped out of his self by risking his life. By nature neither a killer nor an opportunist, he would not join the Arrow Cross, so he stood up for us Jews, fired by all the rage brimming in his angry heart. He sustained his act as long as he was invisible behind the door, and he kept the enemy at bay with the power of his words.

What might have made him do it was a recognition that those Nazi thugs suddenly acquired an ultimate say over life and death. With guns in hand and with the mighty German war machine behind them, they could do anything they wanted — or so they thought, without reckoning with Mr. Kanalas. How satisfied Mr. Kanalas must have been with his two victories. And how right he was.

Did Mother's offer of money infuriate him as the standard bourgeois putdown of a man from the lower classes who was so clearly due recognition and respect? Did he not deserve more, far more, than a bundle of banknotes handed out through a window? He must have expected an invitation to come inside the apartment, sit down and talk, as old friends do, sharing a cup of coffee and something to eat, perhaps a family meal. But how could he have known of Mother's great fear of being near a person with alcohol on his — or her — breath?

In a collision of signals, he struck back in the most forceful way he knew: with words that lashed and stung even if the victim knew that they were unfair and untrue. Mr. Kanalas won his final, devastating victory by turning his back on us and refusing to give us a second chance.

Kanalas, which means "spoonmaker" in Hungarian, is a name typically Gypsy, acquired because carving wooden spoons was a craft Gypsies once practiced in the countryside. Gypsy friends tell me they have never met a person named Kanalas who was not a Gypsy, and after they hear Mr. Kanalas' story they smile and recognize him as one of theirs. They say that his success in finding us after the war was a characteristically Gypsy feat, as some Gypsies have an uncanny ability to track down the people they feel they must find for one reason or another.

Could he have been a Gypsy, another target of Nazi racial cleansing? Yes, probably. Both he and his wife were as swarthy as many Gypsies, and in prewar Hungary Gypsies often worked as janitors. While in the provinces tens of thousands of Hungarian Gypsies were rounded up and sent to Auschwitz, in Budapest the authorities usually left them alone, particularly if they had regular jobs. If Mr. Kanalas was a Gypsy, that fact might well have turned him against the Nazis, and his rescue of Jewish families could have been his way of fighting a common enemy.

If he was a Gypsy, did he become our protector, the chieftain Gypsies call *rom baro* in their language, and did he defend us with all the ferocity and the finesse of a tribe accustomed to the *gadjo*, the hostile non-Gypsy — be they the police or criminals — trying to break into its camp, into its homes? Then, when my mother tried to pay him off, did he exercise his right to rage, a freedom Gypsies believe they are born with, while we cowered in our middle-class restraint, unable to respond?

However, Mr. Kanalas' origins too seem destined to remain a secret. If still alive, both he and his wife would be well over a hundred years old, and a witness who remembers them is increasingly unlikely to come forward.

Unpaid Debts

For the rest of her life Mother was often tormented by memories of Mr. Kanalas. She felt she failed to live up to our family tradition: a good deed is incomplete unless the beneficiary expresses appropriate gratitude to the benefactor. The tradition stems from our ancestors' kabbalistic belief: generosity of the spirit, as all flow of positive energy, must form a circle or "a magic ring," in which each element feeds, inspires, and supports the other. (A magic ring is the opposite of a vicious circle, in which each element contributes to making it worse for every other element.) One parallel is a blessing recited, for example, on coming upon a tree of exceptional beauty and thanking God for that privilege. Such a blessing links up the Creator, the created object, and the human observer, and allows a sharing of their vital forces. But energy does not flow without a blessing, which is, after all, no more than an acknowledgement in an ancient ritualized mode that the circle needs to be completed.

In 1994, with her mind retaining only scattered memories of her eighty-nine years, Mother talked about Mr. Kanalas' call on us nearly fifty years earlier, on Rose Hill. Sitting up in her hospital bed, she had tears in her eyes reliving the janitor's ill-fated last appearance. "We must go and visit Mr. Kanalas right now," she announced in a firm voice, suddenly thrusting herself into the present. "Now is my last chance to make amends."

However, as she went on talking about "the debt of life" we owed Mr. Kanalas, she soon lost track of who he was, and the person she insisted on visiting right away turned into Rozhika, her stern yet beloved old teacher from her native village. Throughout her life my mother was a good student, able to learn new crafts and to adapt to new demands, and she always credited Rozhika for teaching her how to study. But the tattered fabric of that memory also prompted tears. During Rozhika's one and only visit with us in Budapest, in the same apartment building where Mr. Kanalas served as the janitor, Mother shut her out of the kitchen while preparing a festive meal of welcome. An honored guest, Mother insisted, must not lift a finger but be waited upon, and sit in the dining room like royalty while the hostess does what needs to be done in the kitchen.

The teacher, then in her seventies, had never married and lived by herself in a small town not far from Huszt. She had different concerns to voice: she was, after all, just like one of the family — was she not? — thus entitled to help out in the kitchen.

As I know from explanations from the time she was still well, Mother, born into wealth and a well-stocked pantry, was ashamed to let her old teacher find out how shabby our kitchen was and how little food we had. Their tiff, another collision of signals, turned into a dispute as jarring to listen to — and just as painfully repetitious — as a cracked record. The dinner that followed was delicious, as Mother could do magic with a cup of flour, a couple of eggs, some stale bread, and a few potatoes, and Father was at his most charming and courteous when such qualities were called for. But the atmosphere was irreparably strained, and our guest left for her hometown abruptly. As Rozhika's life ended in Auschwitz a few months later, Mother never had a chance to make peace with her.

In the hospital in Budapest in 1994, Mother's past and present merged, and she could also shift the conventional boundaries of space as she wished. For instance, in the course of a visit with her, she would decide that she was a child and the houses of her native village began just beyond the pair of the two tall junipers in front of her barred window. No visitor had the heart to tell her otherwise.

The chasm between the dead and the living filled in, and everyone who ever mattered to Mother was at her beck and call. She always loved having company; now she could invite and entertain whomever she pleased. She believed that her doctor — a handsome, courtly gentleman she was always happy to see — descended from the gentry of her native county; at other times she thought that he was the police chief of Debrecen, the town where she had lived before moving to the capital.

Depending on the drift of the conversation, the caprice of her memories, or the requirements of whatever came to her mind, she addressed me as her father, or one or the other of her older brothers (all buried long ago), or my eldest son Shamu (who delighted her by learning Hungarian), and only occasionally myself. One afternoon she greeted me with a mischievous smile and eagerly revealed the reason: she had had a most extraordinarily wonderful day. She got up before six o'clock that morning, sneaked out of her parents' house, and ate the most delicious pears from a tree, far out in a wheat field, that she was not supposed to pick. But she was sure that I, whom she addressed as Father, would forgive her.

I said that my grandfather had forgiven her long, long ago.

In the days when she was well and her brothers were still alive, she had often talked about a pear tree, grafted by a gardener in the village. It probably sprouted from a stray seed spat out by a laborer, but because the rootstock and the scion came from two different species, talmudic law questioned if the fruit was kosher. For an Orthodox Jewish family, the grafted pear tree became something of a tree of knowledge, though not of good and evil. My mother's father was a tolerant believer who explained to his children a talmudic rule but would not necessarily punish them for breaking it.

In the cast of characters who played key roles in her life, my mother relied on her father as the beacon of inspired knowledge as well as a source of unconditional affection. In contrast, Mr. Kanalas lurked in the darkness menacingly, summoning bitter remorse and unresolved guilt.

Our obligation to him weighed on her as her largest unpaid debt.

An irrepressible doer and therefore an optimist, Mother would not and could not concede that the damage she caused by trying to pay off Mr. Kanalas with money might be beyond repair. (After all, wasn't her eating the forbidden pears forgivable?) Her stream-of-consciousness about the urgent need to visit Mr. Kanalas and her teacher Rozhika concluded with an expression of her absolute certainty that only after she had a chance to apologize to the janitor — which would be surely followed by a similar reconciliation with the teacher — would her mind be "whole again." Then she would not have to stay in the hospital for one more day and could at long last go home. But, as my father, who had died many years earlier, said it: an original fault, such as the one in a crystal goblet, cannot be corrected. The crystal is destined to break.

I often find myself thinking of Mr. Kanalas. From time to time he appears in my dreams in a rage, refusing to listen to my appeals to reason and my plea for reconciliation. After I wake up, all I am left with is his unanswerable, bottomless bitterness. My lingering uncertainty about his motives and purposes frustrates and shames me, and it seems to me sad, even tragic, that we do not even know his first name; nor are we certain about the branch of the human family tree he came from. (Mother used to say that she doubted if we had ever known those facts, or could be sure about them, which saddened me even more.) Unless a surprise witness appears, I will never be able to do more than speculate about this dark angel from my childhood.

Rabbinical tradition defines the essence of angels as fire — the most volatile of elements — and maintains that angels sustain themselves in fire. Thinking of Mr. Kanalas, I am drawn to a statement a rabbi made nearly two thousand years ago: no man can endure the sound of an angel's voice. In our century, the poet Rilke trembled at the thought of angels and declared every one of them *schrecklich* — terrible and terrifying.

My obligation to Mr. Kanalas has been gnawing at my conscience too, and an urge to complete the circle begun by his good deed — and the circles of other angels — was the root reason that compelled me to write about him and other rescuers of Jews. I now suspect that it was my parent's failure to express our gratitude to Mr. Kanalas that has given me the patience I often possess in dealing with people whose anger gets the best of them. I am driven to try and discover what is underneath the uncontrollable rage I may eventually find justified whether or not I agree with it.

Angels — whether an East European lumpenproletarian or a handsome North European patrician like Raoul Wallenberg — are harder to understand than killers. Nazi killers killed for the thrill of killing — the hot, drunken, and, to me, incomprehensible thrill of emptying a gun into a live body until it moved no more. On the other hand, each rescuer had his or her reason and method to save lives.

Kabbalists have written that angels have no control over their actions; nor are they fully aware of the wider implications of those actions. Each is sent to earth with one specific assignment, and after it is completed, the remainder of their lives is inconsequential — as are their character, gender, and appearance. For us ordinary mortals, angels are as impossible to know and to understand as God's inscrutable grand plan.

I envy the self-confident visions of such intact faith.

CHAPTER FOUR

The Secrets of the Mother Book: Erzsebet David

When it seems like the night will last forever
And there is nothing left to do but count the years
When the strings of my heart start to sever
Stones fall from my eyes instead of tears.

Robert Hunter and Jerry Garcia: *Black Muddy River*

Erzsebet David was always in love, and always with the wrong men. Tears often rimmed her blue eyes, obscured though they might be by thick lenses. As fragile as a delicate porcelain figurine, she seemed to stand on a perilously narrow shelf. Her close friends, among them my mother Anna and other members of our family, often expressed the fear that sooner or later she would fall off and shatter.

But documents show that in the workaday world, Miss David served the Hungarian government as an exemplary administrator who received a bonus each year. She was promoted several times and eventually ranked as one of the highest-placed woman in what was otherwise a man's club. In the shadow of Adolf Hitler, her job, always sensitive, became critical, though she was but a proverbial cog in the smoothly running mechanism of the civil service that successive regimes in Budapest — and, before 1918, in Vienna — could rely on to implement policy, whatever it was. "An order is an order," other civil servants liked to repeat, thrilled with the feudal fealty the words echoed. Disobedience was an unheard-of scandal, nothing short of treason.

Known to her friends by the nickname pronounced Erzhi, she had that ponderous Central European look, perceived by Americans as dour, of a person too freighted with serious thoughts to make an effort to appear light-hearted. Her smile, when it came, did not linger. It appeared momentarily like sunlight that peeks through an opening in rolling dark thunderclouds. She accepted disappointment as the principal ingredient of the human condition; living seemed a burden to her much of the time. During the war, she had no trouble in acknowledging the merciless efficiency of the Nazi killing machine — inexplicable to most Hungarians and denied by many as hostile propaganda that cannot possibly be true — just as a luckless person accepts that a truck should happen to run over her or a best friend.

Even as a child I often heard, or overheard, conversation about the mystery of the great love of Erzhi's life: a married man of her father's generation and possibly a friend of his as well. A well-known, highly respected liberal, he met her surreptitiously, usually in the capital city of Budapest where he lived. But it happened more than once that he failed to appear at the agreed-upon time, and after waiting for no more than half an hour — after all, something unavoidable could have held him back — she went back to the railroad station and boarded the next train for the provincial town of Debrecen, where she lived. The four-to-five-hour journey seemed a slow, interminable trudge through the boring, flat Great Plain, and upon arrival she found people in her town even more coldly indifferent than she remembered them.

But happiness eluded her even when her lover showed up on time and things went well between them. After her return home, she appeared lost, like a vessel adrift, and no one at the helm. She asked herself: *Now* what am I going to do?

Did Erzhi cry more when their love bloomed, or after it wilted which happened more frequently? I asked my mother Anna some years ago, and she said she found it impossible to tell. According to her, the affair began when Erzhi was very young, perhaps not even twenty; and though it endured for many years, there never was an hour when it did not weigh on her mind. It served both as a reason and as an excuse for her not taking very seriously any of the other men who entered her life from time to time, Anna my mother theorized. They were not potential husbands, Erzhi decided sooner rather than later, and she dreamed about a lifelong marriage to a valiant man who lived up to her high and unalterable standards. Mother, met most of the candidates and described some of them as "waifs" and "weaklings" who "provoked" Erzhi's compassion, and others as "attractive scoundrels" who took advantage of her gullibility in matters of the heart. One man would accompany her to the theater where her favorites were *Hamlet* and *Macbeth* and other Shakespearean tragedies of relentlessly unfolding destiny. (She refused to waste her time on the frothy French farces and their Hungarian imitations then in fashion.) Or she would spend a few days with someone else at a quiet resort in the mountains, Hungarian or Austrian, celebrated for its "healing waters." Though nervous about encountering someone who knew her, the couple went for leisurely strolls along the serpentine path leading to the hilltop with a picture-postcard view of dense woods and church steeples, with high mountains as the backdrop. Several times a day she took long, dutiful draughts of the water rich with foul-smelling minerals, as recommended by resort management. In the evening they listened to the local orchestra's medleys from Mozart's *Magic Flute* and *Don Giovanni*, in a rhythm that was either intolerably slow or ridiculously fast. Only waltzes by Johann Strauss and Franz Lehar were played to the right beat. But she did not like to dance. She thought of herself as hopelessly clumsy.

Longing for the sight of the sea she imagined would reveal new and unexpected vistas, she regretted her confinement in a landlocked country and felt it a misfortune. Though on several occasions she booked a train ticket for Venice, something unforeseen, usually some illness or another, would come up at the last minute, and she never did catch a glimpse of the sea. She was also drawn to bridges where she liked to linger rather than to cross, to paths strewn with withered leaves, and to fields swaddled in pristine snow. She preferred autumn's hues of resignation to spring's rainbow of vigor. White, the uniform of mourning in the Orient, was her favorite color.

The years passed without her meeting a man who would have proved worthy of her sentiments, except of course for that peerless soul in Budapest, her first love, a pious Roman Catholic for whom divorce was out of the question.

The question may be asked: How do I know all this about Erzhi? The answer is that she was one friend my family, and especially my mother, never stopped mentioning in conversation. On one occasion, for instance, out on a stroll with Uncle Shumi who was talking about an unmarried cousin who did not have much luck with women, he suddenly switched the subject. "I sometimes think," he said, "that Erzhi thought of being alone and unhappy as her ineluctable fate that she couldn't or wouldn't fight."

Erzhi was a newcomer in Debrecen, the country's second city of not much more than 100,000 inhabitants, and proverbially conservative and introverted. It was controlled by merchant dynasties that carefully understated their wealth and power, and by rich farmers no longer engaged in farming who did not mind showing their affluence though usually only among their own kind. They were hardworking, parsimonious, somber burghers of a city proud of its special role in Hungarian history as a "free town" under the king and beholden to no feudal lord, as well as an overwhelmingly Protestant redoubt called "the Calvinist Rome" and a center for visceral nationalism unalterably opposed to the Roman Catholic Habsburg rule. The people of Debrecen called themselves *civis* — the Latin word for citizen — and liked to describe themselves as "thick-necked Calvinists," suggesting staunch convictions, dogged tenacity, and a readiness to take up a stance of opposition, no matter how quixotic. They judged a person by his or her father and grandfathers, or by someone well known farther back on a family tree. They were aware of Erzhi's ancestors who included a founder of Hungarian Unitarianism in the sixteenth century, a man of courage and spirituality bearing the same family name. Such pedigree gave her prestige, but the townspeople did not like her reluctance to discuss it. "Erzhi was too independent-minded, too brainy, too complicated." Uncle Shumi once said. "Most people kept their distance from her."

Debrecen natives tended to be wary of all newcomers as "restless folks who couldn't make it elsewhere" and who might conceivably try to change the tried-and-true ways of a settlement dating back to the twelfth century. The town also baffled generations of poets and artists, who felt lonely and rejected living within its confines, and depicted its sullen silences and smoldering contrariness.

Until the nineteenth century the town's merchants and guilds protected their privileges and refused to permit Jews to spend a night within city limits, let alone settle there. Fear of competition figured as one principal reason; anti-Semitism was another. But in 1840 a new law passed by a reform-minded parliament permitted the settlement of Jews in any part of the country. Reluctantly, Debrecen gave up its tradition of exclusion, though the town council insisted that an applicant for residence must produce a certificate of high moral standing issued by a local magistrate and prove that he has the means to support himself and his family.

Nevertheless, in just one generation, many of the Jewish newcomers became enthusiastic loyalists of Debrecen, and in 1901, sixty years after accepting its first Jewish citizen, the town elected a Jew to parliament and re-elected him for nearly twenty years. Between the two world wars, Jews across the country admired Debrecen's Calvinist bishop, Old Testament scholar Dezso Balthazar, as the most devoted friend of Hungary's Jews. Had he not died in 1938, he would have certainly taken the leading role in opposing the spread of Nazi influence in Hungary. Still, Balthazar did not speak for all of Debrecen. The town also provided the base for perhaps the strongest Nazi-like movement in the country.

Erzhi never felt at home in Debrecen, members of my family later recalled. As she objected to inherited privilege and power, she avoided opportunities to rub shoulders with the ruling class. She reflexively distrusted the town's leading citizens, easily identified by their imperturbable demeanor and dignified gestures, deliberate and unemotional. "Sober" was one of their favorite praises, which they did not award easily. They liked to begin sentences with the clause, "according to my calculations," and they sized up people by their financial worth, which they usually estimated with uncanny accuracy. In the winter they were enveloped in thick, nearly black double-breasted greatcoats with wide collars of wolf fur — the mantle of prosperity only the select few could afford — which they paraded on the street when snowflakes swirled in the air and the bone-chilling wind from the Carpathian mountains drove everyone else into taking refuge next to the home fire of a dark green tile-stove. Their tight-cut blue serge suits, starched white shirts, and immaculate silver-gray cravats seemed like uniforms they took off only at bedtime. Their wives, in plain woolen dresses either navy blue or gray, stayed at home, sending out their servants to shop and do errands. Many of them did not even venture out for the Sunday afternoon ritual of strolling up and down Market Street, between the train station and the Great Temple, the Calvinist church where parliament, fired up by the oratory of the revolutionary leader Lajos Kossuth, approved the dethronement of the Habsburg dynasty in 1849.

Almost a Member of the Schwarcz Family

Erzhi was one of the first people my mother Anna met and befriended after moving from her native village to Debrecen in 1927 with her six siblings and their widowed mother Roza Schwarcz. In their twenties, neither Erzhi and Anna could rely on their family resources. They had to earn a living. Anna welcomed the chance of "going out into the world" and tried a number of crafts such as weaving carpets and sewing dresses before she found a clerk's job with a small insurance company where she worked her way up to the position of a bookkeeper. Erzhi was a colleague at the insurance company before she joined the civil service in 1934. Inseparable throughout the 1930s, the two women exchanged weekly letters after Anna married Aladar, my father, and left Debrecen with him in 1938, the year after my birth. But for the next several years we went back for visits two, even three times a year.

Erzhi adored my maternal grandmother Roza, and was a frequent guest in her home. I remember walking into Grandmother's living room after my afternoon nap —- I was four or five — finding them, along with my mother, crying softly while sipping their favorite mix of coffee and fresh milk, and eating shortcakes filled with slices of tart apple, sprinkled with powdered sugar, and still warm from the oven. Why they were crying I never learned. When years later I asked Mother, she said that usually either Grandmother Roza or Erzhi had something to cry about and that both "enjoyed a good cry." At times, I found them carrying on a lively conversation, and more often that not it was my mother, cheerful and talkative, who did the speaking. I felt that Aunt Erzhi, as I was told to call her, was shy and sad but loving — and almost a member of the family. I don't remember a time when I did not know her or did not hear her name mentioned.

Years later Mother explained that Erzhi was "melancholy" because she was an infant when her mother died and a young girl when her father passed away. A judge and a scholar of the law, the father had a reputation as a man of rectitude, duty, and distance, in the grand nineteenth century mold. His last job was in a senior judicial position in Debrecen.

An only child, Erzhi had no relatives she kept in touch with. When speaking of her, my mother never failed to point out that "poor Erzhi was left completely alone in the world after her father's death." Originally, the family came from Transylvania, a historic Hungarian domain lost to Romania after the First World War. "You see," Mother explained, "Erzhi was an orphan several times over."

It now seems to me that as a lifelong victim, Erzhi nurtured an affectionate pity for individuals and groups that society singled out for contempt. A descendant on both sides from Unitarian stock, she had in her the smoldering fire of that small Protestant minority, a combative back-to-the-simplicity-of-the-Bible sect in Transylvania during the halcyon days of the Reformation in the sixteenth century. While not interested in religion — her own or anyone else's — Erzhi detested those who propagated the hatred of any one denomination or its followers.

My family always thought that Erzhi's father's prestige must have helped her in securing a sought-after, solid government job attached to the mayor's office, with responsibilities for the birth registry for Debrecen, the capital of Hajdu County. But it had to be due to her skills and conscientiousness that even though a woman, she became by age forty-three, in 1942, a special assistant reporting directly to the mayor. Precise, courteous, and pugnacious, Miss David had a reputation as a well-organized administrator who knew how to extract information that was often sensitive for the many different kinds of people she dealt with.

In Hungarian, the register of births is called "The Mother Book," which refers to the Roman law's maxim that only the mother is certain, as well as to the mother's obligation to report her newborn to the authorities. For more than a century, The Mother Book served as the basic, authoritative state ledger where a child's name and birth date had to be accompanied by the parents' names, birth dates, occupations, addresses, and, of course, religious affiliations. Later on in life, a certified copy of that entry was required when filling out other official documents, such as school admission papers, conscription forms, professional licenses, and passports.

Throughout the 1930s, parliament passed discriminatory legislation against Jews; to be exempt, all Hungarian citizens had to obtain certified copies of their ancestors' entries in The Mother Book. Two Jewish grandparents doomed a person as Jewish. (In German Nazi law, one grandparent sufficed.) But public officials were disgraced if the records showed some Jewish genes. In 1939 a far-right journalist tracked down entries in The Mother Book proving that the pro-Nazi prime minister, Bela Imredy, had a great-grandfather who was born Jewish but converted to Christianity at age seven, in 1814, along with his parents. The prime minister was forced to resign but continued to play an important role in pro-Nazi politics, and his distant Jewish ancestry did not save him from execution as a war criminal.

In each county capital, those in charge of administering The Mother Book had responsibility for issuing copies of the birth certificates of forebears as far back as the late eighteenth century. Every adult had to take those papers to another government office which then determined if one was Christian or Jewish and issued the appropriate identity card, which folded in two and was small enough for a jacket pocket.

In the ideal case, the birth certificate showed that the bearer's four grandparents were untainted by Jewish blood and thus not subject to the increasingly severe restrictions of the new, Nazi-inspired laws. Today The Mother Book is still the fundamental state ledger administered by the same government agency, and its custodians continue to receive, as Erzhi once did, the kind of respect reserved for judges. However, there is no longer an entry for religious affiliation.

In and out of her office, Erzhi spoke up against the social stigma attached both to "a fallen woman" and the child she gave birth to. She argued that a man should be held accountable for a child he sired, regardless of the circumstances. Hers was very much of a minority view in a culture that regarded men as hunters and women as their quarry — and rooted for the hunter. She was helpful to unwed mothers, especially to servants thrown out of households where a member of the family was responsible for a pregnancy, a fairly common occurrence. Erzhi took the trouble of not only finding out the father's name — which was a discretionary part of her job — but she tried to obtain some compensation for the servant, or at the very least secure another job, both of which went beyond a registrar's call of duty. Privately, Erzhi also helped out with referrals, loans, and gifts of money.

As so many others from upper-class families which had seen better days "in the happy time of peace" before the First World War, Erzhi insisted on keeping up appearances and conducted herself as if no change had taken place in Hungarian living standards. My mother Anna thought that Erzhi's wardrobe was limited but immaculate. Though modest in dress and not bothering to pay attention to fashion, she permitted herself one sumptuous exception: silk. She liked its sheen and shimmer, its subtle refractions of light and color, and she enjoyed restoring the fabric to its full glory by wielding her iron filled with smoldering charcoal. For special occasions — and visiting friends and going out for Sunday afternoon promenades qualified as festive — a silk dress was warranted. Silk was the fabric in which Erzhi felt most comfortable, Mother said. It seemed to lift her above the dust or the mud of the everyday. Putting on a fine silk dress almost made her feel as if all was well with the world.

By local standards Erzhi should have been content. She held a prestigious job and earned a good salary, both rare for a woman in the period between the two world wars. Women of high social standing nodded to her on the street, and their men tipped their hats, though most of them were reluctant to strike up conversations with her.

As expected of a well brought-up woman, she moved with a kind of hauteur and grace. But she was lanky, and she even stooped a little when not in public view, and her face did not pass the test for conventional beauty. Her thick glasses, which she wore in the office but usually not on social occasions, further discouraged men. Besides, Mother added, Erzhi had no independent wealth or influential relatives, at least one of which she would have needed to attract suitors of her social standing.

In her youth she had a touch of tuberculosis and a host of other medical problems. A chill north wind sweeping through the streets of Debrecen signaled to her a clear and present danger. She worried that the clothes she wore were not warm enough, and she feared an imminent further decline of her health. On occasion, she would sigh and say that without her doctors and pills she would have been dead long ago. Frequently ill, she spent much time in the hospital. My mother, who took pride in what she called her "sturdy peasant health," made fun of Erzhi and joked that despite her delicate constitution, or maybe because of it, she "would live forever."

Mother suspected that at least at times Erzhi must have been "acting ill," which amounted to something of a cultural obligation. A woman of sensitivity and refinement was expected to be "delicate" and devote a certain amount of time every year to the ritual of ailing and recuperation. Her friends were obligated to play their parts by paying bedside visits, bringing her the latest gossip, along with bouquets of roses or carnations or meadow flowers, or little packets containing bite-size cakes of chocolate and hazelnut, or, during fall and winter, dollops of chestnut puree blanketed with whipped cream.

But even when not ailing, Erzhi did not have much energy. She complained that she worked much too hard, and her body and her mind could not cope with the stresses of having to concentrate on doing the flawless job expected of her. Returning home at the end of the day, she was exhausted. On work nights, she could rarely be coaxed into taking a stroll or visiting a friend.

Erzhi lived alone in a tiny apartment she rented, a short walk from her office, in one of the town's hundreds of simple, one-story houses, whitewashed inside and out, that faced the street and went on toward the back yard for a hundred feet or more. Perched on a chair with flowers carved into every square inch, one of the few family relics salvaged from her ancestral home in Transylvania, she looked out a window that faced the dusty yard along the length of the house. People in her social position did not live in the one room that faced the street. It would not have been proper for her to peek out from behind a curtain to watch people walk by, or to sit by a wide-open casement window, with elbows planted on the sill, and engage in conversation neighbors in other windows or acquaintances passing by on the cobblestone streets shaded by leafy trees. That sort of gregariousness was for the common folk.

Erzhi saw her immediate environment as sinking deeper into penny-pinching misery and provincial boredom. According to my Uncle Shumi who liked to make literary references, she was looking for evidence of chivalry in the redemptive Arthurian mode, practiced by a knight worthy of a seat at the Round Table who stalked the streets of Debrecen or rode his horse on the country roads around it. When visiting Budapest, she thought she sometimes spotted a beauteous Queen Guinevere beckoning to a man from a geranium-studded balcony. But nowhere did she recognize a Sir Lancelot.

My other uncles mentioned that Erzhi disliked Gypsy music, perhaps because she felt cheated out of the sweetness of life it celebrated, and she found its dominant mood of melancholy "trite." She admired the vast neo-baroque parliament building by the Danube, a majestic edifice with gold-and-red chambers and vaulted corridors that would have warmed Rudyard Kipling's imperialist heart. But she had the taste of a bitter almond in her mouth as she looked at the politicians puff on their cigars while predicting Hungarian military victories and pronouncing the Hungarian soldier "the unequalled absolute best in the world." Excess and self-deception, she felt like crying out, foolish lies from the beginning to the end. Of what use are the ancient pretensions, romanticizing either the people's Asian, nomadic origins with Attila the Hun as an antecedent, or Hungary's transformation into the eastern outpost of West European Christianity — or both? What was that famous "special role" Hungarians claim to play in Europe? Just exactly what was the meaning of the phrase, repeated like a prayer, that the nation was "destined for greatness from its earliest beginnings"? Hungarian history offered long stretches of abject submission to foreign conquerors and brief intervals of independence. As for the present, it looked hopeless to Erzhi. If the Third Reich emerged victorious from the war, it would swallow Hungary. If the Axis collapsed, Hungary would also lose, no matter how reluctant a partner it might have been to Germany. She made no secret of her conviction that the nation was led by greedy scoundrels under Hitler's thumb and by a foolish, self-centered, narcissistic upper class confident that somehow it would always arrange to receive "a special treatment," whether from Germany or the Western Allies, because they would all sympathize with Hungary's "special predicament." No one bothered to take into consideration what Stalin might have had in mind. Unmistakably, Hungary was careening toward another historic catastrophe.

As early as the 1920s Erzhi began studying Germany's extreme right, fearful of the fanaticism that fueled the growth of Nazi power. At the time when most Hungarians shrugged and dismissed the new chancellor of Germany as "a comic actor" or "the former house painter" or "a ridiculous little upstart" who would be soon thrown out by "serious Germans," she cited passages from his book, *Mein Kampf*, which she had read carefully from cover to cover, and said that his ravings must be taken at their face value. Again and again she told members of my family that a large number of Hitler's compatriots were hypnotized by his boasts of the German race as the *Herrenvolk* and that once rearmed, they would fight wars to realize his vision of world domination.

She argued with those who maintained that the Nazis marching at night in torch-lit parades and conjuring up pagan Germanic war cries were only foolish romantic escapists from the drabness of industrial civilization. Nor did it seem to her as harmless playacting when the Nazis' Hungarian imitators, who received funds from the Reich, gave their children pre-Christian names, toyed with the notion of returning to the pagan rite of sacrificing white horses, and dreamed about restoring the glory of *Magna Hungaria*, which would encompass all the neighboring lands that ever fell under the rule of a king who wore St. Stephen's holy crown. She did not celebrate when Hitler returned to Hungary parts of Transylvania, where her ancestors had lived. To the contrary, she said, the future that Hitler's so-called generosity foreshadowed was grim, and Romania would surely regain those lands after the war, which indeed it did.

While my Uncle Levente agreed with her, other Hungarians, Gentiles and Jews, smiled at her theories condescendingly and parroted folksy proverbs such as "one does not eat porridge when it's piping hot," she declared that Hitler was determined to implement his polemic calling for the extermination of all Jews. She also recalled that in the first edition of *Mein Kampf*, Hitler condemned Hungarians as Asiatic interlopers who had no role to play in Europe. Yes, that reference was dropped from later editions, but she angrily dismissed arguments that Nazi slogans, as harsh as they may sound, would soon be tempered by plain common sense and could be further whittled down by negotiation, that Nazi leaders once in power could be made to see the exaggerations of their early ideas, or in the worst case they could always be bribed. After the war broke out in 1939 Erzhi claimed to know for a fact that ordinary German soldiers — and not just the deeply indoctrinated SS — killed civilians mercilessly, and that they not only followed orders but did it with joy, believing that they were doing the right thing by *Das Vaterland* and *Der Führer*.

Mother remembered Erzhi as the first person who talked to her about Hitler. Erzhi hated the Nazis as evil, unredeemably and non-negotiably so. If they are not stopped, she declared, they will kill all the Jews as well as those who are out of sympathy with Nazism. She also detested right-wing Hungarians who kept praising the Germans' "iron will" and "invincible military" and expected that their worship of the Germans will somehow pay off. Posing as populists, they hoped to take advantage of social injustice and unrest among the poor in the countryside and in the cities, and to replace the regime of Regent Miklos Horthy and his aristocratic friends ensconced on Castle Hill in Budapest.

After the war, Mother and her siblings recalled how Erzhi confronted them: "Don't you see that it is a struggle for survival?" But she did not get more than a courteous hearing from, say, Mishi who typically did not want to be late for a meeting with his date at 8 p.m. and still had to borrow money for dinner from one of his sisters. Nor did Erzhi make headway with one of his cousins whose mind was on the job of selling his harvest of wheat or wine to a buyer he was scheduled to see that evening.

Listening to Erzhi's ideas disturbed my mother, she said to me years later. While Erzhi's mastery of her facts suggested a well-briefed government administrator, Mother recalled, her sentiments were those of an overly anxious friend who was an honorary member of a Jewish family. Mother could not change Erzhi's radical pessimism, and she feared that Erzhi's "hysterical certainties" reflected mental instability. On the other hand, Mother said to herself, Erzhi claimed to know what others only feared; she articulated what others kept to themselves. Nevertheless, in the final analysis, Erzhi could not be right. For a congenital optimist such as my mother, it seemed as if her friend had come from another world. Mother often asked her: "Why don't you think bright, happy thoughts?"

Mother acknowledged that she remained unconvinced that it was the reality of facts, rather than subjective unhappiness, which informed Erzhi's assessments. All along, Mother was firmly convinced that Erzhi's ideas originated with the love of her life, that mysterious man in Budapest, and Mother blamed him for filling Erzhi's head with dark foreboding about the world — in addition to making her life miserable in other ways as well. But not even Mother knew who that man was, though she had some suspicions — it occurred to her that he could be a high-ranking official in the all-powerful Ministry of the Interior — and she would never forgive Erzhi for refusing to let her in on the secret.

Mother liked each of her friends to be "an open book" to her. Erzhi was not only a half-closed book, but Mother did not understand the language that book was written in. No matter how many times Erzhi tried to explain, Mother remained baffled why the Nazis, be they German or Hungarian, should hate the Jews as much as they said they did, and, even more important to her, why a Gentile like Erzhi would jeopardize her job and, in the end, her life, in helping a people not her own.

For both of them, films offered an escape. It was a matter of heated debate in the family whether it was Erzhi or my mother or one of our relatives who should be given credit for inventing a special system of rating movies: whether a person needed one, two, or three handker-chiefs to soak up her tears. It goes without saying that the highest rec-ommendation was "a three-handkerchief movie," such as *Gone with the Wind*.

Strolling on Market Street

Erzhi enjoyed meeting and making friends with our relatives, then numbering well over a hundred, most of them living in small towns and villages within a few hours of a carriage ride from Debrecen, the big city of northeast Hungary, and visiting one another frequently, usually dropping in without prior notice. While they all loved their soft-spoken Aunt Roza, "a woman of consummate kindness" as one of her grandnieces characterized her, most of them were related to her husband Karl Schwarcz who had died in 1921 and whose memory they all treasured as a loving relative and an innovative farmer. But the village estate he built up collapsed after the First World War, and after 1927 his widow was reduced to a modest household in Debrecen consisting of most of her seven children, three of whom married in the 1930s. There was no telephone in the house, but there were extra beds for relatives in the boys' room and the girls'; whoever visited was fed and entertained, taken to theater and soccer games, and for strolls on Market Street, the broad main thoroughfare with trees and benches in the middle.

On a crisp sun-filled Sunday afternoon in spring, Erzhi would join my mother and a few of her cousins to walk for an hour, as far as the edge of the town, up to the woods called the Great Forest, sit in the little pastry shop called the Palm Tree, enjoy one or more of the three flavors of ice cream (chocolate, vanilla, and lemon), and then walk back to Roza's house. They marched arm-in-arm, in lockstep, taking up the width of the pavement and splitting into two groups when passing someone or letting someone pass from the opposite direction. These walks, my mother said, were somtimes too brisk for Erzhi, though she obviously enjoyed the togetherness.

Erzhi loved the theater of the male relatives bouncing into Roza's living room with broad smiles on their faces and saluting everyone with hands high up in the air, ready for embraces. They kissed the ladies' hands and then the cheeks on both sides, starting with Roza, of course, then her three daughters, with the eldest always first, and then going around the room to greet everyone else. Hugs and kisses with female and male relatives were not just airy, symbolic contacts, though intense and heartfelt, and after meeting Erzhi a few times, family members included her as well. The women were smart and stylish, but less boisterous and less free in their choice of words and stories than the men; they were expected to be ladylike, and they were that. They relished the role of walking around the room and offering, with gracious gestures, trays of sweets such as crescent-shaped almond cookies dusted with vanilla-scented powdered sugar.

My uncles and aunts remembered Erzhi as impressed with the unconditional affection that members of the Schwarcz family had for one another and with their readiness to accept their relatives' relatives and friends as their own. She was touched by their emotional links with ancestral lands that some of them still owned or at least rented, and by their unswerving loyalty to the country which, as they often declared, had been good to them. But most of all, she was buoyed by their cheeriness which reflected the Schwarcz tradition of unshakable confidence in the future. Years later Uncle Mishi recalled her saying that she appreciated the Schwarcz faith in the fundamental goodness of people that unfortunately she could not share.

My mother and her female contemporaries thought that Erzhi must have been in love with some of the men. After all, woman relatives said with a knowing smile, opposites attract. (The men, proud of their discretion, would not condescend to discussing such matters, and they were masterful in eluding direct questions from inquisitive relatives.) Mother's older brother Mishi, a handsome, light-hearted raconteur and an inveterate skirt-chaser, was everyone's prime suspect. Another candidate was eldest brother Shumi, serious and responsible. My mother was quite certain that Erzhi had been in love with Shumi for a long time, though neither Erzhi nor Shumi encouraged that impression. Or, she said, perhaps Erzhi had liaisons with one or more of the numerous cousins. Mother suspected that Erzhi must have fallen for one of the attractive but unreliable relatives always on the lookout for adventure, and she was embarrassed to reveal her secret even to her best friend.

I have sometimes thought that the affairs existed only in Mother's imagination. A born matchmaker and an enthusiastic gossip, she enjoyed pairing people and thinking up hypotheses about their secrets. Talking about Erzhi, which was often, she once said: "I do wish that Erzhi had had some good moments in life. God knows she deserved at least some good moments." But Mother also recalled that Erzhi was "a very serious, somber person" who did not visit Grandmother Roza because some handsome relatives were often around. "Erzhi was always eager to discuss things that truly matter," Mother said.

From the pedestal of her civil service post, Erzhi saw dishonesty and betrayal all around. Uncle Levente, a journalist who probably relied on her as a source, recalled after the war how she laughed bitterly when members of the extended Schwarcz family expressed their confidence in "the chivalry of the Hungarian nation." But she did not make a face when hearing story after story about the deep Jewish roots in Hungary. Yes, Jews had settled in the country before it became Hungary, when it was a province of the Roman Empire. Yes, plenty of Hungarians, including some serious scholars, firmly believed that perhaps two of the seven nomadic tribes which in the ninth century crossed the Carpathian mountains from the east were from the Khazar Empire, the one nation in history that converted to Judaism, though eventually it was defeated by neighbors who later founded the Russian state.

Erzhi listened politely. She too had studied history, an academic discipline considered far more important than mathematics or biology in a country where everyone was trained to be proud of one thousand years of statehood. But she felt that collecting precedents was a way of avoiding the need to confront the dangers of the present and the threats of the future, and on occasion she lost her patience with my relatives who tried to dismiss her warnings. She pleaded with family members to try to emigrate before it was "too late." Her recommendation was to have a few of the young and most resourceful men go first, find jobs, and then send for the others.

"I know the name of every flower in a meadow," one of the Schwarcz cousins is quoted as having replied to Erzhi, and after the war no one could tell me for certain who that might have been, as any one of them could have expressed that thought. "Why should I leave for a foreign country? Who can say that I don't belong here?" After every new law designed to restrict Jewish participation in national life, there were always a few relatives who said that, certainly, it would be the last such legislation, and some believed that the restrictions were designed "to take the wind out of the sail of Nazi demands." They displayed pride rather than pragmatism. After the government expropriated all agricultural land owned by Jews, one cousin countered: the state could steal the vineyard that his grandfather Yankel Schwarcz had planted and pruned to perfection, but no one could ever take away Yankel's glory as the first in Szabolcs County to produce high-quality wine from its notoriously poor, sandy soil.

Nevertheless, Erzhi's advice did have an impact on Uncle Anti, Mother's then unmarried younger brother who emigrated to Uruguay around 1934. My mother, his favorite sister, was supposed to follow him. But Anti got homesick and returned after two years, arriving just in time for the enactment of the first comprehensive, Nazi-like legislation restricting Jewish participation in every aspect of economic and cultural life.

To my family, Erzhi sounded like Cassandra, the shrill seeress in Greek tragedy who prophesied war and Troy's destruction. Such a role was unpopular in Hungarian society dedicated to comfort and still citing Emperor Franz Josef's dictum: "Staying calm is the citizen's first duty."

The time came, in the early 1940s, when family members other than Roza and my mother were reluctant to invite Erzhi. Forgetting her manners, Erzhi had been raising her voice at Saturday night and Sunday afternoon get-togethers. At first, she might express her preference for silk. But then she said that she was not interested enough to engage in lengthy arguments with my mother or a cousin praising "artificial silk" — what rayon was called in Hungary — the product

of factories then fashionable and offering more durability and shimmer than silk and so much easier to iron. Erzhi would say something
curt and unpleasant about the superiority of authentic substances to
ersatz products invented by people who want to make a profit.
Another incident was remembered by Aunt Mara, my mother's
younger sister: when someone expressed the hope that airplane traffic, then new in Debrecen, would stir up the stagnant, oppressive
summer heat of the Great Plain, Erzhi seized that crazy rumor as an
opening for voicing her fears about the Luftwaffe and the German
military buildup and the dangers they posed to Hungary and the rest
of Europe. While the British and the French were seeking "peace in
our time" and the Hungarian government was cozying up to Berlin,
Erzhi discussed German preparations for a most destructive, univer-
sal war.

Throughout the 1930s she kept talking about how much worse
things were getting for Jews in Germany. "But Germany is not
Hungary," was always the answer. She countered that the beginnings
of the anti-Jewish legislation in Hungary constituted a multi-staged
bureaucratic sequence. Restrictions on Jews practicing their profes-
sions and running their businesses would soon continue with curfews,
limitations on freedom of movement, and ghettoization. After the
war broke out, she cited the experience of Jewish communities under
German occupation, and she spoke about the transports to the so-
called labor camps. She was certain that eventually in Hungary too
there would be no more compromises and no exemptions, and everybody with Jewish ancestors would have to go to those camps. When
someone recalled the hoary Habsburg tradition of "live and let live,"
she retorted that the precedent was flawed because the German Nazis
were fanatic killers and not flexible Austrian Habsburgs, the German-
speaking neighbors and former imperial masters whom Hungarians
were familiar with. Finally, she did not agree with her Jewish friends
and well-meaning Gentiles that Hungary's government would or
could shield the country's Jews from the Nazis.

After Hungary joined the war on Germany's side in 1941, Hitler demanded strict measures against Hungary's Jews, the last large Jewish community still functioning in Europe. Hungarian resistance to German pressures stiffened after 1942, when Horthy appointed a covertly pro-Allied prime minister, Miklos Kallay, also known to be sympathetic to Jews. His father had been a friend of Roza's late husband and a frequent visitor to the Schwarcz estate in the village of Gyulaj, along with several other members of the Kallay clan who claimed descent from one of the seven chieftains leading the conquest of Hungary in the ninth century. Erzhi pleaded with Roza to turn to the prime minister for advice, which she did most reluctantly, as she did not like to make demands on people. According to Uncle Shumi, Kallay's response recognized the tender ties of the past by calling Roza "my dear aunt" (in the affectionate sense, of course), but his advice was to leave the country as soon as possible, and he implied that he could not stand up against the Germans for long.

As a measure of his distrust of the Hungarian government's allegiance to the Axis, he sent the Wehrmacht to occupy Hungary on March 19, 1944. To evade arrest, Kallay sought asylum in the legation of neutral Turkey, and his pro-Nazi successor quickly began the deportations of Jews from the easternmost parts of the country. Gathering Jews in ghettoes and then packing them into sealed trains bound for the Reich's concentration camps was presided over by the Hungarian gendarmerie, the superbly organized, well-paid, and totally reliable enforcement segment of the civil service.

Roza's weekly postcards to her daughter Anna in Budapest reported that "dear Erzhi visits us faithfully" and "strengthens our spirit in these trying days."

Visitor to the Ghetto

In May 1944 the Jews of Debrecen were ordered into a ghetto that they were not allowed to leave — only authorized personnel could visit them. But Erzhi was a ranking civil servant, then the deputy director of The Mother Book. The administrator who was known never to raise her voice in the office would bully her way into the ghetto and intimidate the guards, whether ordinary policemen or elite gendarmes. She claimed she had work to do in checking out details for The Mother Book.

Hidden under her dress were copies of birth certificates of Christians, each properly authenticated with her so-called masculine signature: decisive, bold, and illegible. Once she found someone who was born in about the same year as the person described in the birth certificate, a match was made, and a Jew could escape from the ghetto at night, confident that if he or she later ran into police or gendarmes, Erzhi's document would suffice. Escape was dangerous but feasible, particularly during air raids that sent the guards scurrying for the safety of underground shelters. Next, the fugitives had to find friends who would hide them, at least for a few days, before they could leave town.

Erzhi looked for people she knew and offered them the documents. A few jumped at the chance. A birth certificate seemed safe enough; its bearer simply had to memorize a birth date and those of the parents, plus their occupations and addresses. A certificate that identified one's religion as Calvinist or Roman Catholic was strong proof, and military and police patrols had no particular reason to challenge it. If they detained someone and checked with the office of The Mother Book, the answer would have been that yes, such a person was properly entered into the mother book, and the names and the dates were correct.

Erzhi cautioned them that staying in Debrecen was dangerous because in a small town someone hostile to Jews may recognize a familiar Jewish face on the street. It was far safer to find a way to reach Budapest, the big city where no one was likely to be able to identify a native of another town. The fugitives could claim that their home in Debrecen had been bombed and were lucky enough to escape with the clothes on their backs and their birth certificates.

As an administrator of people and papers, Erzhi knew precisely how she could help. When I last spoke to them about Erzhi, my mother and her brother Shumi did not know if she relied on anyone's advice or encouragement, and they did not think that she tried to bring together likeminded people to organize a network. But, I have since learned, she maintained contact with Calvinist pastors helping Jews, and she supplied their protégés birth certificates. Recent research by the head of the Debrecen Jewish community, Peter Weisz, revealed that she had a most important helper, her colleague Istvan Varga. Moreover, she had a number of people she could turn to with a request that they hide Jews, and her contacts probably included some of the unwed mothers and their children whom she had helped over the years.

She had no doubt that she was doing the right thing, and the fear of being caught and imprisoned did not hold her back. For once, she found she was not tired after her regular work hours. To the contrary, she had the energy to visit with people in the ghetto and to search out Gentile friends and acquaintances to find out if they might be willing to hide Jews. She later told my mother as if the assignment to help Jews had been "just waiting for her."

However, most Jews were afraid to take the risk of going illegal. Oblivious to what awaited them in the so-called labor camps in Germany, they were paralyzed by the fear of getting caught during the escape from the ghetto, or unmasked later by anti-Semites on the street, and then jailed or shot. Others told her that as responsible, law-abiding citizens, they could not imagine themselves doing something illegal, even if the law happened to be cruel and unreasonable.

Erzhi countered that using a Christian birth certificate was the best way to evade certain death in a concentration camp. But most Jews did not believe that such camps existed.

According to Uncle Levente, Erzhi was among the few people in Hungary who knew of the extermination camps early on and did not doubt their existence and purpose. In the spring of 1944, she was one of the few dozen people in Hungary informed by anti-Nazi contacts about a report by two Jewish escapees that outside a Polish village called Auschwitz, people were killed by poison gas and then cremated by the tens of thousands. She did not question the authenticity of the

Above left, Erzsebet (Erzhi) David before the war. Above right, Erzsebet David with an unidentified friend in Debrecen after the war. Below, Istvan Varga, Erzsebet David's key associate in her rescue work.

report that the Protestant anti-Nazi underground passed on to Regent Horthy, himself a Calvinist, and to key members of the government and the churches. She cited the facts mentioned in the report as she begged Jews to dodge their guards, jump off the train, run for their lives, hide — try anything to escape deportation.

Years later Uncle Shumi told me that he knew from Erzhi and some eyewitnesses that when her arguments were still rejected, Erzhi sometimes broke down in tears. Nevertheless, she systematically copied the treasures of her office records, and she was undiscouraged in her attempts to give them away in the ghetto she visited nearly every day for several weeks — until it was emptied by late June 1944, with its inhabitants packed into cattle cars bound for the death camps.

Erzhi failed with the older members of my family, even though she had arranged for hiding places for some of them, first of all Grandmother Roza and her eldest daughter Elza, and a few cousins, descendants of Great-Uncle Yankel, my grandfather's brother. They told her that they could not see themselves endangering the lives of the good people who offered to hide them. Some of them shuddered that if caught, how humiliating it would be when shown to be lying. As for younger relatives who might have taken the risks, they would not leave their aged parents behind. Yet another factor that immobilized them was that they depended on the men in the family to make decisions. But men between eighteen and fifty-five years of age were away, serving in labor battalions, and not many women were as brave as my mother who defied the government in refusing to move into the ghetto. But then we lived in Budapest, a metropolis with more than a million inhabitants, not in Debrecen.

"For your grandmother, carrying a forged document was out of the question," was my mother's curt statement to me many years later. She added: "And not only for the obvious practical reasons." When on another occasion I pressed for an explanation, she snapped: "You must understand. For your grandmother, using someone else's identity paper was out of the question. Simply out of the question. Period."

I think I understand. By the time my mother was sixteen, her father was dead, his estate lost just as the First World War was lost, and she had to learn how to survive in a hostile environment. But her mother, though in reduced circumstances, continued to live by the rules of a world that was still whole in her mind — the world she had been born into. Her reasoning in rejecting a forged birth certificate did not get as far as her breaking the law of the land or risking humiliation if caught in an escape attempt. She could not accept the notion that any temporal power could force her at age seventy-two to begin pretending that she had another name belonging to another person and that she was born to parents other than Milka and Naftali Kaufmann. She was their cherished only daughter, given the Hebrew name Rachel after the beloved of biblical Jacob — which was turned into Ruchl in Yiddish and Roza in Hungarian — and when she married she became Mrs. Schwarcz. How could she give up those names?

When my mother reached the end of her life in 1995 and could no longer recognize the people closest to her or where she was, "What is your name?" was the one question she could still answer. When the fabric of life has unraveled, whether in the external or the internal world, we hold on to our name as the last length of thread.

It was neither fear nor pride that made Grandmother Roza reject Erzhi's offer. To her way of thinking, using someone else's birth certificate would have meant that she would have to deny her faith, the family she grew up in, and the family she married into, as well as the children she raised, and the extended family whose matriarch she was. All her life she conducted herself in accordance with a code, observing the minutiae of Jewish tradition not just obediently but wholeheartedly. She could not imagine acting as if she were someone other than herself. Wasn't taking on another identity an abandonment of one's own? To her, dissembling was unthinkable. She could not live with a lie, no matter how necessary, or temporary.

Trusting to God and His unfathomable ways, Grandmother did

not fear for herself. She worried only about her family, a few of whom were with her in the ghetto. Then she did as ordered by the authorities: board a train going to a labor camp somewhere in Germany — whatever that meant. If boarding the train meant death, it meant death. She might have surmised that it did. But I doubt if she thought of her death as something as lofty as martyrdom.

When approaching death, the devout have an advantage.

According to the Talmud, first-century sage Rabbi Akiba was arrested a few days after the Romans prohibited the study of the Torah. In jail, he was surprised to meet an acquaintance, Papos ben Yehuda, and asked what brought him there. Papos said: "Happy are you, Rabbi Akiba, that you were arrested because of matters of the Torah. But woe to Papos who was arrested because of matters of no worth!"

Erzhi sent a trusted friend to deliver Christian birth certificates to my parents in Budapest. The messenger, I now know from the research encouraged by Peter Weisz of the Debrecen Jewish community, was her colleague Istvan Varga. In his briefcase, Varga carried a sheaf of documents, as we were not Erzhi's only contacts in the capital.

Concerned that at age six I might have problems learning a new name, Erzhi located in her files someone with the same first name as the one given to me at birth, and with a last name beginning with the letter "F," as in my true name. Thanks to the birth certificate, I became Karoly Farkas, a Calvinist and the son of Calvinist parents, and my father was listed as bearing that same name, a solidly Gentile custom. By occupation, he was a butcher. (My father, already in a labor battalion, could not make use of the birth certificate Erzhi prepared for him. My mother had no way of getting it to him.)

I still have my document; it is in an envelope in my desk drawer. My mother saved it, not only as a memento from the war and of Erzhi's heroism but as proof of another identity that I might — who knows? — need again one dark day. After I left Hungary following the revolution of 1956, my mother gave it to a trusted friend traveling to

With this birth certificate furnished by Erzebet David, the six-year-old author took on a new identity as Karoly Farkas, a Calvinist child from the city of Debrecen.

Vienna who mailed it in a registered letter to my new address in the United States. My roommates at Harvard — one from Texas and the other from New Jersey, both of them majoring in political science — were incredulous when I explained to them that Nazi patrols had once scrutinized that carefully folded piece of coarse paper, then worth more than an original work of art by a leading artist. Without it, a patrol would have sent me off to an Auschwitz-bound transport or marched me down to the Danube for a quick disposal.

On the basis of what they heard from friends in Debrecen, my mother and her brother Shumi believed that Jews used several dozen of Erzhi's birth certificates, and most of them escaped deportation and survived. However, one person was caught on the street in Debrecen, after a passersby identified him as a Jew he knew well and alerted a policeman who promptly arrested the suspect. The man soon confessed that the birth certificate he presented was indeed not his. The police summoned Erzhi and asked her if she knew how the Jew obtained the document signed by her.

Erzsebet David acknowledged that she had given the birth certificate to the man.

She was arrested on July 3, 1944 and taken to jail. As the Soviet troops were approaching from the east, prosecution proceeded with haste. She was tried within days, in the same courtroom once presided over by her father. Apparently concerned that some of her contacts in the local police might help her escape, the prosecutor made certain that she was placed in the special custody of the more reliable gendarmes.

Not for a moment did Erzhi deny what she had done. Instead, she denounced the laws and the ideology behind the persecution of Jews.

The prosecutor found her behavior scandalous and pronounced her guilty of the crime of abusing her authority as a senior official of the civil service. She stole documents belonging to the state. She defamed the memory of her father, a great judge and a patriot. She violated the sacred trust of the state; she broke the law in attempting to help the escape of the vermin Jews that the country was at last trying to get rid of. It was expected that Erzsebet David would be sentenced to death.

To gain time, her lawyer appealed on a technicality: her dismissal from the civil service was not done according to the rules. The record reflects that the court reprimanded the mayor, Laszlo Csoka, who was tardy in submitting the papers necessary for her prosecution, which was probably the mayor's way of delaying the process. Also charged was her colleague Istvan Varga.

In early August, an Allied air raid dropped bombs on a number of targets in Debrecen, most of them factories supplying the military. (According to a local story which is on its way to becoming a legend, one of the American pilots was a Debrecen-born Jew who knew the city and led the squadron.) One structure that received a direct hit was the law court and the adjacent jail where Erzhi was held. The bombs and the fire they set also destroyed some of the documentation relating to her case.

Though wounded, bleeding heavily, and barely able to walk, she managed to climb out of the ruins and escape, as did her co-conspirator Varga. Both found hiding places with friends who took care of them.

After the Red Army occupied the city in October 1944, Debrecen became Soviet military headquarters, and then the seat of the new, provisional, anti-Nazi Hungarian government. Erzhi was exonerated and reinstated in her old job. But, Uncle Shumi later reported to us, she limped, looked much older than her forty-six years, and could no longer maintain in public that proud, ramrod-straight bearing of hers. She spent more time in than out of the hospital. It was unclear if her illnesses had to do with some of her old medical problems or with the injuries she suffered during the air raid that also liberated her. The doctors also could not tell whether her condition was improving or getting worse. Nor could her visitors decide whether she was truly ill or just ailing in her usual ladylike manner.

My mother said she heard that Erzhi smiled, albeit faintly, only when visited by someone whose life she had saved with a Christian birth certificate. But when she talked about her rescue work, she focused on her failure in convincing most people to accept her documents. Again the tears came, just as they did when someone in the ghetto turned down her offer.

Mother, who exchanged frequent letters with Erzhi, could not imagine that she was seriously ill and thought that she must have been drained, physically and emotionally, and needed a long rest. Many years later Mother confessed that she did not travel to Debrecen to visit her friend because she did not want to go through the agony of hearing Erzhi say, "Your mother could be alive today," and listening to her repeat the same question in every one of her letters: "Why did your mother refuse the birth certificate I begged her to take?" Erzhi could not fathom the reason, and Mother did not want to explain, or perhaps could not explain.

Then one morning in September 1948, without any prior intimation of a crisis, Erzhi died in her sleep in the hospital, at age forty-nine. My mother learned from mutual friends in Debrecen that the doctors could not identify the cause of death. "Erzhi died of a broken heart," people who knew her said in conversation with my mother over the years. My mother, who could not forgive herself for not paying a final visit to her friend, used to sigh deeply and softly added a correction: "multiple fractures of the heart."

The small Jewish community that survived in Debrecen arranged for her funeral, in the so-called "common" or nondenominational cemetery. Nobody related to her could be located, but scores of Jews attended, many of them beneficiaries of her documents. The head of the Jewish community called her "our second Esther" — a reference to the woman who saved the Jews of Persia two thousand years earlier, the archetypal rescuer in Jewish tradition.

Despite its scant resources, the community commissioned a splendid five-foot tall white marble monument to mark her grave. Underneath a carving of a grief-stricken female figure, a fine sentimental poem titled "Farewell" was etched into the stone following Erzhi's name, her occupation, the date of her death, and the motto, "She loved everyone else more than she loved herself."

Who wrote the poem? No one in my family seemed to know. My mother — who visited Debrecen in the late 1970s and spent several frustrating hours looking for the grave and could not find it — speculated that the author might have been that secret lifelong love of Erzhi's. Uncle Shumi, who included in his family album photographs of Erzhi and her tombstone, said he did not know and could not even guess.

Combining modernistic rhymes with traditional religious phrases, the poem refers to her "snow-white soul" as "an ornament of God's seat." It declares that angels would be sending to some "mysterious distant infinity" "the faint smile of her now-cold lips" as a form of sunshine. It mentions "her tired heart" and "her many hidden wounds." The last line addresses Erzhi with a thought perhaps meant as a consolation: "This earth was not your world."

Of the many letters I sent out inquiring about Erzhi, one was answered by a contemporary of hers, a lawyer who responded by asking his professional researcher/investigator to look up Erzsebet David's papers in the Debrecen archives. The researcher's report arrived in the mail after I completed the first draft of this chapter, and it contained a few surprises and a shattering revelation.

Erzhi's mother's maiden name was Laura Vallerstein, an ethnic German name, probably belonging to one of the many thousands of craftsmen who over the centuries migrated to Transylvania from Saxony. Their genes might have accounted for Erzhi's blond hair, blue eyes, and a demeanor recognized in those days as "Aryan."

The researcher found the gravestone and noticed that the poet's name does appear at the bottom, in tiny letters. It was a woman whose name no one I asked ever heard of. The researcher also reported that according to cemetery documents, in 1975 someone paid the considerable fee to the authorities so they would not eliminate the grave for another twenty-five years, as such recycling cemetery spaces is standard practice in Hungary. The researcher copied the person's name, and it was Shumi's. He died in 1988 but never mentioned the matter to his sister Anna. She thought that the cemetery authorities must have removed the grave and sold the site to someone else.

As a result of Peter Weisz's lobbying efforts, in 2001 the city of Debrecen recognized Erzhi's rescue work. Her tombstone was cleaned and the gravesite is now carpeted with flowering plants. Moreover, her name and those of her helpers headed by Istvan Varga are etched into a large marble plaque on the wall of City Hall. She is now honored as Debrecen's heroine.

My researcher offered another finding I read several times to make sure I was not mistaken: Erzhi's death certificate stated the cause of death as "poisoned by sleeping pills." The researcher explained that the term is a standard legal reference to suicide, which the Hungarian language borrows from the Latin *suicidium* — the murder of one's self.

I shivered as I asked myself why a woman who saved so many lives would take her own. From everything my family knew and perhaps imagined of her, she saw the protection of human life as an obligation that did not end with the war. Was she just worn out with this world's misery? Did the future hold nothing but loneliness for her? Was she bereft of those to whom she felt the closest? Or is all of this wrong?

Could the physician simply have proffered a speculative diagnosis? People familiar with Hungarian medical practice say that a doctor who conducts an autopsy is most unlikely to sign an unsubstantiated claim on an official document, though he or she may choose to keep the results confidential. As in Erzhi's case no relative could be found, the doctor was under no obligation to disclose the clinical finding to anyone. I am certain that my mother, who could not keep a secret, did not know. I am not so sure about Shumi who always felt duty-bound to protect the privacy of his friends.

In all the many family conversations I heard — and overheard — about Erzhi, no one ever hinted about her overdose of sleeping pills. Taking her own life seems to have been the last of Erzhi's many secrets.

Her suicide was confirmed to me in 2001 by Istvan Varga's son, by the same name, and Erzhi's godson. The story he heard from his parents was that Erzhi went home from the hospital and took a supply of sleeping pills with her. When she did not show for work next morning, a colleague was sent out to check on her. No one answered the buzzer but the colleague discovered that the door was locked, and the key inside. He called the police who broke down the door, found her barely alive, and took her to the hospital where she died within minutes.

Suicide is not a closeted secret in Hungary. Many Hungarians admire suicide as a courageous exit, as a strong person's way of defying fate. Such defiance has been shared from conscience-stricken statesmen to cancer patients and spurned lovers, to teenagers feeling oppressed to Jews ordered to board Auschwitz-bound transports. Suicide as a hero's denouement has made Hungary a leader in that sad statistic among the nations of the world.

Mother had the habit of summoning the spirits of family members and friends by talking about what they liked — for instance her brother Mishi's preference for a rose of a certain dark red tint he once presented to the women he courted, or her brother Shumi's fondness for a pickled cucumber not too sour but with plenty of dill which she used to prepare in large jars every summer. Her séances were sentimental rather than spiritual. Her invocations had power. During one stroll through a village a few years after the war, she called attention to a flock of storks flying directly above us. She sighed while relating how much like Erzhi it was to admire that dramatic large white bird of the countryside, a bird not hunted but respected. Across Hungary's Great Plain, villagers called the stork "God's bird."

Graceful when gliding across the sky or perching atop utility poles where they compose their wondrously intertwined nests, storks are pitifully awkward when they make the mistake of coming down to earth. Once they decide that their time is up, villagers say, they die while flying. They soar higher and higher, and their hearts break suddenly as they fly into the clouds, higher than they ever flew.

CHAPTER FIVE

Man of God, Man of Action: Gabor Sztehlo

...hide the outcasts,
betray not the fugitive;
let the outcasts of Moab
sojourn among you;
be a refuge to them
from the destroyer.

Isaiah 16:3,4

One subzero morning toward the end of 1944 in Budapest, a Lutheran pastor opened the front door to his apartment and found on the doormat a wicker laundry basket with a bundled-up infant. A slip of paper tucked under the blanket offered the only identification: "She is called Zsuzsika." The pastor had no doubt that the infant was Jewish and that her parents had her smuggled out of the ghetto or perhaps from a train bound for a concentration camp in Germany.

At a time when Gentiles were afraid to let Jewish relatives or friends enter their homes and averted their eyes when approached by an acquaintance wearing the six-pointed yellow star, the pastor was setting up homes for children destined for the death camps. His name was Gabor Sztehlo, then thirty-five years old and little known outside Hungary's Lutheran Evangelical Church, a modest, unassertive

Pastor Gabor Sztehlo in the early 1930s.

The author in the summer of 1945 with pet rooster Maxie.

minority denomination of some 300,000 souls, many of them of ethnic German stock.

The law, decreed early in the spring, forbade Gentiles to let Jews into their homes or to meet them socially. Nearly every week that followed brought additional restrictions that denied Jews opportunities to earn a living, virtually imprisoning them in ghettoes or apartment buildings marked with the six-pointed yellow star. By October 15, Germany installed the Arrow Cross Party in power, and the Arrow Cross militia searched apartment buildings and stopped passersby to check identity documents. They arrested people whose faces they thought looked Jewish or anyone whose papers did not appear to be in order. They took the suspects to one of the Arrow Cross centers throughout the city where they were tortured, sometimes murdered, or packed into trains bound for Auschwitz. Many hundreds were marched to the Danube and shot on its embankment so they fell into the river that carried away their bodies. Hungary's own Nazis took pride in inventing such a quick and efficient way of disposing of corpses.

Informers queued up around Wehrmacht headquarters at the Hotel Astoria, then, as now, one of the most luxurious in Budapest. The Germans did not bother to check the names and addresses of the people accused of hiding Jews — just one denunciation sufficed to send a person to jail or to a concentration camp, or to have him or her shot.

Nevertheless, Pastor Sztehlo had to spread the word about his sanctuaries for Jewish children so they would be brought to him. The two propositions — letting Jews know about his network and keeping informers deaf and blind — were mutually exclusive. From a practical point of view, a project of renting and running, staffing and provisioning houses for Jewish children seemed hopeless, even absurd. It would have been an impossible mission for anyone, but especially for a naïve village pastor who had lived his life among the God-fearing faithful of small Lutheran congregations. Sztehlo had no experience in clandestine assignments and no familiarity with government officials and other potentially important, slippery city folk. The punch-drunk killers and the greedy opportunists he had to outsmart were strangers to him. A plain-spoken, tight-laced moralist, he was temperamentally unsuited to offer a bribe or to bargain with a Nazi who might be tempted to negotiate a deal in the expectation of evading postwar retribution or getting his hands on some money.

When Sztehlo started out to rent houses for Jewish children, the first person he got in touch with, a lawyer, demanded an immediate advance of 4,000 pengo in cash, a large sum that equaled the pastor's half-year salary. As he recalled years later in his memoir, he first thought of all the lawyers he had known, most of them in his family — his father, grandfather, and a brother — and concluded that he should trust their young, well-spoken if slick colleague. The location, which he inspected with the lawyer on a bright sunny morning, offered ideal isolation on a picturesque Buda hill, on a street named Snowflower. Counting the rooms of the villa and adding up the square feet, he reckoned that he could easily place thirty children there. Though he worried about the largeness of the amount, he paid the lawyer's price.

The pastor had a bad taste in his mouth. On the way back to the streetcar stop, the lawyer pressed him for information on the tenants, and somehow he let it come out that they might include some Jewish children. He was furious with himself for that dumb slip.

At the agreed-upon time, in mid-afternoon, the pastor pressed the buzzer to the lawyer's apartment. He was to sign the lease and take the keys. But the lawyer claimed he had never set eyes on the pastor. The befuddled Sztehlo could only stammer about their joint inspection of the villa and the advance of 4,000 pengo. The lawyer shouted that the pastor was "a liar" and "a stooge of the Jews," threatened to call the police, and slammed the door in his face.

Sztehlo later described himself as "choked with shame." He also worried that the lawyer would denounce him to the Gestapo or the Arrow Cross, and the whole rescue project would unravel before it began. He wept when he explained his "terrible misjudgment" to the elderly Jewish man who had entrusted him with the 4,000 pengo, perhaps the savings of a lifetime. The pastor cried aloud: as an ignorant bungler, wasn't he unfit to save people? Shouldn't he quit and stop endangering his family, his church, and the planned rescue operation?

His memoir makes it clear that though he could writhe in self-doubt for hours, even days, in the long run he would not concede defeat. He had a habit of getting up after each bad fall, determined to try harder the next time. He was a fighter with irrepressible energy. Done with his tears and anger, he wrote, he returned to his prayers, and he recited the Psalms on how good it is to be near Him. A bull of a man, Sztehlo had a stubborn resolve to do right by his God.

Photographs show him as broad of beam and as solidly implanted in the earth as an oak tree. A nearly continuous horizontal line of massive eyebrows divided his squarish face. A shock of thick dark hair, a broad, angular forehead, and piercing dark eyes conveyed vigor and determination. But he was also open and gregarious, relishing a good meal and the company of friends. Among those who remember him, what first comes to mind is his cheery welcome of a smile, a rare treat in those days of snarling distrust. "His smile dissolved our fear," recalls Pal Foti, one of his protégés. Years later Otto Orban, by then a leading poet in Hungary, defined the critical tension in his erstwhile guardian: "Though he turned toward God, the earth seemed to pull him back."

People closest to him speak of his baritone and his love of J.S. Bach's music. "He had a strong voice, and when he sang, he was totally absorbed by the melody, as if nothing else existed in the world," says his daughter Ildiko. An image treasured by those who huddled with him in the cellar during the Red Army's siege of Budapest was his radiant face while singing Bach chorals. With the building above them shaking from the explosions that came from all directions, his strategy was to have everyone sing to overcome the fear of imminent death. "As long as he was with us," remembers Foti, "none of us was afraid." In his memoir Sztehlo confessed that never before or after could he feel Martin Luther's favorite choral, "A Mighty Fortress Is Our God," as literally true as in those days in the cellar. He wrote: "Never in my life could I say, confess, and pray those words as I did then."

The Year of Hope and Hopelessness

In a foreword to his memoir he described his mood swings in the period from March 1944 to March 1945: "For me, that year was like a dream. I lived through it as if dreaming: crying and laughing, hungry and well-fed, struggling and happy, full of trust and deprived of hope, freezing cold and cozily warm. I did what I had to do as though unconsciously, performing those daily tasks that flowed from yesterday into today and from today to tomorrow, but without my being able to see the precise outlines of the day after tomorrow. It was a dream yet also living reality that cut into the flesh. I could call it a bad dream because it showed how much human misery and meanness could exist on earth, but it was also a wonderful dream because God's evident love did not abandon us. To me, the dream revealed man's immeasurable sin and the infinity of God's love, and that is how I received the answer to the painful questions I and others posed."

It is a fact that Sztehlo rescued more Jews than any other Hungarian: the lists of names add up to a figure just short of two thousand, three-fourths of them children. What is astounding is that in the thirty-two homes he founded and managed, not one of his protégés was lost — not to the Nazis, nor to the bullets and bombs which left tens of thousands of civilians dead, reducing much of Budapest to rubble. "Each morning he prayed that those he protected stay alive," recalls his cousin, Sara Sztehlo. "At the end of each day he thanked God that they did."

Yet nothing in his life before the German occupation of Hungary in March 1944 suggested that one day he might rescue Jews. As age eighteen, Sztehlo defined his life goal in his application for divinity school: helping Hungary's "impoverished common people" by improving their material and spiritual lot.

In his twenties, he won a two-year fellowship to study theology and pastoral work in Finland. He not only learned the language — difficult even for those who speak Hungarian, which is only distantly related to Finnish — but acquired an appreciation for the Finnish Lutherans' pietistic "awakening," an introspective spiritual self-examination that struck him at first as alien to the average extroverted Hungarian. He also admired Finnish educational institutions dedicated to raising the cultural level of the rural population, and he decided to emulate Finnish methods in Hungary. But unlike some other pastors, his colleague Emil Koren wrote in his biography, Sztehlo did not antagonize his conservative, viscerally patriotic parishioners by promoting a foreign model. He was a teacher aware that the most effective form of teaching is setting an example.

Upon his return home in 1932, he was sent to the countryside where as a novice pastor he soon made a name for himself in the Lutheran church by building several small communities. He spent much of his time visiting with his parishioners, trying to answer their questions. He also raised funds for building a church and supervised its construction.

For ten years, his church regarded Sztehlo as a model village pastor, and his wife Ilona, whom he married shortly after he was ordained, earned the reputation of a model pastor's wife. They cared about the lives of their parishioners and helped them to deal with their everyday problems. Mr. and Mrs. Sztehlo had no doubt that this was what God had intended them to do.

A straightforward account of Sztehlo's internal odyssey is his memoir that he wrote in a confessional mode following his first heart attack in 1962. It was not meant for publication. He wrote it for himself and "perhaps for others interested in drawing conclusions from the past."

Unlike other clergymen recalling the Second World War, Sztehlo did not defend the churches by repeating arguments such as the one about the paramount need to avoid making the angry Nazis even angrier. Nor did he endorse the pious logic, promoted by those with a guilty conscience in the periods that followed the Nazi downfall – and later the communist collapse — contending that everyone has suffered, all suffering is equal, and forgiveness is indispensable for "social peace."

Sztehlo began his memoir by acknowledging that until 1944 he rarely glanced at a newspaper and never read an anti-Nazi opposition paper. He was only vaguely aware of the world war. Even the shock of the German invasion of Hungary produced little more than a concern, which he acknowledged was the same as his colleagues': "Can we continue our work?" Was "holy simplemindedness" the reason for such a narrow, shortsighted approach, he asked. "Unfortunately," he answered, "it was worse than that: sinful ignorance. Or selfishness, a life seeking only its own salvation. A characteristic of the church in 1944."

While Hungarian Protestant pastors knew of the arrest and deportation of some of their anti-Nazi German colleagues, Sztehlo noted, "we also knew that we should not talk about such things." The wisdom of silence was embellished by a naive expectation: since Hungary also had internment camps, where the detainees were either communists or Arrow Cross members, "we assumed that the German camps were not much worse, and it did not occur to us that their purpose was the liquidation of the Jews."

Sztehlo knew of only two Lutheran colleagues in Hungary who were aware of the impending catastrophe even before the German invasion and who did something about it. One was a village pastor, father of two children, who refused to serve in the military or to take part in the ceremonial "blessing of the arms" before the troops went off to fight. As a punishment, he was sent off to a labor battalion organized for the politically unreliable. The second pastor was of Jewish origin, a father of four, who assisted the anti-Nazi guerrillas in Slovakia. The Germans arrested him in his church and shot him in front of the altar.

Only the beginning of the deportations from the Hungarian countryside, in May 1944, prompted "many clergymen in every denomination to recognize their duty," Sztehlo wrote. "But in the first days of the German occupation we were barely stirring from our sleep."

Knowing what we know now, we find it hard to understand why so many thoughtful and decent people failed to recognize the signs of the Nazi determination to conquer the world. Speaking for himself and his colleagues in the Lutheran church, Sztehlo's explanation rings true: "We were not trained to fight in the temporal world and for its unfortunate victims. We fought far more for the rights of our church and its positions. Whatever advantages the Roman Catholic Church achieved, we too had to have them. Equality in treatment, equal rights: beautiful principles! . . . We were full of pride, disguised by Christian humility, whenever we managed to make life just a little difficult for other churches." Sztehlo left the sharpest words for his conclusion: "the strange world of the churches" was "devoid of the spirit" and "only humanly inspired."

Most of the Christian clergy sought to maintain a kind of self-containment that belonged to the golden age of the Catholic Church, the Middle Ages. Sztehlo too kept an emotional distance from the world war, even though Hungary was in the center of a maelstrom, both courted and threatened by Hitler's Germany but threatened openly only by Stalin's Soviet Union which did not think it worthwhile to woo a future victim. The Nazis used the bait of the historically Hungarian territories — the peace treaty after the First World War awarded two-thirds of Hungary to its neighbors — to coax a wavering government into joining the Axis. At the same time, those who took the trouble of reading Nazi ideology knew that Hitler's New Order left little or no room for Hungarians, whom Adolf Hitler once condemned as Asiatic intruders not entitled to play a role in his Europe.

"I did not like the Germans, and war repelled me," Sztehlo wrote. "I found their slogans alien to my way of thinking, and I condemned what the Nazis were doing. . . . But I did not fight them deliberately; I did not have enough hatred burning in me — not until I myself saw what they were doing."

Sztehlo was shaken when he saw German soldiers patrolling Buda-pest streets after the Wehrmacht invasion of the country in March, 1944, which followed Hitler's decision that he could no longer trust Hungary, a nominal ally, to remain with the Axis. Sztehlo was shocked when he noted the joy in the eyes of some of his fellow Hungarians. A few even tried to speak with the German soldiers who were, he noted, "unapproachably somber." Other passersby seemed to ignore the presence of the soldiers and "minded their own business which they regarded as more important than any military move-ment." He did not doubt the gruesome rumor: as the German tanks and trucks rumbled through Budapest, they did not stop when they bumped or hit someone by accident but rolled right over that person. He understood the message: the Wehrmacht show was a demonstra-tion of its superior might as much as the readiness to use that might without the slightest hesitation.

Sztehlo knew enough to be hostile to German nationalism. German was spoken as the second language in his parental home, and German culture was part of his family heritage. His maternal ances-tors had come from Switzerland and Austria. Nevertheless, members of his extended family proved impervious to the call of pan-Germanism. His cousin Sara Sztehlo says that the Sztehlo ancestors lived in the Czech lands and followed the teachings of Jan Hus, burned as a heretic at the stake in 1415 and considered by many a forerunner of Martin Luther. The Sztehlos escaped Catholic persecu-tion by settling in what was then northern Hungary and is now Slovakia. "Since the middle of the 1600s, the Sztehlos provided many pastors to Hungary's Lutheran Evangelical Church," says Sara Sztehlo, the family historian. "But they also excelled with their talents and industry in other intellectual pursuits. As lawyers, judges, physi-cians, engineers, architects, and artists, they brought honor to the family name."

Sara Sztehlo suggests that her cousin Gabor inherited something more important from his mother's side: "His mother, Martha Haggenmacher, had a tender, generous heart and a capacity for unconditional love. She came from a wealthy Swiss family. Even in her old age — she died in 1969 — she regularly visited the homes her son organized, and led afternoon sessions of sewing and repairing bed linen and other household objects. She often brought along with her many Sztehlo relatives, including my mother. When Martha visited Switzerland and her relatives, she raised funds for Gabor's homes. Warm and compassionate, the Haggenmachers knew how to set up an enterprise. But they also knew how to give themselves to a cause and to ensure that what they created would endure. Some of Gabor's wonderful genes came from his mother's family."

Defining himself as "a servant of God," Sztehlo had an almost monastic way of dividing the world into a part that had spiritual content and another that did not. While he kept aloof from politics that he held responsible for creating injustice and inhumanity, he was passionately involved in providing help to victims of those policies.

Was he otherworldly? "It depends on what you call otherworldly," says Magda Koren, biographer Emil's wife and a teacher who first worked with Sztehlo in the 1930s. "Gabor was fully engaged in this world. But his ever-smiling, light-hearted optimism had a special, not-of-this-world quality."

Sztehlo stood apart for yet another reason: he was a rare independent. Though a product of an acutely class-conscious and ideologically fragmented society, he did not belong anywhere socially or politically. Except for the Lutheran church, he was not part of any institution or grouping or circle of likeminded friends. "I saw one goal ahead of me: to educate, to organize," he wrote in his memoir, and "to realize what great minds devised but could not translate into practice." For the first decade of his professional career, that goal was to raise the educational level of the peasantry, the poorly educated, peremptorily dismissed, and looked-down-upon majority of Hungary's population.

Sztehlo impressed his superiors as an exceptionally hard worker — celebrated as a sterling Lutheran trait — as well as an unusually successful evangelizer. He was able both to inspire and to organize his parishioners and students. They flocked to his churches. But it must have also helped his standing in the church organization that he came from a solidly successful family respected in the church, and that he had an unpretentious version of the manners of the upper middle class.

Nevertheless, he was not a gentleman in the proud, much-celebrated Hungarian mode. He disliked the posturing and pretensions of the ruling class and condemned its lack of concern with the peasantry and other less fortunate elements in society.

A Surprise Assignment

When it came to choosing him for the extraordinarily sensitive and unquestionably illegal task of assisting Jews, it did not seem to matter that he had never before affiliated with Jews or shown interest in the so-called Jewish question. His bishop, the autocratic Sandor Raffay, first plucked Sztehlo from his job of organizing and educating peasant youth and put him in charge of ministering to the faithful in Budapest hospitals, which was a promotion complete with a substantial raise. Then in a seemingly offhanded way, the bishop handed him the assignment that would change his life.

In his recollection of the fateful meeting with his bishop, which took place a few days after the German invasion of March 19, 1944, Sztehlo wrote that Raffay seemed strangely preoccupied throughout the conversation and did not look at him while informing him of his transfer. When Sztehlo asked what he owed the honor of the promotion, the bishop said that it was a decision of the presbytery, prompted by two earlier decisions: to close down the peasant youth project and to fill the long-vacant post of the chaplain for patients in Budapest hospitals.

At this point of the conversation, Raffay looked at Sztehlo with "piercing eyes" and said that he had "one more thing" on his mind. He asked if Sztehlo had heard of the organization Good Shepherd. Without waiting for a response, the bishop explained that though he had been asked to participate in the work of the Good Shepherd, he did not have the time. He was thus appointing Sztehlo to represent

the Lutheran church in that Protestant group whose Calvinist director had asked him "to do something for Christian children of Jewish
origin. There are many of them; they are without a home, or someone to take care of them. They would have to be collected, and some
sort of a safe haven would have to be set up for them."

The bishop's instructions to Sztehlo were terse: "Rescue the children. I can't give you advice, but go to the Good Shepherd office and
look around. Report to me what you find; if you need something, let
me know. I'll help you if I can."

Dutifully, Sztehlo said he understood the order and expressed his
gratitude for the assignment.

With a curt "go now, and get to work," the bishop dismissed him.

Closing the door, Sztehlo felt ashamed of his ignorance. He knew
nothing about the Good Shepherd, and he asked the bishop's secretary who informed him that it was an organization that had been
sending food, clothing, and money to those in labor battalions, nearly
all of them Jews of military conscription age.

But Sztehlo reminded himself that the bishop said his work would
have to do with a children's home. With some bitterness he recalled
that only a year earlier the bishop had contemptuously rejected his
request to set up a home for war orphans of the Lutheran faith. "You
don't know about such things," the bishop said sternly. "That sort of
a thing is not for you." (Nevertheless, the persistent Sztehlo was able
to help a close friend of his set up such a home.) A year earlier, the
bishop had also rejected his application to serve as the new director of
the Protestant orphans' home. Sztehlo asked himself: "So why is he
now entrusting me with the rescue of children?"

Sztehlo was deeply ambivalent about his bishop. "An archetype of
the Protestant high clergyman and the Hungarian gentleman,"
Sztehlo summed him up in his memoir. "He communicated calm,
conceit, and decisiveness, yet he was neither decisive nor purposeful,
but wrongheaded and stubborn. And that was precisely the impressive and the tragic characteristic of the Hungarian gentleman: he
always projected more than what he in fact had in him."

His harsh judgment notwithstanding, Sztehlo felt he had to recognize that the bishop had baptized, confirmed, ordained, and married him. He noted: "My life was in his hands until his death." Nevertheless, coming from a man as gentle and as spiritual as Sztehlo, the concluding sentence contains the ultimate rebuke of his bishop: "But he was never my spiritual advisor."

A studiously careful historian, Pastor Koren did not have many kind words for Bishop Raffay. "It is clear to me that Raffay did not want to be outdone by the Calvinists," Koren told me in 1995. "He didn't want to take the initiative to set up the Good Shepherd organization — perhaps he was afraid — but once the Calvinists set it up, he didn't want the Lutheran church to be left out of it."

Sara Sztehlo thought differently. "Even the coldest, driest, most vain individual can be moved by the misery of others," she said. "And even if such an individual does not confess the true reason, sometimes he does what he must do."

At the time of assigning Sztehlo to rescue work, did Raffay have an inkling of what Sztehlo could do? The bishop knew his protégé well enough to expect that once the idealistic young pastor realized that the children who needed to be saved were Jews, rather than Christians of Jewish origin, he would focus on those with the most crying need, regardless of the religion they professed or their parents adopted in the hope that conversion might save their lives. Yet the bishop could not have foreseen the size of the network the pastor would eventually build.

But why did the bishop not mention what he knew well, that Protestant children of Jewish origin made up a tiny minority in both groups. Did the bishop think it was best for the sensitive Sztehlo to find out for himself what his Christian duty pointed to and let him run the operation the way he saw it fit? Most likely, I'd like to think, the bishop knew Sztehlo well enough to expect that he would move beyond his formal assignment and perform the task with his natural zeal and customary persistence. On the other hand, the prudent and politically savvy bishop might have prepared for the worst-case scenario, giving himself plausible deniability in case his subordinate was caught in the unlawful act of sheltering Jews and a police investigation tracked down the source of his assignment.

It is safe to say that all of these considerations entered the mind of Raffay, the brilliant son of a boot maker — a proverbially lowly occupation in the Hungarian social hierarchy — who first became a teacher of theology, then a New Testament scholar, and finally the head of the Lutheran church and a member of the Upper House, Hungary's equivalent of Britain's House of Lords. "He reached everything he had set his mind to," Sztehlo wrote, with just a tinge of disapproval. "He was proud of everything he had achieved, but he was even more proud of the fact he had accomplished everything on his own, rising high from way down." And pride was not a quality Sztehlo appreciated.

In the years that preceded the Nazi takeover, Raffay was never known as a friend of the Jews. He frequently called for "curbing Jewish power" and considered Jews "an alien element" in the nation. He gave voice to a brand of nationalism that focused on recovering the territories that Hungary lost after the post-World War I peace treaty. Social justice or resisting the Germans were not on his agenda. But retrenchment seemed prudent in 1944, as the Red Army was driving the Wehrmacht westward, along with what was left of Hungary's army. Assigning Sztehlo, one of the brightest young pastors in his church, to the rescue of Jews suggests that Raffay, like other Christian clergymen and Hungarian nationalists, realized that the alliance with Germany had been a terrible mistake and that Hungary would not only fail to recover its lost lands but would damage the nation's reputation in the world. Perhaps Raffay, like other enlightened nationalists, might have come to understand that decades could pass before Hungary recovered its good name, besmirched by the deportation of most of its Jewish citizens.

"Bishop Raffay trusted Pastor Sztehlo," Koren told me when we spoke in 1995. "Raffay knew that once he appointed Sztehlo, he did not need to worry about the project. Sztehlo would take care of everything, relieving Raffay of responsibility. Raffay knew what Sztehlo would do with non-converts. His instinct told him. He did not have to be told. He knew that with Sztehlo, the question would never arise whether the children were Lutheran or Jewish. In his monthly reports, Sztehlo never mentioned the question. He didn't need to. And Raffay simply closed his eyes to Sztehlo overstepping the modest bounds of his mission."

To Sara Sztehlo's thinking "a home for Lutheran children of Jewish origin was the billboard — something of a cover the church had to use because it was against the law to hide a Jewish child. In the church, you did not need to spell out what was being done, and those who knew the truth did not talk about it."

Raffay died a disappointed, broken man shortly after the war. Many of his fellow countrymen accused him of riding the nationalist wave, and his church was critical of his autocratic management. He did not claim credit for what Sztehlo had done, and he did not offer to explain why he chose an inexperienced pastor for such a dangerous assignment. Nor did Sztehlo spend much time in trying to understand what precisely his secretive, elusive, and manipulative ecclesiastical superior had in mind for him to do — and for what reason. We will never know the truth.

A Partner Enters

As Sztehlo was studying the files of the Good Shepherd in his room, another young Lutheran pastor and a coworker from the peasant youth association, knocked on his door to bring him a message: a Swiss Red Cross official who had just arrived in Budapest wanted to see them urgently.

The day after the interview with Bishop Raffay, Sztehlo was to meet his future partner who was outspoken and purposeful. Friedrich von Born, described by Sztehlo as "a middle-aged, elegant, large gentleman," surprised the two pastors with a series of blunt questions: Just exactly what is the Lutheran church doing to help Hungary's Jews? Has it developed a plan, a strategy, to rescue them? Are the two pastors and their superiors aware that now that the Germans are in military control of Hungary, Nazi-style ruthless elimination of Jews would begin immediately?

"Somewhat shamed," Sztehlo wrote, he responded by citing the statements in defense of Jews that Bishop Raffay and his Calvinist colleague had just delivered in the Upper House. Von Born was fully aware of the statements, as he was of earlier less public efforts. Not wishing to discuss them, he pressed the two young pastors: what will happen next? Von Born expressed his conviction that "the final hour" arrived and that the Germans were determined to carry out the deportations that meant one thing: extermination.

Years later, Sztehlo wrote that he felt "very ashamed for the poorly-informed and helpless churches." But in his response to von Born at the time he contended that though Raffay would help the Jews wholeheartedly, he was incapable of doing so by himself. Sztehlo cited the work of the Good Shepherd in supplying food and warm clothing to Jews in the labor battalions. He mentioned his new assignment to help Jewish children. Von Born listened to every word but did not respond.

As the two pastors left, it suddenly occurred to them that they only knew that von Born came from Switzerland and supposedly looked for them on the recommendation of a friend of theirs, a Hungarian pastor. But von Born did not talk about the organization he represented. Could he have been a German spy, a Gestapo agent provocateur, pumping them for information? They were angry with themselves for telling him everything they knew and planned.

The two friends parted company in a low mood and agreed that they would not talk about their meeting with anyone.

"I did not feel optimistic that day," Sztehlo recalled in his memoir. "With awakening conscience I began to watch developments, and I began to notice things. I saw many people in queues of various types trying to hide, with their briefcases and other objects, the yellow stars they wore." His first visitors arrived in his office — how quickly the word spread about his project! — some wearing the yellow star, others without them. "So many tragic, desperate lives!" Sztehlo wrote. He was depressed every time he thought of the conversation with the Swiss gentleman. He began to feel ambivalent about his assignment. "I was troubled that I did not see things clearly," he noted. "Many days had to pass before I recognized what my task was."

Melancholy, the national neurosis both feared and cherished, had him in its vise. "We were two poor, naive clergymen," he recalled his state of mind. "How could we have taken up such an assignment?"

But Sztehlo was too much of a man of action to be immobilized by doubt for long. In a few more days, after the bishop's secretary handed him his letter of appointment to the Good Shepherd, Sztehlo went to its headquarters and introduced himself to his new coworkers, three Calvinist pastors of Jewish origin. "It was good to meet with people whose hearts were filled with obedience to God," Sztehlo wrote in his memoirs. "I felt that God spoke on that day."

His memoir suggests — and Koren confirmed for me — that it never occurred to Sztehlo that he could decline or dodge the bishop's assignment; nor did he weigh the potentially disastrous consequences if he was unmasked. In the prophet Isaiah's words, he was "swift to do righteousness." It was only years later that he asked himself what made him do it: "Was it faith? Blind fanaticism? I don't know. I think our eagerness to act blurred our sense of reality to such an extent that the impossible too appeared to us as a road we could walk."

In the 1990s the poet Otto Orban asked: "Did he not understand what everyone understood only too well? Or was it he who really understood, thanks to his character which had a stubborn, uncompromising streak?"

Chaplain in the Suicide Ward

As Sztehlo began work as chaplain to Budapest hospitals, he entered yet another scene of "the Jewish tragedy," as the Holocaust was then called. Visiting the special ward for failed suicides who filled two large rooms with fifty beds each and several small rooms, he found that some ninety percent of the patients were Jewish, as defined by the racist new law. Many of them had converted to Christianity long ago, sometimes more than a generation back, and in some cases even their neighbors and friends did not suspect their origins. But when the law ordered them to document their ancestry, they found themselves branded as members of a contemptible minority, and they were unable to live with the humiliation of having to wear the six-pointed yellow star. (Police records listed 1,572 suicides on the day that the law required the star to be worn.) Others were brought into the ward from the ghetto because they slashed their veins or swallowed an overdose of sleeping pills, rather than to board a transport to camps in Germany.

The converts were afraid to talk to Sztehlo because of Christianity's condemnation of suicide as a mortal sin. Observant Jews distrusted him because he was a Christian clergyman.

Sztehlo found only very few Lutherans, but that did not trouble him. The pastor who had once lived within the tight circles of his flock decided that his new duty lay in comforting all the patients in the ward, regardless of their religion. "God did not reject you," Sztehlo told those few who indicated that they accepted him as a chaplain. "The time to approach Him is not when we are pure, but when we see and feel that sin has stained us." While feeling personally inadequate to cope with the magnitude of the suffering he witnessed, Sztehlo kept citing divine love and forgiveness. Twice a week for six months, he delivered that most Christian message even though he knew it was not well received. But he could not think of anything else to say. Like heaven's winged angels in the Jewish as well as Christian tradition singing "Holy, holy, holy" in God's presence, the pastor could only praise the God he served in his tradition-sanctioned way, regardless of the circumstances and the mindset of the traumatized people he was supposed to comfort.

Ever the innocent believer, he was surprised that faith in placing one's life in God's hands was very rare in the suicide ward. On the other hand, he could not fathom "a fanatical, blind confidence" he witnessed in a few patients who thought that now they would survive the war simply because their suicide attempt failed. In still other patients, he observed a deep, seething hatred for the Christian world. He did not condemn the hatred, nor did he try to diminish it. Instead, he decided that "hatred can give someone life-affirming power. I was astounded in the presence of that fact. The human hatred which brought about racial discrimination gave birth to a new hatred; sin begat sin, and the reaction was not less intense than the action which had caused it. The most terrible part was to see in this the judgment of God who weighs sin by the measure of its growth."

Sztehlo was not reluctant to talk to those who looked at him with eyes smoldering with hatred. He wrote: "I could read the eyes which said, what do you want at my bedside? The love that your lips speak is false! You too belong to those who sowed this hatred on the earth. You too have a part in the murder of my brothers and sisters, my parents, and my children!"

At the end of his long paragraph trying to translate the language of the angry eyes, Sztehlo noted: "There were of course a few such patients with whom I had several very long conversations, and in the end we could shake hands."

After spending time every day with as many as nine patients during each of his three-hour visits in the suicide ward, the pastor found himself emotionally and physically drained. "Often I envied the nurses who provided care and food to the patients," he wrote. "I felt I ought to do a lot, but I was helpless in this world of hatred."

The experience tested his faith. No comparable blows had struck him before — or after. "I fell into a life-and-death struggle," he wrote. "It was an agony of conscience that drew blood." But his relentless life-affirmation prevailed, and after the war he felt vindicated whenever he ran into people who emerged alive from the suicide ward that, paradoxically, turned into a safe haven where Jews could and did hide from the Nazis.

Looking for "the lesson" taught by his chaplaincy — that bonus of a moral that pastors and rabbis alike hope to gain from painful experiences — Sztehlo decided that he "needed the tough education" of having to defend God's role in a time of war and of having to find ways to prove by his own example that, despite appearances, God was still in control of the world. He concluded: "The wounds I received at that time were blessed, as were the blows, because they carried in them the promise of a life obedient to a merciful God. Because God still lived and functioned in that time despite every human mutiny, accusation, and denial."

In the year 1944 in Budapest, few people risked facing the shadow of death by visiting patients in a suicide ward. Common sense argued against deepening one's despair by looking up unfortunate victims of their own despondency. Why pile on misfortune on misfortune? Besides, what could caring relatives and friends say? That it was a pity that the suicide attempt failed? Or, to the contrary, that life was worth living? Or that the patient would now surely survive what people then called "the tightening Nazi noose"?

For the patients, a Lutheran pastor burning with the Christian fever of caritas was an apparition from an alien spirituality that few if any had ever had a glimpse of. His stated desire to give comfort must have baffled those he approached. I can imagine a few patients thinking him an amazing man, while others perhaps asked: Who needs a Christian clergyman preaching to us Jews? Someone could have jested: Do the pastor's feet really touch the ground?

Negotiations with the Arrow Cross

In July, Miklos Horthy, Hungary's head of state, issued orders to stop the deportations, which was soon followed by a German-sponsored Arrow Cross attempt to topple him. He and the ghetto that was the other target of the Arrow Cross were saved by a colonel, Ferenc Koszorus, whose troops were hidden in the Budapest area. Nevertheless, rumors persisted that the Arrow Cross was on the verge of taking over. Sztehlo and a coworker from the Good Shepherd engaged in negotiations an Arrow Cross official, a lawyer by profession, who boasted of his close links with the party's top leaders.

Sztehlo described the lawyer as a sleazy man in his fifties, a chain smoker and a heavy drinker, dressed in a rumpled suit and a dirty shirt. The fastidious pastor noted with disdain that the lawyer's office was a filthy, disorganized little room where he also slept and cooked his meals. The lawyer claimed to be in favor of a "humanist solution to the problem of the Jewish plutocracy," and he encouraged the clergymen by criticizing anti-Jewish violence and "the excesses of a few" Arrow Cross members. He spouted vague generalities that were difficult to understand, but it seemed the better part of wisdom to hear him out. He stirred hope in Sztehlo with "brilliant quotes" from classical literature in Latin, German, and Hungarian. Almost apologetically, he explained that "fiery patriotism" made him join the ranks of the Arrow Cross, and he spoke nonstop for hours and hours. He impressed Sztehlo as something of a liberal Nazi, a rare breed even in those days of waning Nazi self-confidence. Or he was just muddle-headed, a poor fool, a victim of his own ill-conceived, inconsistent ideas, drunk even when sober. In any event, the two pastors could not find anyone else in the Arrow Cross machinery who would talk to them, and the two clergymen fell for his promises.

For a month, Sztehlo and his coworkers hoped that the lawyer would provide access to key Arrow Cross officials who could be bribed or talked into permitting a Protestant children's home while turning a blind eye to some of its residents being of Jewish origin. In the end the lawyer did indeed talk to his friends in high places, and Sztehlo and his Calvinist pastor coworker received invitations to Arrow Cross headquarters. The meeting did begin as scheduled, but the two clergymen were soon thrown out and threatened with a bullet in the head unless they dropped the project of the children's home. Once again Sztehlo realized he had blundered. They wasted precious time and, worse, they might have tipped off the Arrow Cross. He jotted down the lesson learned: "You cannot negotiate with despots."

The Good Shepherd closed down its office, and its organizers moved to apartments where Arrow Cross thugs were unlikely to find them. Sztehlo joined his wife and their two children who had remained in the countryside. However, after a few weeks he was back in Budapest ready to start again, and his family followed him.

Having learned about the Good Shepherd folding up, von Born of the Swiss Red Cross sent a message to Sztehlo to come and see him immediately. Von Born offered money and provisions once Sztehlo set up the children's home originally authorized by his bishop. With the prestige and the resources of the Red Cross now behind him and inspired by von Born, Sztehlo plunged into the project.

A coincidence helped to speed up the project. Elizabeth Haggenmacher, von Born's newly arrived secretary from Switzerland and a key person in the tightly-run little bureau, turned out to be Sztehlo's cousin on his mother's side. She was a toddler when they last met, before the war, and now Sztehlo took heart in their surprise reunion. In his enthusiastic recollection of the two meetings with Cousin Elizabeth he perceived that nothing is incidental in the seeming chaos of wartime: people who needed to meet to make good things happen found one another, and events coincided in ways that suggested that what truly matters in life may in fact be preordained, an important concept in Protestant theology. "God's love is greater than our imagination," Sztehlo wrote. "He could intervene in ways that we would never dare to think."

The first children's home was launched on October 5, 1944 on Buda's Gellert Hill overlooking the Danube, in a lovely villa belonging to the beer magnate Otto Haggenmacher, another cousin of Sztehlo's mother. Within days, he opened other sanctuaries, most of them villas in the hills of Buda; some rented, others handed over to the trustworthy pastor for safekeeping. Within days Sztehlo selected the staff, most of them known to him from the Lutheran church; prominent among them were his old friends, Magda and Emil Koren. Each home operated under the emblem of the Swiss Red Cross, which was displayed prominently above the main gate. The organization's Budapest director, von Born, used his imposing personality and negotiating skills in convincing the Hungarian foreign ministry and even the Arrow Cross that "the homes for Protestant children" enjoyed diplomatic immunity due to their "extraterritorial status." Like Raoul Wallenberg's scheme of provisional Swedish citizenship for

Now the French ambassador's residence in Budapest, Csaba utca 20, was a home for supposedly Protestant children, one of 32 set up by Lutheran Pastor Gabor Sztehlo in 1944.

The drawing room of the French ambassador's residence today. In the winter of 1944-45, it was the room where children, including the author, played.

Budapest Jews, von Born's phrases represented a piece of bold fiction without any basis in international law.

The Street Named Csaba, House Number 20

Equipped with Christian birth certificates sent to us by Erzsebet David, our family friend in Debrecen, my mother Anna and I walked out of the house where we had been living for about a year and where the janitor, Mr. Kanalas, saved us from two Arrow Cross raids. But Mother did not think we could rely on him again. She carefully removed the six-pointed yellow stars she had stitched to our coats, packed two small suitcases, and we left for the other end of the city.

Our hearts were pounding. I knew that by not wearing the yellow star, we disobeyed the law and that we were fugitives with false documents. "Remember that your name is Karoly Farkas, the same as your father's," Mother told me softly as we walked through the nearly deserted streets toward the streetcar stop. "We have just come from Debrecen to get away from the Russians. We are Calvinists, as were all our neighbors in Debrecen. We are going to a home for Protestant refugee children."

As the streetcar took us from Pest across the Danube to Buda, I witnessed murder for the first time in my life, a few days before my seventh birthday. From the bridge named after St. Marguerite — a thirteenth century nun and a Hungarian king's daughter — we could see how people with guns lined up a group of prisoners by the water's edge and shot them so they fell into the river. I knew without asking my mother that they had to be Jews. Mother pretended that she saw and heard nothing, which is how other passengers reacted as well.

When we got off the streetcar, it was raining hard and noisy, and my heart was pounding. The raindrops sounded like something solid as they hit the cobblestones. They both had the color of the lead bullet tips that children collected. I too had a few of them, but some of my friends filled shoeboxes.

We climbed a steep street of fancy villas and spacious gardens surrounded by tall wrought iron fences painted shiny black. It was a neighborhood I had never seen. Mother looked nervously at the house numbers. "Twenty — we are looking for the number twenty," she said several times, reminding herself, even though numbers were always her friends, and she could keep in mind strings of them. Several times she assured me that everything would be just fine. She said that a recommendation from Uncle Levente, her sister Mara's husband, meant that we would be very well received. We had nothing to worry about. "Your name is Karoly Farkas," she repeated, "and now tell me where we came from and why." I did, and she said I was a good student.

Number 20, on the street named Csaba after the eldest son of Attila the Hun, was perhaps the most beautiful villa in the block, flanked by tall, spreading trees. It had a large, intricate wrought iron gate, tall and wide. Mother rang the bell. After a while, a woman came out of the house, walked over to the gate and asked who we were. As soon as Mother said that we had come from Debrecen and that Levente Thury sent us, the woman quickly opened the little gate next to the big one. "Welcome to your new home," she said with a friendly smile. "We have been expecting you."

As we walked into the building, the woman introduced herself as Deaconess Margit Huszar, and she invited us to hot chocolate, a luxury we had not tasted for many months. She had a lovely smile, and I could see that she and my mother would become friends. She showed us to our room, which was small but neat. I heard the sound of children talking and laughing, and I asked Deaconess Margit if I could join them. She looked at my mother and asked if we first wanted to say something about ourselves. Mother showed her our documents and told me to explain to Deaconess Margit who we were. I rattled off my name, my parents' names, our religion, and our former residence. Deaconess Margit said that I was a smart boy and that I could go and play with the other children if my mother agreed. She did, and I found the children, some older and others younger than me, and a few of them about my age, and I soon stopped thinking about what I had seen from St. Marguerite Bridge less than an hour earlier.

There were only a few mothers in the house but more than twenty children, with new children being brought over nearly every day, and my mother assisted by cooking and taking care of the youngest of them. Margit *neni* — or Aunt Margit as we children called her — taught us songs and games, and read us poems and fairy tales.

I regret that I do not recall any of her words, or the color of her eyes, or even the timbre of her voice. What I do remember in this haze is her great kindness. She reminded me of Grandmother Roza, and when I mentioned that to my mother she did not protest, as she would usually do, saying that no one could be compared to her mother.

A few weeks after our arrival we all had to move into the cellar. For the next three weeks we children were seldom allowed to go upstairs as the thudding, hissing, and whizzing of shells and bullets did not stop. The grownups who listened to BBC knew that the Soviets surrounded the city, and it was a matter of days before they would capture it. But German and Hungarian radio stations kept announcing that Hitler ordered the Wehrmacht to defend Budapest to the last man, "as if it were Berlin." Radio Moscow quoted Joseph Stalin's order that Budapest will be conquered regardless of what it cost in lives.

The older boys took pride in identifying the many sounds of war. Machine guns are exchanging fire from one end of our street to the other, they said, tanks are rumbling up on the hillside, on the street above us. They asked, did you hear that boom? Now that came from a Russian tank. A few of the older boys claimed they could tell the difference between the whoosh of Russian artillery pieces nicknamed Stalin's Candle and the dull thunder of the Germans' big guns named after women.

As we huddled in the cellar, Aunt Margit and her two or three coworkers, all women, never lost their calm. Their words and faces conveyed the confidence they had in God that He would get all of us out alive. Aunt Margit told us that she was certain that in a few days we would be allowed to play hide-and-seek in the garden, go sledding on the steep slope of our street, and walk over to the famous lookout point nearby to enjoy a beautiful view of Pest.

Prior to the city's siege, children were not allowed to leave the villa, not even to go out into the garden. Now I know that Sztehlo issued strict orders to keep us inside, afraid that neighbors and passersby might observe us playing outside, suspect that some of the children were Jewish, and report us to the local Arrow Cross unit.

The neo-baroque villa where we stayed, now the residence of the French ambassador, belonged to the Hungarian foreign ministry that used to stage lavish parties there. Through his contacts Sztehlo heard that as the war stopped the parties, the space was left empty. He negotiated a loan of the villa, apparently unconcerned that several top Arrow Cross officials, including cabinet members, requisitioned other houses on the street. Or perhaps he thought that Arrow Cross thugs would not dare to intrude in their leaders' own neighborhood.

Sztehlo's staff also told the mothers not to discuss among themselves their true identities. We had to act the roles of the people our identification papers said we were. I now know that if someone arrived without a Christian document, a specialist in another Sztehlo home had the equipment to forge a good one, which was quickly arranged. Our protectors wanted each of us to have proper papers in case of an Arrow Cross or a German raid. Sztehlo, whom my mother and I never met, kept in touch with the staff on the telephone and through couriers who also delivered food. Though he made the rounds of the homes he set up, he did not visit ours during our stay there.

Aunt Margit spent time with each of the children to make sure we knew our cover stories. According to my birth certificate, my father was a butcher, and she asked questions about his shop, and I invented a place of business near Market Street, the main street everyone who has been to Debrecen knows, and I bragged that he made the best sausages, which was impressive because sausages from Debrecen had the reputation as the tastiest in the country.

Aunt Margit praised me when I told a good story, and she suggested answers to her questions when I could not come up with one. She made it all seem like a game we played, but she pretended that all the stories we made up were true. She had me switch back and forth between Hungarian and German, and I was delighted when I made her laugh with some detail about my father's ways of getting the farmers to sell him their best pigs. The truth was that Father used to sell grinding stones which he always insisted were "the very best there is in the world," and he did at times trade them with farmers for food. I used his salesman stories as raw material. When I repeated my versions to Mother, she looked frightened but did not question the need for making them up.

Though our home on Csaba street was never raided, one day German soldiers came in a car. With friendly smiles, they invited half a dozen children, "poor refugees from the Russian beasts," to a formal lunch to be given by their commanding officer at headquarters. Deaconess Huszar tried to talk the Germans out of the invitation, claiming that the children under her care were still emotionally disturbed by their experiences of fleeing the Russians. The children are not normal, and they might misbehave, was her final argument, but the Germans said it didn't matter. They had orders to deliver to their commander half a dozen refugee children, and our home had enough of them to choose from.

Mother started trembling like a leaf in the wind when Aunt Margit told her that because I spoke German I would be one of the guests. There was no appeal, Mother soon realized. So she focused on warnings such as to sip only the tiniest sips from my glass during lunch so I won't have to use the bathroom. Her fear of revealing my circumcision was great, and she told me to wet myself rather than to go to a bathroom where German soldiers might also be present.

A day or so later, the Germans came back to pick us up in a big car. Some of the children, particularly the older boys, were very tense. We had never discussed that all of us were Jewish though some of us guessed it. Nor had we ever said aloud that we were hoping for a German defeat. But this time, we knew that we had to be very careful not to hint at our true identities or our feelings about the war. We talked about the chance to eat a lot. Thanks to the Red Cross, we were well fed in our home, but there was little or no meat and not enough food for second helpings.

The commander's lunch was delicious, and soldiers in white gloves served us. I cannot forget the huge piece of fried liver across my plate, with a mound of potatoes next to it, and onions all over both. It's my favorite, I told the Germans, and indeed, it is a dish I still like. Dessert was ice cream which none of us had ever eaten during winter, and we kept saying so.

The commanding officer asked us about our flight from the Russians and the homes we lost. I spoke about my father's sausages and his dealings with pig farmers, and the German officers around the table laughed.

We did notice that people were taking pictures of the lunch table and that one of the cameras was very large. But only some of the older children suspected that we were being filmed. After the war, Uncle Levente told us that he had seen me on a newsreel. The film emphasized the hospitality of the German commander and the festive table spread for "the poor refugee children." Fortunately, I appeared only briefly, saying something about my father's sausages, but it was enough to make my uncle's heart stop beating for those seconds. He asked, "What if someone who saw the newsreel identified you and reported you to the authorities?"

As soon as we finished eating, we were taken back to our home. The ride was uneventful, and none of us felt like talking. I don't remember discussing the event with the other children.

I thought of the lunch as a game, a parlor game in which our team had to win. I do not recall being nervous, and I could not understand why both my mother and Aunt Margit did not laugh but cried instead when I told them what I had said to the Germans about the fried liver and my father's sausages. I remember feeling thrilled that I fooled the German officers. I was proud of the stories I made up, but I also knew that my mother wished that I had not opened my mouth.

Since then I have always looked back at the lunch as a small victory — a very small one — deceiving members of the Master Race who believed they knew everything and could tell a Jew instantly.

I was very much aware that the Germans were out to kill us, but I thought of my birth certificate as a license to be another person until the earth swallows them all up. I doubt if that image came from the Bible but perhaps I did overhear a relative referring to a biblical precedent or uttering the curse, "May the earth swallow up our enemies." The earth splitting open and then closing in on the Nazis was the picture I had on my mind ever since I remember thinking about the war.

Encounters with the Enemy

The Russian army advanced into the hills of Buda on Christmas Eve, 1944. In one Sztehlo home, on a street named Bogar, a German lieutenant who had known that the villa was a children's home knocked on the door in the middle of the night and told the woman in charge to clear out as the Wehrmacht intended to set up a defensive line in the villa and its yard. According to Gabor Vermes, then eleven years old and now a history professor at Rutgers University, everyone dressed in a few minutes and crawled out of the house, assisted by German soldiers. Fortunately the night was dark, Vermes says, and no one was hit by the shots fired by the Russians, only 100 to 200 yards away. The woman in charge, remembered only as "Aunt Lujza," phoned Sztehlo who suggested that they come immediately to his home, more than a mile away. The group, with fifteen or so children, trooped through the knee-deep snow and arrived safely in the Sztehlo apartment where Ilona Sztehlo, Gabor's wife, waited for them with hot caraway soup.

There was not enough space for that many children in the apartment and things got even worse when the intensity of the fighting forced everyone into the cellar. There was no other place to go. Nor was there enough food. Nevertheless, in the days that followed Ilona Sztehlo somehow found something to feed each guest, as well as her own two children, then both under ten. Vermes still shudders remembering that some evenings German officers visited the Sztehlo home and the Sztehlos fed them too. The pastor seemed unruffled and had the children form a choir singing German songs to entertain the guests. In his memoir Sztehlo wrote that one officer pulled him aside and told him that he could tell that the children were Jewish but that he would not do anything because he hated Nazi racism. (Reading that passage, I thought that only someone with the aura of Sztehlo could elicit such an extremely rare admission by a German to a Hungarian.)

Sztehlo felt he could handle the Germans, Vermes says. But he was worried about the Arrow Cross and especially concerned about Laszlo Endre, the police chief whose declared goal in life was to cleanse Hungary of its Jews. He made friends with Adolf Eichmann of the SS, who said of him: "Laszlo Endre wants to eat Jews with paprika." He boasted that in May and June 1944 he scored "a world record" by deporting 500,000 Jews in sixty days.

In the 1930s Sztehlo happened to have two very unpleasant encounters with Endre, then the equivalent of a deputy chief executive in the same county where Sztehlo served as a village pastor. In one case, Endre illegally disrupted a local election and arranged that a crony of his get a job as the government representative in the village. Sztehlo was among those who protested to the authorities in Budapest, and Endre knew that. On another occasion, at the graduation exercises of the school Sztehlo ran for village youths, Endre walked out in protest because the valedictorian spoke of the need for land reform and social justice. Endre retaliated by denouncing Sztehlo to the authorities and demanded that he be stripped of government subsidies.

Sztehlo suspected that Endre had a fairly clear idea, through his network of informers, that Jews lived in "the homes for Protestant children" protected by the Swiss Red Cross. In early December 1944, Endre's men caught two boys between the ages of ten and twelve, residents in one of the homes. Taken to Endre's office, the boys were told by Endre himself to carry back a stern message to Sztehlo: unless he disbanded his shelters immediately, Endre would go to the pastor's home and beat him with the famous bullwhip he was known to use for humiliating his enemies.

There is no single explanation for what made Endre hold back. He might have been too busy organizing the transports to the death camps. Others think that he feared that if he showed up with his bull-whip, the impulsive and physically powerful Sztehlo would confront him. People who knew Endre say that he was a coward.

Nevertheless, he could have dispatched his thugs to raid a Sztehlo home. He did order them to attack a building near Sztehlo's head-quarters that housed both a Jewish old-age home and a hospital. They shot everyone, including the parents of two young Sztehlo protégés. Perhaps Endre meant that raid as yet another warning to Sztehlo, though in a few more days Endre joined the Arrow Cross cabinet in its flight to Austria.

During the last days of December, the Wehrmacht requisitioned the villa on 20 Csaba street, and all of us were summoned to the pala-tial dining room. We saw that a framed photograph of Adolf Hitler had replaced a painting of a Hungarian village, once at the place of honor. A German officer strode in and told us that the Wehrmacht needed the upper floors for fighting the enemy. He ordered us to move into the cellar temporarily, for those few weeks required to push the Russians back to Russia. As he spoke, the sound of gunfire came from all directions.

About two weeks later, during a sudden lull in the shooting around our villa, a few children sneaked upstairs. We could not find any Germans. After we tiptoed into the dining room, where we used to play, two German soldiers burst in. They paid no attention to us; they uttered not a word. The bigger of the two walked over to the wall, locked his hands and hoisted onto his shoulders the smaller soldier who quickly unhooked the Hitler picture, put it under his arm, and jumped to the ground. In a second, they were both gone. I think we all knew that the action meant German retreat, but none of us said anything. We were trained to keep our mouth shut.

Soon the firing resumed and we scurried down to the cellar. About nightfall we heard the big wooden entrance door crash on the floor. That door had been left unlocked in the hope that it would not anger the Russians who, the grownups learned, suspected resistance whenever encountering a locked door.

Then came the sound of gunshots inside the house, and a lot of shouting in a language we did not understand. The men of the Red Army poured into the building and stuck their bayonets into every wardrobe and under every bed, looking for German soldiers. Finding none, they ordered us to gather in the dining room. In fractured German, a captain told us that the villa was now Soviet headquarters, but the children and their mothers were permitted to stay in the cellar as long as the women cooked and washed for the officers.

Then he gave a signal, and one tall soldier standing by the wall locked his hands for his short buddy to step on them and then onto the shoulders. He hung a framed photograph of a thick-mustachioed man on the same hook where Hitler's portrait had been. "This is your new father," the captain said, pointing to the picture, "Yosif Vissarionovich Stalin." He promised that our new life would be "*sehr wunderschön.*"

Two Women Go Out for a Walk

By the beginning of February, the Russians conquered the city, and the fighting shifted to the west of the capital. January 26 was my cousin Levente's fourth birthday, and Mother, who loved surprises almost as much as she loved her nephew, wanted to visit his family — her sister and brother-in-law who lived on the other side of the hill, a little more than a mile away. She relished the thought of knocking on their door, bringing with her a birthday cake she had baked out of a few ingredients, her specialty.

Deaconess Margit had a different errand in mind. She was anxious to contact Sztehlo to tell him about the Russians taking over our home and to find out what she would have to do next. She said to my mother: "Don't be afraid, Anna. The Lord Jesus will be with us." But they turned down my pleas to tag along.

They waited for a day that was quiet, though thuds of artillery fire did come from far away. Their first several hundred yards were uneventful, my mother later told me. After weeks of confinement in the cellar, the two friends enjoyed being outdoors on a chilly but sun-drenched day that seemed perfect for a stroll. The bombed-out buildings they saw all around shocked them, but they gave themselves courage by talking about their plans after the war.

The streets were deserted; no one was to be seen. Suddenly Mother heard gunshots from nearby. She felt as if "a few pebbles" hit her, and as she fell down, she caught a glimpse of her friend already flat on the ground. Then Mother lost consciousness. When several days later she came to, she found herself in a hospital room. A nurse came by and said that as many as seven bullets sprayed her, from her left shoulder down to her right leg, but, miraculously, without injuring a vital organ, and that all the bullets had been taken out and she would live.

Mother asked where her friend Margit Huszar was. The nurse said that only one bullet hit Margit but it went right through her heart.

Incredulous, Mother asked: How do you know?

Two young Russian soldiers carried you here, the nurse explained, and you were bleeding heavily. Two other Russians brought in a lady whose papers identified her as Margit Huszar. She did not bleed. She was dead.

Margit did not suffer, the nurse tried to comfort my mother who was by that time sobbing, the bullet must have killed her instantly.

In the years to come, family members discussed the story as "Margit's murder" rather than my mother's survival of seven bullets, which they cited not as a miracle but as proof of my mother's strong constitution and "that Schwarcz will to life." Though they did not know Margit, they always referred to her as "that dear Margit who should have been allowed to live."

Was the person who fired the volley Russian, German, or Hungarian? And why did he aim at two women?

Later, when my family talked about the shooting, most everyone first guessed that a vengeful German soldier hiding among the ruins of a house must have pulled the trigger. Knowing that sooner or later he would be found and shot by the Russians who took no prisoners in Budapest, the German decided to take a few locals with him. But on second thought, many family members thought it at least equally possible that the shots were fired by a crazy Russian, perhaps even one of the good Samaritans who then helped to carry the two women to the hospital. The reason? The Russian dialectics of the head and the heart: shoot first as Stalin ordered, then repent as Christ said. Still others argued that the culprit might have been an Arrow Cross thug still on a killing spree and with some ammunition left.

Half a century later, it seems to me yet another possibility that a man belonging to any of the three nationalities could have taken savage delight in punishing two women who by walking boldly in the sunshine dared to mock war, the most serious among the games of men.

Mother came to think of the seven bullets that hit her as though they were her war medals. However, she objected with uncharacteristic anger to all discussions about the national identity of the person who had done the shooting. She said it was irresponsible to ask a question that would never be answered with certainty; such questions should not be asked at all. "War is war," she declared, "and a soldier fired his gun at Margit and me. We should not play a parlor game of guessing his reason or his nationality."

At times she could get so upset about the arguments that she even forgot to mention, as she usually did when telling the story, that she never did find out what happened to the birthday cake she baked for her favorite nephew.

A Series of Miracles

Deaconess Margit was the one person killed among the scores of individuals who joined Sztehlo's staff. Moreover, the pastor lost no others who sought asylum in his thirty-two homes. A modest man, he permitted himself pride in that statistic which was indeed extraordinary, even incredible.

"We lived through a series of miracles," wrote Sztehlo who envisioned all humanity as nestled in God's palm. To him, God could never be angry or jealous but only loving, and the survival of all his protégés confirmed his thesis.

For a preacher, setting out to prove God's compassion and loving-kindness at a time of war would have been absurd, if not hypocritical. But Sztehlo was not only a man of God but also a man of action, and stubborn and fearless at that. As Koren observed, "He acted before he preached."

It was as if Sztehlo had attempted to undo the Holocaust by gathering all the Jewish children he could find, establishing one sanctuary after the other for them and seizing every chance to obtain yet another villa. He ignored reality: that his bishop had commissioned him to organize only one home and that with each new home he increased the odds for the Nazis to discover what he was doing. In addition to picking up about a dozen infants left at his front door and accepting children brought to his homes, he drove a Red Cross car at times into the ghetto, collecting a carload of children whose parents could no longer be found. By any so-called rational calculation, the Nazis should have uncovered his project and shot him, or shipped him to a concentration camp, and at the very least captured some of his protégés.

Sztehlo entered another sphere of reality. His gift for spontaneity, which did not become evident until the year 1944, overruled the dictates of ecclesiastical discipline. He came close to turning into a being of pure energy untainted by any thought of material gain or personal advancement — what both Christian and Jewish traditions define as an angel. Or as Harold Bloom suggests in *Omens of Millennium*, he was "a mirror of spiritual aspiration" reflecting "the nostalgias of belief [rather] than a manifestation of faith." Bloom argues that we should be prepared to encounter angels "at the gates of the dream, or on the threshold of death."

For Sztehlo, the war's last year, which Hungarian Jews have since named "The Year of Hate," was the seminal experience of his life. That year, he wrote, "I learned from experience that God leads, protects, and guards me." He could not for a moment fault Him for allowing the war's carnage to take place. Instead, he blamed the hatreds that the free will of His creatures invented.

Sztehlo wrote that the war "taught all of us that created beings should not besiege the Creator with unnecessary questions but, instead, do what He asks each person to do." It might not have occurred to Sztehlo that Jews often question God. Probably he did not know that such questioning is a vital element in Jewish tradition. There is no indication that he ever read the writings of his Jewish contemporaries, such as Martin Buber, who defined a continuing dialogue with God as the essence of Judaism. Sztehlo was no interfaith pastor; he did not come from a culture or a generation that looks for reassurance in finding common doctrinal ground among the monotheistic faiths and studies ways to avoid offending the sensitivities of people belonging to another creed. "God loves us, does things for each of us," he wrote and preached, "and by sacrificing His son, He did the greatest sacrifice He could."

On the other hand, unlike others in his generation and culture Sztehlo did not teach Christianity to his Jewish protégés. "Pastor Sztehlo never wanted to convert any of us," Pal Foti wrote years later. Foti had been a student in rabbinical school who eventually emigrated to England. He added: "It was he who made me go to the synagogue on Yom Kippur, 1945."

"He was a saintly man in the biblical meaning of the term," wrote Koren. "In his eyes, what he dedicated his life to was a sacred cause." Citing the burning bush that Moses saw, Koren suggested that Sztehlo was driven by a vision of similar intensity. "He heard an inner voice," Koren observed. "In serving God, he was burning like fire."

"He was a *tzaddik*, a righteous man," Foti writes. "He and his wife gave me back my faith in my fellow human beings."

New Assignments

Sztehlo was that rare Central European who unhesitatingly, even instinctively pursued the traditional Christian mission of living to serve others. His congregations were underprivileged peasant youth, patients in Budapest hospitals, and Jewish children. His model was Albert Schweitzer. In March 1945, while waiting for family members to claim the children he had sheltered from the Nazis, he proceeded to set up another home, this time for orphans of aristocrats and other "class aliens" the communists singled out for discrimination and mistreatment, as well as for underprivileged children whose parents disappeared in the war. The idea was to teach them regular school curriculum as well as to train them in trades such as carpentry, shoe repair, and tailoring. Sztehlo organized an inspired, highly trained teaching staff but insisted that the children set up their self-government, then a revolutionary idea. They ran their extracurricular activities such as a literary magazine, and made decisions on maintaining and improving their buildings and to help clean up the rubble of war on the streets of Budapest.

There was an overlap between the two groups of Sztehlo protégés. It took several months for Jewish adults to gain enough physical strength to return from camps in Germany, and many of the children in Sztehlo's care kept waiting as long as a year in the vain hope that their relatives might knock on the door. While many of those who found themselves without any family eventually emigrated to Israel, others stayed on in the new children's home that Sztehlo called Gaudiopolis, Latin for City of Joy, where they lived together in surprising harmony with the scions of Hungary's most famous historic families, as well as with the strays and abandoned youths Sztehlo picked up on the street. But in 1950, the communists, by then firmly in control, closed down the home. They would not trust a clergyman as an educator of young people.

Sztehlo returned to his prewar work as a congregational pastor, this time in the outskirts of Budapest. But he found ways to help the new enemies persecuted by the government. They were members of the prewar ruling classes, many of them old and frail, whom the communists punished collectively by confiscating their Budapest homes and deporting them to the poorest sections of the countryside where they had to do manual labor to survive. Sztehlo obtained a motorcycle with a sidecar, delivering food and medicines to them. The government warned his church that such pastoral help was illegal, as deportees must confine themselves to contacts with the parishes near their new residences. Despite warnings from his church superiors, Sztehlo persisted in assisting victims of the new dictatorship.

After each of the churches negotiated an agreement with the new people's republic, Sztehlo adopted an unusual, private stance. "He accepted neither the path of 'joint progress' with the state, nor did he defy the state by a policy of confrontation," wrote Koren in his biography, published in 1994. "He decided to save what can be saved, especially in the domain that became his specialty: helping those who needed help."

Sztehlo discovered that the communist regime did not want to bother with the handicapped, the retarded, and the elderly, so once again he devoted his energies to raising funds and establishing one home after the other for his protégés whom he recruited regardless of their religious affiliations. He even talked the government into providing some social-welfare funds. "He searched for a chance to help," Koren explained. "He looked around where he might be needed and where he could do something for others. He was happy when he recognized the results of his labor in the smiles of others." Sztehlo's irrepressible compassion made all the difference for his protégés, each of whom, in the words of one Gaudiopolis alumnus, "walked around convinced that he or she was the most important person to Sztehlo."

He was convinced that he could turn the retarded and the handicapped into well-balanced, contented, "happy" individuals. This was his declared objective that he pursued with his usual persistence, and his optimism infused the training program he designed which has since received much praise among his professional peers.

Could it be that Sztehlo was so absorbed in his projects that he was unaffected by the 1956 revolution — the finest hour of the century's Hungarian history — and its brutal suppression? Koren, who raised the question also asked by others, did not believe that to be the case.

Could he have confined himself "to the cocoon of serving the unfortunate?" Koren asked, but then, uncharacteristically, avoided a direct answer. "With his limitless love, he grew to the point that he towered over everyone," Koren wrote, using a rare hyperbole. "He was larger than the rest of us."

For Sztehlo, faith was not an option that could be adjusted or negotiated; instead, faith was the center to which everything else needed to be adjusted. He was a wholesome and wholehearted man, undivided in his loyalties. He would not harness his soul to a cause unless he believed in it fully. All his causes were just and right; unlike so many others in his generation he did not fall for any of the numerous inviting traps that promised salvation, or at least professional and material opportunity. God is loving-kindness and He loves every one of us, he kept preaching throughout his life with a single-minded insistence reminiscent of Don Quixote. The darkest statement he allowed himself to commit to writing was that during the Second World War he observed a clash between "the immeasurable human sin" and God's "infinite love" — and he omitted to mention which side scored higher.

Sztehlo's saint-like dedication, bolstered with the organizing skills of a captain of industry, not only led to his many disagreements with church and state officials — "Gabor was not a good politician," Koren said — but also to conflicts with his family. While he was beating the odds in carrying out his commitments to the unfortunates on the margin of society, those closest to him found it hard to live with him. He could no longer convince his wife Ilona, an enthusiastic helper in 1944, to give him at least moral support. The beloved surrogate father of many could not satisfy his own two children. Teenagers by the mid-1950s, son Gabor and daughter Ildiko demanded "a better life" with critical elements such as education, freedom of expression, and recognition for their talents.

"The tensions became very, very difficult for us," says Ildiko, now a nurse in a small town in Minnesota. "As children of a clergyman we could not hope to get into a university. We saw no future for ourselves. My brother and I felt we had to leave Hungary, even without our father. Our mother agreed." In the exodus that followed the Soviet suppression of the 1956 revolution, the three of them left for Switzerland.

Faced with a heartrending choice, Gabor Sztehlo did not hesitate. He could not desert his flock, he said. At that time, he managed sixteen homes which, Koren mentioned in passing, was a higher number than any of the other churches maintained in Hungary. Koren the faithful friend recalled in his biography that Sztehlo answered the question, "why don't you too leave for Switzerland?" by sweeping his hands around while declaring that he "could not make a mockery" of the love with which his protégés surrounded him.

The following is a commentary from Andras Rac, one of his 1944 protégés who kept in touch with him and argued with him much of the time, urging him to bend, to seek an accommodation with the regime and his own church, and begin to recognize reality: "Gabor was not an easy man to deal with. But the errors of such a passionate man are worth more than the old, comforting verities."

Ever the optimist, Sztehlo thought that he would soon be allowed to visit his family. But the government repeatedly refused his application for a passport. Finally, he was told that he could leave but only if he agreed never to return to Hungary — which was the deal suggested to dissidents by the regime of Janos Kadar, so easily awarded with the adjective "liberal" in the Western world. Sztehlo turned down the offer. He said he had people to take care of in the country of his birth.

Five years passed before he received permission to visit his family. But the contrast was too sharp between the years of tension followed by the serenity of a new life in Switzerland. A few weeks after his arrival, he had a heart attack. Though he recovered, his family and the doctors argued that he should not return to Hungary. The church assigned him to a small parish in Hasliberg, 9,000 feet up in the mountains, a place of spectacular beauty. Later he moved to Interlaken at a lower elevation, which the doctors thought would be better for his heart. Once again, he served as a model village pastor, and his wife as a model wife of a village pastor.

"Gabor loved mountains, and he adored the mountains of Switzerland," says his cousin Sara. "He could have been on a hike all the time — climbing when he had the strength and sketching the scenery when stopping for a rest." Though he took up drawing late in life, he became quite accomplished. Filling sketchbook after sketchbook, his drawings were precise, realistic renditions, unimaginative as art but faithful to every ridge and dell.

Though the landscape captured him, he never felt entirely at home in Switzerland. Daughter Ildiko says, "He missed Hungary terribly."

But once outside Hungary, the Sztehlos could visit with their erstwhile Jewish protégés, many of them scattered through Western Europe. In Hungary, Sztehlo was not in the habit of talking about what he called "that one year" in his life, from March 1944, when the Germans took over in Budapest, to March 1945, when the Russians completed their conquest. He did not show any sign of feeling offended when no institution — not his church, not the Jewish community — gave public recognition to what he had done. They were not permitted to do so. Nor did he track down the two lawyers who double-crossed him; he claimed he had forgotten their names.

During the Stalin era — which survived the tyrant by several years — one had to be careful to raise the issue of "those persecuted during the war," as the official phrase euphemistically described Jews. It was even riskier to mention the people who helped them, because the party line insisted that the underground communist organization was the Nazis' number one critical target as well as the one and only authentic anti-Nazi force. There could not have been a noncommunist anti-Nazi hero, particularly not a man from the clergy and therefore a sworn enemy of the people.

It would have been unwise for my mother or Uncle Levente to get together with Sztehlo. Those were the days when people outside the communist party tried not to draw attention to who they were or had been, and they did not endanger their friends and ideological confreres by holding reunions, thus giving grounds for charges of anticommunist conspiracy. The propaganda and intimidation effort was so overwhelming that Mother had the impression in the 1950s and

1960s that Sztehlo had died. Nor did she mention Sztehlo to me. Only in the 1980s, when the government allowed the publication of a few articles about him, did she seek contact, through the Lutheran church, with Sztehlo's wartime staff. She knew only vaguely that the home where she and I were given asylum was one of several Sztehlo organized. We were amazed when we learned in the 1980s that he saved close to two thousand people.

Honored in Jerusalem

Sztehlo was delighted when in 1972, following testimony from his former protégés who had settled in Israel and the West, Yad Vashem — the Jerusalem institute for the study of the Holocaust — recognized him as a "Righteous Gentile." He received a medallion and a certificate bearing a quote from the Talmud: "He who saves a life saves the entire world." The following year the Swiss government nominated him for the Nobel Prize for Peace. The Budapest authorities forbade any mention of the honors in the Hungarian press; even the Lutheran church was ordered not to print in its newsletter any reference to the pastor.

Sztehlo hoped that his doctors would soon allow him to accept an invitation from Yad Vashem and plant a tree in the Jerusalem grove memorializing Christian rescuers.

He returned to preaching. Koren visited him and thought he was effective because members of the congregation felt that Sztehlo was addressing each of them personally. One of his sermons delivered in the tiny church of Interlaken in the Swiss Alps was devoted to Thomas, the little known apostle famous for his doubting that Jesus bodily rose from the dead. In a plain, robust German, Sztehlo paid Thomas a personal tribute.

"But he is not a doubter," Sztehlo began. "For us, he is a true witness." Arguing the way a stonemason composes a dry wall or a classical musician builds a theme with point after counterpoint, Sztehlo pieced together Thomas the man: "Doubting pains him, isolates him from other disciples, and brings him close to despair. But the disciples bring him back into the community. They will not abandon him. His suspicions set conditions: he wants to see the Resurrected One himself and put his fingers in His wounds. He wants reality, and he looks for reality. But what does that mean after Jesus Christ's death and the incomprehensible resurrection?"

In answering the question, the preacher seemed to join his flock. "We simply cannot do anything but to hold to the immediately tangible as our standard," he declared. "We can't be fed with 'fine words'." He portrayed Thomas as "the kind of man who stands with both feet on the ground. He heard how Jesus described the future. Now is the time for the realization of that future. But, instead, what is expected is the death of Jesus. Thomas cannot accept that. It's not possible that Jesus tells a lie! As a realistic man, Thomas cannot rest."

Sztehlo suggested that people such as Thomas have an important role to play in the company of Jesus that should not be limited to those in a state of grace. Perhaps in talking about Thomas the aging pastor recognized himself. During the Second World War, he too tested his faith and its "fine words" against the harshness of reality. He too had his problems with his bishop and with church politics, and for long he had entertained some fundamental doubts similar to those of Thomas, though he did not publicly express them. He too searched for the elusive, potentially painful truth rather than the solidity and the comfort of grace. Already past one heart attack and warned about the likelihood of another, the pastor was getting ready to meet his Maker. He might well have been telling himself that once entering that promised land of heaven he would pose those questions he answered throughout his life with an old-fashioned pastor's didactic self-confidence, delivering the triumphant affirmatives of a received faith.

A meticulous craftsman, Sztehlo sought earthly harmonies. After he retired from most of his pastoral duties, he found a hobby that harked back to his youth as a builder of churches and an organizer of sanctuaries for Jewish children. He spent endless hours constructing elaborate model ships out of scraps of wood he sandpapered until they were smooth and lustrous, and made for a perfect fit — and symmetrical.

No longer engaged in the world of action, Sztehlo began a voluminous correspondence with his former protégés, now scattered all over the world. The mailman in the village of Emmenthal got into the habit of delivering the letters during Sztehlo's morning walk, and there was always a thick bundle of them which he liked to read while resting on a park bench.

One clear, glorious spring day in May, ten days after the sermon on Thomas, the mailman returning from his rounds in the afternoon was surprised to see the old pastor still sitting on the same bench where he had read his letters in the morning. Concerned, the mailman walked over and discovered that the man was no longer breathing. He rushed to phone a doctor who appeared in a few minutes but concluded that some hours earlier the pastor had suffered a fatal heart attack. Gabor Sztehlo left this world while reading letters from people whose lives he had once saved.

It took another decade after his death in 1974 for the Budapest government to remove Sztehlo from the list of unpersons and permit a carefully curtailed recognition of his unique achievement in Hungarian history. The 1984 publication of his memoirs, though authorized a print run restricted to 2,000 copies, made an impact, and it was followed by a television special that discovered him for the nation as a hero of the Second World War. At commemorative meetings and in newspaper articles, church officials and journalists began to characterize him as "an apostle of love" and "a rescuer of children."

With Mikhail Gorbachev's rise to power in 1985 and the onset of glasnost across the Soviet camp, Sztehlo's friends and former protégés asked the Hungarian government for permission to set up memorials to him. In 1986, the Lutheran church on Budapest's Castle Hill was permitted to display a bas-relief that showed Sztehlo's face and a likeness of the tree that his son, also named Gabor, planted in his honor in the Garden of the Righteous Gentiles in Jerusalem. The memorial was unveiled in the presence of Lutheran and Jewish officials, government representatives, and former Sztehlo protégés.

One of the speakers, Susan Ungar, came from New York. She introduced herself as the infant in a basket left on the pastor's doormat in that terrible winter of 1944 and identified only with a slip of paper, "She is called Zsuzsika."

Survivors' Feast

On a brilliantly sunny October afternoon in 1995, I am a guest of Sara Sztehlo, Gabor's cousin, and her husband Lajos Keszthelyi. Their book-lined apartment is in a building perched on Rose Hill, one of the verdant hills of Buda. Around their dinner table are four other Jews rescued by Gabor Sztehlo. Also present is his wartime coworker and biographer, Pastor Emil Koren. He is the oldest person around the table, and out of respect and affection we all call him Emil *bacsi* — Uncle Emil.

Spread out on the lace-edged white tablecloth is the favorite Hungarian meal for a family reunion, a sumptuous version of the English high tea: a banquet of crusty, freshly-baked cheese biscuits and an assortment of pastries that makes dinner redundant. We praise the chocolate-and-coffee layer cake — a trademark triumph of Central European confectionery — which Sara slices and serves on fine china. Her husband Lajos, a biophysics professor, pours the wine into intricate lead crystal goblets and the coffee into dainty, fragile porcelain cups. Inherited from grandparents and great-grandparents, the heirlooms are exemplars of good craftsmanship, as well as survivors of bombing and plunder, of wars, occupations, and revolutions, and of mass flights across borders altered by two world wars. I cannot resist clinking the crystal with a silver fork to listen to its soprano tinkle. A shaft of sunlight the color of acacia honey enters the room. Mesmerized, I watch the rainbow refracted endlessly by the crystal's flawlessly symmetrical facets.

Ours is a survivors' feast, a celebration of life that seems to us far more precious because it was wrenched from the hands of killers. The reunion is joyous, yet at times it has us on the verge of tears. We know that survival is a favor we may never comprehend. Yet many of us believe there had to have been a purpose, a reason we were saved. No, we cannot account for the gift of life — and some among us contend that it was due to nothing more than the luck of the draw — yet we all agree that it calls for thankfulness. We must remember those who kept us alive, and we should not give up looking for the meaning of such generosity.

Nor can we ever allow ourselves to forget how exceptionally fortunate we are, the lucky few saved from the cattle cars and the river Danube, and we pay our respects to the memory of the great majority, including parents and siblings and other relatives of those present, who perished. Mixing guilt with pleasure, shifting from flaring anger to tender remorse, we talk about our shared past. We also smile and laugh a lot. While we disagree about the value of psychoanalysis and the roots of Hungary's post-communist malaise, no difference of opinion that truly matters tears us apart, and we thoroughly enjoy one another's company. It is as if we were members of one extended family, a happy family. We are, in a way, Gabor Sztehlo's children.

He was "our second father," Andras Rac declares, and everyone agrees. (No one around the table needs to be reminded that the Arrow Cross militia shot Rac's parents in a raid on a Jewish old-age home not far from Sztehlo's apartment.) "I wish he was here to tell me how to settle arguments with my kids," continues Rac, a wiry, rough-hewn sculptor with powerful hands. "Gabor knew how to deal with children, more so than anyone else I have known."

"How I wish he were still with us," Balint Fuzeki says wistfully. He is a smooth, handsome Freudian psychoanalyst with a great shock of wavy gray hair. "I miss him," says softly his cousin Sara. There is a rare second or two of silence. Then we drink to Gabor Sztehlo's memory, and the toast is "*l'chaim, l'Sztehlo*" — to life, to Sztehlo. Without a doubt, a part of him is with us in the room. His is the radiant presence of a pure soul who delighted in the company of friends and the pleasures of the palate. More than a memory to be cherished, he is an elemental force that not only saved but also blessed our lives. It occurs to us that on a level of reality we cannot fully understand, he is our host, we are his guests.

Sara's face and personality remind us of Gabor's: the prominence of the cheekbones, the decisiveness and the grace, and the sparkle in the eyes. The other center of attention is Uncle Emil who at age eighty-one sits ramrod-straight. A figure out of a nineteenth century oil painting, he radiates integrity. His carefully weighted words roll forward in formations; his sentences reflect the symmetries of an ordered, self-sufficient inner world. He is factual, straightforward, lucid, and rational. No myrrh and no frankincense. Listening to him, I sense the spirit of European Reformation, a movement that taught simplicity in all things, embraced the language of plain people while saying "no" to pomp and corruption and conceit, and called for a return to the Bible, to the sources of the faith.

Pastor Koren is respectful of the Talmud's wisdom, but gently rebuts the mysticism of the Kabbala. It is the Old Testament that brings us together, he declares, and, above all, the Psalms of the immortal King David. For once, I won't enter into an argument. I don't dare to step where an angel won't.

Koren cautions against "mythologizing" Sztehlo. He argues: "If Gabor were here with us today and hear us talk about him as an angel, he would say, 'come on, are you kidding me?' He would laugh. He'd say things such as 'I am not that important to God.' He was a down-to-earth man." Rac backs up Koren: "Gabor was not an angel or a saint but a human being. Very human. An extraordinary human being, but a human being like the rest of us."

Koren indicates no outrage when telling the story of how one of their postwar bishops once got angry with Sztehlo and rudely told him to get out of the room. "They had a disagreement," Koren notes, matter-of-fact. Though he sided with Sztehlo, he did not feel that as a war hero Sztehlo should have deserved special consideration.

Koren does not like to think in terms of signs and wonders. He acknowledges that not losing a single one of the Sztehlo protégés to the Nazis was a great achievement. "Gabor worked very hard for that," Koren says, "but we were also lucky. Very, very lucky." Could it have been an instance of divine grace? Well, he is embarrassed to say that he would not know what to say about the possibility of such a thing.

When pressed on the issue, Koren concedes that it might have occurred to Sztehlo that "God held back the hands of our enemies — but Gabor would not have said that aloud." Instead, what mattered were Sztehlo's dedicated work, his energy, and his circumspection. As for Laszlo Endre, Koren thinks that "it just happened" that the Hungarian Eichmann did not send his minions to raid the homes Sztehlo had set up. No need to read anything more into that. Endre was a very busy man, after all. There were many people on his enemies' list, and he did not have enough time to kill all of them. Right?

The subject that brings a broad smile to Koren's face is the Garden of the Righteous Gentiles, the Jerusalem hillside where trees honoring Sztehlo and him now grow. He regrets that because of health problems neither he nor Sztehlo before him could travel to Jerusalem to plant the saplings with their own hands; they had to send their children in their places. He shows photographs of the trees, taken by visitors over the years. He points to a branch of his tree that broke off; he finds a more recent photo showing the tree healed and sprouting another branch. To him, as it must have been for Sztehlo too, a tree is living, tangible reality, a form of life that may be touched and its beauty admired, whereas angels and miracles are mere metaphors designed to satisfy our sweet tooth for a felicitous phrase, for the equivalent of an ornament such as a silk bow or a gold swag.

Earlier in the year Koren had emergency surgery that doctors warned could easily take his life, and they told him that he must not travel any more, not even to visit the trees in Jerusalem. He is most unhappy about the doctors' order but does not fight it. As we part, he says without a trace of self-pity, "I am not getting stronger, but it is good to know that our trees are growing."

A few weeks later, we meet again. I am in Budapest because my mother died, three days short of her ninetieth birthday. Sara Sztehlo comes to the funeral; Koren excuses himself. He is afraid of the icy paths in the Jewish cemetery he knows well. The funeral is set for

Friday, early afternoon, so it does not interfere with the Shabbath. Sara Sztehlo and Koren invite me to Sunday services in the 150-year-old Lutheran church on Castle Hill, just across the famous Vienna Gate of the medieval walled city, where the old highway to Vienna begins.

In Lutheran liturgy, it is the Sunday of Eternal Life, and the sermon delivered by a pastor born since the Second World War calls on his congregation to stand up to life-threatening challenges and not to fear death because life continues in heaven. Sara and Uncle Emil had asked the pastor to read from the pulpit my mother's maiden name, Anna Schwarcz, as among those who died in the year behind us and were "close to members of the congregation." I appreciate the gesture, and I know that it would have pleased Mother.

Wearing a black overcoat and a black fedora, Uncle Emil is in a pensive mood. He is concerned about his wife Magda, in the hospital for minor surgery. "But no surgery is minor when you reach our age," he says. He asks if he may take my arm for safety as we take a short walk on the cobblestone street that is icy in the shade and slushy in the sun. He is worried about slipping and breaking a bone; he apologizes for not attending the funeral of my mother whom he had met once, years ago, but whose "sparkling eyes" he remembers well.

He says he thought about my questions concerning Sztehlo and came to some new conclusions. "Gabor was an instrument of God," he says. "You are right that we can't just say that his success in saving two thousand lives without losing a single one was due entirely to luck or to his doing his best. Yes, he was doing his best, and his best was very good indeed. But God helped him. Well, yes, you could say that it was a miracle and that Gabor was an angel — not a biblical angel with wings, but a man who carried out what God wanted him to do. Yes, Gabor did overcome his limitations, and he did step out of his self — and God was with him."

He asks if I am satisfied with his new explanation, and a smile spreads across his face when I tell him that it has the ring of a higher truth. He talks about the foundation he and Sara Sztehlo set up, with help from "the Sztehlo children" and from the Lutheran church, for the benefit of yet another Sztehlo project begun after his Jewish children scattered: a home for handicapped youngsters, a number of whom just left the home at age eighteen and who now need help to be trained as auto mechanics and electricians so they could start living fully independent lives.

CHAPTER SIX

The Matter of Honor: Levente Thury

Language of furtive smiles,
of shining tears secretly shared,
language of loyalty, of faith never surrendered,
password of hope,
language of freedom snatched behind the prison guard's back

Gyula Illyes, The Wreath

When the Germans invaded Hungary on March 19, 1944, a seemingly endless file of tanks, armored carriers, and trucks rumbled through the streets of Budapest in a show of force that went on for hours. They crushed whatever did not get out of their way — a two-wheel pushcart, an unwary bicyclist, a pedestrian trying to cross the street. Hungarians hankering for a separate peace with the Allies got the message: nothing can stop the warriors of the master race in their plan to subdue a reluctant ally.

No resistance movement existed at the time. However, Hungarian who refused to let the Germans roll over him was Endre Bajcsy-Zsilinszky, a member of parliament from the left-of-center, anti-Nazi Smallholders' Party, journalist and editor-in-chief of a newspaper teetering on bankruptcy, and a World War I veteran decorated for "the highest level of heroism." (His memorable action: covering with a carbine the withdrawal from Belgrade of 800 enlisted men of the Austro-Hungarian army across the Danube. Under constant fire, Lieutenant Zsilinszky was the last to board the boat that took the troops back to safety.)

As a politician, he began his career in the 1920s on the far right, with "the preservation of the Hungarian race" as his agenda. He kept company with a stiffly conservative, *Junker*-like crowd, anti-Semites all, and most of them military officers who helped acclaim as Regent — the head of state substituting for the king — a tall, handsome, and pompous admiral, Miklos Horthy. But little by little Zsilinszky moved to the left and severed his ties with his former associates. By 1930, he was demanding power to the peasantry, and soon he became one of Hungary's most outspoken opponents of Nazi Germany and its local subsidiary, the Arrow Cross movement.

In the early 1940s, after Hungary joined the war on the side of the Germans, Zsilinszky intervened on behalf of Jews mistreated in labor battalions. In one instance, a Hungarian commanding officer ordered Jews to wade into the icy waters of the Danube to dismantle rafts. Outraged, Zsilinszky spoke to highly placed friends and had the commander removed, and called national attention to "the hundreds, perhaps thousands of sadists" in the military. In 1942, he created a front-page scandal by denouncing a Hungarian general who had ordered his troops, supposedly liberating an historically Hungarian territory Yugoslavia acquired after the First World War, to massacre 4,500 Jews, Gypsies, and Serbs. Zsilinszky was the one member of parliament who risked speaking up and calling for an immediate investigation. Though shouted down and called a traitor by the parliament's far right majority, he staked his prestige on getting the commanders prosecuted and the massacre condemned. Surprising people on both sides of the controversy, the court found four of the officers guilty.

In 1944 Zsilinszky was fifty-eight years old. Gyula Illyes, the nation's unofficial poet laureate in the 1950s and 60s, remembered his "splendid shoulders in a well-tailored jacket; a flawlessly symmetrical bow tie on a powerful neck; an immaculately white shirt on a convex chest; perfect cuffs. Everything about him was strong and clean."

The drama of Hungarian resistance began on March 19, 1944, Sunday morning at 8:45 when the buzzer sounded in the Zsilinszky apartment in Buda. His wife Maria opened the front door's little window that allows a peek at a caller. Speaking German-accented Hungarian, a man in civilian clothes asked to see Mr. Congressman. He is still asleep, she said, and won't get up until eleven. She closed the window. The buzzer sounded again. When she opened the window, the man thrust his hand through it and tried to open the door from the inside. As she forced the man's hand off the door handle and shut the window, she noticed that the unwanted visitor had companions: three men in black SS uniforms. From behind the door, the civilian shouted that they were from the Gestapo and must see her husband immediately.

She woke up Zsilinszky who phoned the chief of Hungarian police but was told by his assistant that the Germans had just taken over police headquarters. Zsilinszky showered, shaved, and dressed with the same deliberate tempo as on any other day, though by this time the buzzer was buzzing nonstop. Then he reached for his revolver and checked if it was loaded. It was. As Zsilinszky was about to leave his bedroom, he heard the Germans forcing their way through the front door by shooting at its lock.

Seeing a man's shadow through the translucent glass of the bedroom door, Zsilinszky fired at him. The Germans opened up with their submachine guns. "Glass from French doors, windows, and mirrors shattered, flying through the apartment," his wife Maria Bende Zsilinszky wrote years later. As the Germans approached the bedroom from the other direction, through the bathroom, a bullet punched a hole in the boiler, and water began to spurt all over.

Though hit in the stomach and the shoulder, Zsilinszky tried to shoot the intruders. Soon he ran out of bullets, and Maria whispered to him "surrender!" He threw his revolver into the living room. The

SS men ran into the bedroom, jumped at him, tied his hands behind his back, and forced him to walk out of the apartment and down the steps to the street. He was bleeding heavily. Before the Germans pushed him into their car, he shouted to the crowd that had gathered, "Long live independent and free Hungary!"

From the vantage point of *realpolitik* — not to mention military tactics — one man defending himself with a revolver against four attackers armed with submachine guns is an act of folly. The sober-minded might also call Zsilinszky's defiance worse than quixotic because as the man best qualified to lead a resistance movement he risked being blown to pieces.

However, Zsilinszky lived by a different code. He intended the shots he fired at the Germans to echo across the country, which they did, telling his compatriots who submitted supinely to the Wehrmacht's superior firepower that the nation must save its honor and resist the invasion. Years later the poet Illyes wrote: "His front door became the country's front door," marking the first occasion that Zsilinszky "was Hungary." Another time would come nine months later, in December 1944.

The Chivalric Code

A solitary act of defiance regardless of the consequences is at the heart of the Hungarian cult of honor, and the more impossible the goal, the purer and the more beautiful the act in the sense that Immanuel Kant defined his categorical imperative: an unconditional action that expresses moral autonomy irrespective of the circumstances. Or to shift metaphors, defiance without hope of success is comparable to what romantics call the purest form of love: the one that is unrequited.

However irrational such a chivalric code may appear in the bottom-line, zero-sum game of power politics, it throws some light on the enigma of Hungarian survival in a hostile region where neighbors often agree only in their dislike of Hungarians, calling them overbearing when up in the saddle and ornery when down in the dust. Whether the language is Romanian or German, Serbian or Slovak, the historic charge has been the same: Hungarians conduct themselves as if they were God's chosen people.

A subterranean compulsion to stake one's life on a lost cause links the men Hungarians acclaim as their historic heroes. Three years before Zsilinszky fired his revolver at four German intruders, Prime Minister Count Pal Teleki shot himself. As his farewell letter explained, he hoped that his suicide would help in absolving his country of the sin of violating its "treaty of eternal friendship" with Yugoslavia (which he had signed) by allowing the Wehrmacht to pass through Hungary, thus assisting in that invasion. He also hoped that the drama of his exit would give the people of Germany second thoughts about blindly following its Nazi leaders. His suicide did receive a lovely epitaph from Winston Churchill who prophesied that Teleki's spirit would be present at the peace talks after the war. Nothing of the sort came to pass, and the suicide failed to achieve its purpose. Yet to this day many Hungarians admire Teleki as "the man who had the ultimate courage to protest."

Though Teleki was a conservative aristocrat clinging to the privileges of his class and Zsilinszky a populist rebel crying out on behalf of the oppressed peasantry, they shared a loyalty to a code of honor that upholds the sacredness of the given word and defines an individual's life as subservient to the needs of the nation. Refusing to acquiesce in the humiliation of an unconscionable foreign diktat, both men took it upon themselves to save Hungary's honor.

Unpremeditated courage rather than reasoned calculation is the better part of the Hungarian spirit. Hence the preposterous notion, most recently advanced in October 1956, that regardless of the odds, an oppressed small nation must challenge a mighty empire such as the Soviet Union and the irreversible march of history it claims to embody. But unlike those ten days in 1956, when bands of students, intellectuals, and workers put Hungary on the world's center stage for one luminous moment in one thousand years, the failure in 1944 to stand up collectively to a great power led to another national tragedy that recurs like a refrain through the centuries.

The Gestapo wasted no time in stamping out the resistance movement before it could rise. On that same Sunday morning when the four Germans broke into Zsilinszky's apartment, other units arrested more than a hundred anti-Nazis, many of them his friends and political allies. The roundup, which the Germans had long demanded from the Horthy regime, was one of the reasons Hitler ordered his troops to invade the country, a nominal Axis ally of three years.

One of those imprisoned was journalist Levente Thury, then forty-nine years old and the editor-publisher of a daily news bulletin, *News from Abroad*. Based on BBC broadcasts from London and prepared by a multilingual staff, most of them Jews and some of them refugees from Poland and Czechoslovakia, it was the only pro-Allied news service in Hitler's Europe. Hungarian newspapers printed its items because of the concise, factual, and reliable reporting. After Prime Minister Teleki's suicide, his pro-German successor promptly banned it. Nevertheless, Thury was soon able to go back to printing and distributing the news service illegally, as an underground operation. And when the next prime minister, pro-Anglo-American Miklos Kallay took over, the service was legal again. Newspapers made good use of its reporting, giving the public details about the Nazi defeats at Stalingrad and in North Africa, the Allied landing in Sicily, and the fall of Benito Mussolini.

News from Abroad was secretly funded by the British intelligence service that helped launch it in 1939. Thury astonished his patrons by turning a profit. His British liaison noted that making money was most unusual in intelligence operations and quite unnecessary. He said he had no idea what to do with the profit Thury wanted to hand over to him. Instead, the Brit suggested that the news service spend the money on office furniture and lower its fees, so the problem would not come up again.

Thury purchased capacious, densely tufted leather armchairs the color of fine tobacco, the kind favored by members of London clubs for reading newspapers and for encouraging catnaps. But he refused to lower the subscription price, explaining to the British liaison officer that the high fees helped convince editors that his service was not a propaganda effort but a legitimate news business of top quality they should rely on.

Well-informed about the Hungarian press, the Gestapo sent its men to shut down *News from Abroad* as soon as German tanks rolled into Budapest. They seized all the files and then sealed the entrance door. Nevertheless, some of Thury's staff later broke into the office, retrieved the leather armchairs, and hauled them to the Thury apartment.

A World Hermetically Hungarian

Zsilinszky and Thury came from similar backgrounds: born in poor villages, they descended from peasant warriors elevated to petty nobility once they proved their courage in battle. Along with hunger for land, and anger with poverty and foreign oppression, these ancestors left a legacy of defiant independence. Moreover, both Zsilinszky and Thury professed a Protestant faith, which in Hungary had a rebellious flavor, competing with the majority Roman Catholicism that Austria promoted and at times imposed. Thury's father and grandfather were both Calvinist pastors, and he too studied for the ministry before he left divinity school — or was thrown out, as some remember that murky event he did not like to talk about — and became a journalist. Zsilinszky was born a Lutheran; his father was a village teacher, the first in his peasant family to achieve such a status.

Opposed to militarism and to the semi-feudal privileges of a ruling class protected by the Horthy regime, Thury found himself in permanent opposition. For twenty years he wrote for newspapers in Debrecen, then the country's second city and known as "the Calvinist Rome" because of its Calvinist majority, and eventually became editor-in-chief of the local left-of-center daily *Independent News*. In an unpublished essay of self-examination years later, he described himself as serving as "a more-or-less unconscious root of the forces of the times," while working "to affect social reform and to alleviate misery." In the same period, Zsilinszky wrote pamphlets calling for radical political changes that would lift the peasantry out of its abject poverty. He also edited a succession of financially unstable newspapers and ran for parliament, often successfully.

Zsilinszky and Thury were outraged by the injustice of "poverty in a rich land" and by "the routine brutality" with which the government crushed dissent from the left, particularly in the countryside where few witnesses would ever dare step forward. The two men agreed that the nation's historic first task, postponed far too long, was to improve the lot of the peasantry, "the soul of the nation," and to remove it from its "nearly Asiatic misery." But nothing could be done without first distributing land, huge chunks of which were owned by the Roman Catholic Church and a small group of aristocratic families. Looking beyond Hungary's borders, both men were far more worried about a militant, expansionist Germany than the Soviet Union they regarded as weak and divided. But influenced by the fact that historically Russia seldom played a role in Hungarian affairs, they did not expect the Soviet Union to be the country's new master.

Thury had a reflexive empathy for the poor and the unfortunate. One story his friends liked to tell about him featured a barefoot villager entering the offices of *Independent News* in Debrecen and asking to see the editor. Thury's instructions called for an open door for visitors, and the man was shown in. He told Thury that he had traveled to the city to look for a job and spent the night on a park bench. But somebody stole his shoes while he slept, and now he was cold and found no one who would give a job to a barefooted pauper. Thury unlaced his shoes and gave them to the man. "They fit like a glove," the villager said. "Now people won't look down on me, and I will surely find a job."

Thury sent an assistant to his home to fetch another pair of shoes. His colleagues pieced together what happened, and the story became the anecdote that defined him.

In the mid-1930s, the impulsive, silver-tongued politician Zsilinszky and the cheerful, witty intellectual Thury became close friends as well as political allies. Their wives, both named Maria, had been originally assistants in the offices of their husbands' newspapers, and they found each other kindred souls.

Thury's wife, nicknamed Mara, was my mother's younger sister, so he was my uncle by marriage. In her early twenties, Mara fell in love with him, her first boss, whose face reminded her of Gary Cooper's and whom she found "the perfect gentleman." They married in 1934. Thury was the first Christian to join our traditional Jewish family, causing grief and consternation, particularly among older, strictly Orthodox relatives. But he surprised everyone by asking his wife to light candles on Friday nights, a ritual she abandoned only during the war. He also impressed the family with his ability to read Hebrew he had studied in divinity school — his parents had wanted him to become a pastor — and remembered so well that he led a Passover service in his mother-in-law's home.

The Zsilinszky-Thury friendship deepened over many evenings arguing over the destiny of their nation, usually around the dinner table and with some half a dozen friends present. Though the announced objective was to develop a program to defeat the corrupt government by winning more parliamentary seats, the friends found themselves spending most of their time raking the dead fires of the past. When did things go wrong? When did the nation lose its way? Which battle and which king altered the course of Hungarian history that began so promisingly with the House of Arpad? That dynasty was named after the legendary leader of the tribal confederation of nomads who burst in from the steppes of the east, through the Carpathian mountain range. In the ninth century, they conquered what soon became the Kingdom of Hungary under its first Christian ruler, King Stephen, raised to sainthood a few decades after his death. After the male line of the Arpads died out in 1301, foreign dynasties seized the throne. But about the time Columbus discovered the New World, Hungary enjoyed a brief golden age under King Matthias the

Just and became the eastern outpost of the Renaissance. He encouraged trading with neighbors, raised beautiful buildings, and collected illuminated manuscripts, while the country's population reached four million — about the same as England and France at the time. After a brief and mysterious illness, he died in Vienna, which he had conquered.

Three decades later the Hungarians lost to the Ottoman Turks whose huge armies eventually marched as far west as the outskirts of Vienna. In a century and a half, after the Ottoman storm was spent, the Habsburgs quickly achieved control of what was left of Hungary. Which foreign invader inflicted more damage, the Ottoman Turks or the Austrian Habsburgs? The Ottomans did not insist on conversion to Islam but for a century and a half despoiled the country, abducted children, raised them as Turks, and forced them into an elite unit used as the army's vanguard. The Habsburgs turned the ravished land into their eastern buffer but held it back from full recovery. Why did Christendom pay no heed to the Hungarians who fought on the ramparts of Western civilization and begged for help against the Moslem hordes? And, after Austria finally pushed back the Turks, at the end of the seventeenth century, why didn't France and England help Hungarians reclaim their sovereignty from Austria? Was abandonment by its "natural allies" in the west Hungary's inescapable destiny?

Zsilinszky and Thury and their friends agreed that the much-awaited turnabout could have come in the miraculous year of 1848, when revolutions spread across the continent. But after spectacular initial victories, Hungary was vanquished by Austria backed up by an army of Russia's Czar Nicholas I. Did treason lurk in the heart of the general who capitulated to Austria? Or did the fault lie with the overly zealous nationalist leader, the fiery orator Lajos Kossuth, who went too far in dethroning the Habsburgs? Should he have adopted instead a cautious, moderate course of independence in stages? Or was he the once and future "father of the nation" who pursued the right course and whose example must be followed?

Is Hungary a land destined to be in the way of empires determined to trample on its sovereignty and to occupy it as a buffer or as a staging area for further conquests? Are Hungarians doomed to fail in their aspirations? Is there some fatal flaw in Hungarian character — is it miscalculation or recklessness or incurable romanticism — that causes the nation to fall behind the western half of the continent, forever unable to pull itself up from its poverty, backward ways, and provincial insignificance? Are Hungary's tragedies inevitable?

But even if the answers to these questions are yes, shouldn't a true patriot keep fighting for the nation's honor — and his own? Isn't defiance of injustice and oppression the high purpose of life, the examined life, the honorable life, and thus the only life worth living? Is there any other way to live — and to choose death, if need be — but by a code of honor?

Newspaper articles and memoirs testify that these were the unresolved dilemmas that Zsilinszky and Thury and their friends debated night after night, finding themselves reluctant to leave the sacred past and to reenter the profane present.

Some time past midnight, as cups of strong black coffee were summoned to counter the effects of the fine local wine, the mood around the table turned somber. At least one person raised the possibility of the ominous present as a prelude to ultimate tragedy in the near future, the *Endlösung* prophesied by the German philosopher Herder in the early nineteenth century: the death of a nation. The idea was a melodramatic equivalent of the biblical prophet Ezekiel's vision of the Valley of Dry Bones, and it made a deep impression on generations of Hungarians.

Then as now, Hungarian *Weltschmerz* reflected a loser's cultivated self-pity. That native melancholy was a form of sublimated rage over questions also debated in taverns by men of the working class, albeit in somewhat different terms: Why are we always at the bottom, mired in mud? Why can't we ever amount to anything? Who are the people responsible for our misfortune?

In both kinds of assemblies, a person began the presentation of his thesis with the same phrase, "The tragedy is . . ." — as if diagnosing the core national tragedy could help in preventing its recurrence.

The men around the table resented — but on occasion relished —

the picture of Hungary as a provincial backwater of the continent, off the main highways of European thought and action, where most people ate and slept well but where nothing of importance affecting the rest of the world ever happened. Life was decorated with melancholy anachronisms. For generations, the eyes of people from all walks of life glistened with tears when listening to a Gypsy violinist's lament over the fading of a once perfect rose or the arrival of autumn's first raindrops. As far as anyone could remember, the most popular man has been the cheerful cynic resigned to lassitude and defeat who knew all the right clues to laughing and crying — and excelled at prompting both. Yet carriers of the deep gloom of Hungarian history have always commanded respect as patriots. They soared and stumbled, lived and died within a world as hermetically Hungarian as their language, earning the right to what friends called "a beautiful funeral."

The Lesson of the Gray Donkey in Thick Fog

In jail in the spring of 1944, the Gestapo's men beat Thury so severely that he was taken to the prisoners' hospital. Once there, his friends arranged his release by means of a ruse. They delivered a military summons that assigned him to guard a labor battalion, a Hungarian invention to force Jewish men — excluded from the military because of their race — into hard labor twelve hours a day. Corporal Thury soon became his unit's link with the outside world. He put the men's letters in envelopes he sent to his home; he made it possible for their families to send packages of food and clothing. Some of them became his close friends. But even they did not know the secret of how he managed to persuade his fellow guards and their commanding officer to stop administering punishments such as having the men strip to their underwear and stand at attention for hours in subzero weather. "Somehow, his arrival changed things radically for our unit," one of the men told me years later. "I suppose he had a way with people who didn't share his outlook on life. And he was also the rare Gentile who made us Jews feel that we are one hundred percent Hungarians — and without saying it."

However, the Gestapo tracked Thury down and once more arrested him. For weeks, there was no word from him, and his wife Mara feared that the Germans might have beaten him to death.

One day the buzzer sounded in the apartment, and Mara found herself looking at a stranger whose "crooked face" frightened her. But she let him in as soon as the caller whispered that he brought a message from her husband, with whom he had shared a prison cell. "Mr. Editor is well," the visitor said, using a respectful formula. "He recovered from the latest beating, and he hopes to be released soon." That hope made sense, he continued, because according to prison wisdom, if a political prisoner is not killed in the first few weeks, he will eventually be released.

The visitor explained that he himself was a common criminal. His most recent conviction was for armed robbery, and murder too figured on his police record. But, he emphasized, he looked up to Mr. Thury as "a true patriot" and "a scholar." "Mr. Editor taught me a lot about Hungarian history," he said. "I had only a few years of schooling, and I will always be grateful to him. But, Mrs. Thury, may I tell you what *I* told *him*? I said, thank you for explaining to me that we are living through historic times. But then I said that it seems to me that whenever history is being made, it is best for a private individual to become as invisible as a gray donkey in thick fog. I am very sorry to inform you, Mrs. Thury, that I could not make him see my point."

As Aunt Mara told me years later, she could barely force herself to look at the visitor's face, and his matter-of-fact revelations about his criminal past made her shudder. Yet she felt relieved. She found herself in agreement with his judgment, and she wished that her husband had paid attention to the lesson of the gray donkey in thick fog. Strangely enough, for the first time since the war began, she felt reassured that her beloved husband, whom she could not talk out of risking his life, would come out of the war alive.

During the summer of 1944, after the Allied landing in Normandy, Regent Miklos Horthy felt strong enough to dismiss his pro-German prime minister, and the new, covertly pro-Allied cabinet renewed the secret contacts with the Allies and sent an emissary to Moscow. The new government also insisted that the Gestapo hand over its Hungarian prisoners to the Hungarian authorities, which it did, surprising everyone and encouraging the anti-Nazis. Zsilinszky and his friends, Thury among them, were free again.

Following Horthy's unsuccessful attempt to declare the country's neutrality, the Germans promptly struck back and arranged for their Arrow Cross stooges to stage a putsch toppling Horthy on October 15. Zsilinszky went underground and began organizing a resistance movement. He contacted comrades from the First World War and other friends in the military, proposing that at the right moment, Hungarian soldiers commanded by reliable anti-Nazi officers take over certain parts of Budapest from the Germans and disarm the Arrow Cross. He then would get on the radio and call for a national uprising against the Germans.

Thury was among the civilians Zsilinszky asked to take part in the secret organizing sessions of the conspirators. Thury was in his element. Relying on his judgment of character, he approached people he thought might join the resistance. He looked up his many contacts who in turn gave him more.

For the first time in his life, anti-militarist Thury was making friends with professional soldiers. A brilliant idea occurred to him: since the government excluded Jews from the regular army and forced them into labor battalions, a furlough pass in the hands of a Jewish male of conscription age automatically proved Gentile status. No other document, such as a birth certificate or a police paper authenticating a permanent address and Christian religion, would be needed. Thury's new contacts in the military supplied sample passes, as well as the names and locations of units and commanders, just in case questions were asked. A printer friend and neighbor — a devout member of a small Protestant sect from Transylvania that kept Saturday as its Sabbath — printed hundreds of passes. Each was good only for a week or two, and Thury filled in the dates by hand.

Later he confided in his brother-in-law — Uncle Shumi who in turn told me in the 1960s — that he especially liked forging the illegible signatures of the commanding officers, enjoying every flourish and curlicue, the vaunted mark of penmanship and individuality. Though he had never before whittled or shown any talent in crafts, Thury quickly acquired the considerable skills needed to carve letters on slices of potato that had to make do as rubber stamps.

I remember seeing Uncle Levente cutting potatoes at his desk. (My mother and I were in a home, supposedly for Protestant children, run by a friend of his, and we were visiting.) I thought he was on kitchen duty and was surprised to hear him curse the Nazis profusely from time to time. I realized that he cursed when his penknife slipped. But, I asked myself, why was he spending so much time on each potato?

He had many contacts who used the passes, and they in turn distributed them to their contacts. Evidently, the passes did not arouse suspicions. Neither German nor Hungarian patrols questioned the validity of a military document presented by a haggard-looking man — after all, soldiers were allowed brief respites from fighting the Russians.

In the meantime, his apartment, in a quiet residential section of Buda, was open to Jews as well as Gentile anti-Nazis who felt unsafe in their own homes. Besides picking up forged papers and making contacts, the men traded information, listened to the BBC, ran errands, made telephone calls, ate, and slept. "The apartment was always full of strangers," remembers his son, my cousin who is also named Levente, born in 1941. "They came and went. There was a lot of traffic. There were even people hiding in the attic."

He warned everyone that his apartment might be under surveillance. But with every passing day without a Nazi raid he became more and more confident. Fellow tenants in the apartment building did not report him to the authorities. Somehow, Thury even managed to persuade a vocal right-winger feared by other tenants that he too should close his eyes to the traffic of strangers. Not even his wife Mara knew how he did that and surprisingly the two men remained on friendly terms even after the war. "My father had a great capacity to make friends," my cousin has said. "But he did not always choose his friends because he agreed with them politically. He had his own standards, which I do not understand. He could give allowances for strength of character and for painful experiences in childhood that might have led someone astray politically. Yet he was unforgiving when it came to people he thought had sold their souls to the devil."

Thury was a gracious host. Years later cousin Levente and I heard from some of his guests that he made them feel as if they had attended a festive gathering of friends, even something of a party. He reassured the fugitives that the Allied strength was overwhelming and the Nazi collapse imminent. "It cannot be otherwise," he kept saying. "Hitler has got to lose."

One night, a group of young thugs in the uniform of the Arrow Cross pushed the buzzer at the apartment building's garden gate, kept locked after 11 p.m. The janitor's wife, Matild Varga, answered the call. Once she recognized their uniforms, she flew into a rage. "You boys go to Berlin to fight," she shouted at the top of her voice. "You belong in Germany. Not here. Not in Hungary. And now get out of my house." A short, chubby woman in her thirties, Mrs. Varga was not afraid of the thugs, who were armed. Her voice, honed in the Roman Catholic choir where she sang, had a sharp edge, and it carried as far as a city block in the stillness of the night. She did not swear at the thugs — she was, after all, a respectable, church-going woman — but her words apparently shamed them. Surprisingly enough, they turned around and left.

Thury told Mrs. Varga that her action put her in the same class with a heroine from Hungarian history, Ilona Zrinyi, a warrior woman who defended a fortress besieged by the Habsburgs in the seventeenth century (and lost because of treason by her chief lieutenant). Mrs. Varga's complexion, as white as milk, turned red. "Mr. Editor," she said, "you shouldn't say such things. I am a simple woman." On a visit to Budapest some thirty years later, I asked her to remember that conversation, she blushed again. When she responded, she did not use the familiar form of "you," as she did when I was a child.

Bracketing me with my uncle, she said, "You Mr. Editors express yourselves in fancy ways."

Her routing of the Arrow Cross inspired Uncle Levente. "With women like Mrs. Varga, we have a future as a nation," he said at the time to friends, and for years to come he repeated her brave words.

In 1944 Thury exuded optimism. He liked and respected the people he worked with, and he was confident that the military uprising Zsilinszky and the officers planned would triumph. He was never in good health — as a young man he had tuberculosis — and the Gestapo thugs damaged his spleen and liver, and knocked out most of his teeth. His lungs, always weak, were again giving him problems. He coughed a lot, and he had to slow down his walk because of shortness of breath.

But nothing seemed to dampen his spirits in those deadly days of 1944. He was too busy with his assignments to worry about small things like his cough or the deepening lines on his face, which no longer reminded anyone of Gary Cooper. He kept telling his wife that he was recovering from the beatings, feeling just fine, and things were getting better.

"Those were the best days of your uncle's life," Aunt Mara told me in the 1970s. "He was never happier. He felt he was doing the kind of work he was always meant to do. He never seemed to be afraid. He was not even nervous." But she was. She told my mother that she could not sleep, and when she did, she had nightmares of her husband's execution by the sword and their son's kidnapping by the Germans. She kept crying in her sleep and waking up in cold sweat.

He visited my mother Anna and me in the house where we were hiding, officially a center for refugees from eastern Hungary, run by one of his friends, Pastor Gabor Sztehlo. Uncle Levente assured us that the Nazis would soon lose the war and that Allied victory was near. "But how much more time will that take, weeks or months?" my mother asked. "And are we going to come through alive?"

"I'll get you tickets to the trial of the Arrow Cross criminals," he told her. "You, your sister Mara, and I will sit together. We'll go to their hanging too. I'll get the tickets. I promise you." But he was evasive when my mother asked what he thought was happening to family members deported to Germany. When she started to cry, talking about her mother, his response was that he didn't know the facts but that the truth will become known in the courtroom. And the Nazi criminals will hang.

"I'll get you the tickets," became his slogan.

"You say such extreme things," my mother replied at the time, with a deep sigh. Years later she acknowledged: "My brother-in-law Levente kept up my spirits." In the 1960s, in the notes she jotted down about her life, she mentioned "one lovely evening," when her younger brother Anti unexpectedly arrived, on leave from his labor battalion, and their sister Mara hosted a family dinner. "Levente made a toast with beautiful words that all our family would soon be together again, in good health and in happiness," my mother wrote. "Next day the Gestapo came to get Levente one more time."

That was in late November when the Gestapo rounded up all the conspirators prior to the planned uprising. A lieutenant in the Hungarian artillery had infiltrated the resistance movement and delivered the participants' list to the Germans. The Arrow Cross government put the three top military leaders on trial and hanged them. But Zsilinszky's lawyer argued that even though parliament had been disbanded, its members continued to enjoy immunity from prosecution. His trial was postponed. Astoundingly, in this instance the Hungarian Nazi authorities felt obliged to comply with due process, a vestige of the Austro-Hungarian *Rechtsstaat*, "a state ruled by law."

As the Red Army was closing in on Budapest, the Arrow Cross authorities ordered the evacuation of political prisoners. They were crowded into two buses that were to transport them to the western border of the country. In a woody area in the outskirts of Budapest, air raid sirens sounded. The buses stopped, and the soldiers who guarded the prisoners ordered everyone to take cover under the trees. In the confusion, Thury slipped out, as did a few others.

According to testimony pieced together after the war, one of the soldiers approached Zsilinszky. He whispered that he was from Zsilinszky's constituency, the village of Tarpa, and that his family always voted for Zsilinszky. The soldier said he had been talking to a few of his like-minded comrades, also from Tarpa, and they had a suggestion: Mr. Congressman ought to break loose and run into the woods; then they would pursue him and shoot like crazy but only in the air.

Deeply moved, Zsilinszky first expressed his gratitude to the soldier. But then he explained that he felt he must not try to escape his fate. He could not "abandon" his three friends and co-conspirators who had already been executed in Budapest. He said that in honor of their memory, he was obliged to submit himself to a trial and share their fate if need be. The soldier was too respectful to argue.

Late in the evening the following day, the two buses arrived at a prison near the Austrian border. A few days later, Zsilinszky was put on trial for high treason. As expected, the Arrow Cross judge pronounced him guilty of trying to overthrow the government and sentenced him to death by hanging the following day, December 24. In his closing statement, Zsilinszky said he had sought to save his country from destruction and he would do it again. He had no regrets and refused to ask for clemency. The Lutheran pastor assigned to the prison appealed to the judge for delay. The pastor cited the law forbidding executions on a holiday, such as Christmas Eve. The judge dismissed the request. He said: "I want to spend Christmas with my mind at peace."

Again according to the Austro-Hungarian protocol, in the final hours of his life the condemned man was allowed to receive in his cell fellow inmates including co-conspirators. He told them "never to be unfaithful to the cause" for which the three officers had sacrificed their lives. "His serenity was uplifting and astounding," one of his guests recalled in a memorial volume published in 1969. He wrote a farewell letter to his wife and asked to be buried in the village of Tarpa.

Zsilinszky shook hands with the two soldiers who escorted him to the gallows. He urged them to be "good Hungarians." One of the soldiers happened to be another young peasant from Tarpa who kissed his hand. In the prison courtyard, the judge faced Zsilinszky and read the sentence again, as required by law. As the noose was placed around his neck a few hours before Christmas Eve, 1944, Zsilinszky cried out, in his resonant, strong baritone that needed no bullhorn: "God sees everything!" That was the second time "Zsilinszky was Hungary," the poet Illyes later wrote.

Three months later, the prison staff crossed the border to Germany to escape the Red Army. Marching toward Eberfurt, the hangman suddenly took out his revolver and blew his brains out. Was the hangman, too, Hungary? The poet never addressed himself to the question.

Six Post-War Trials

In the first free elections after the war, in November 1945, Zsilinszky's Smallholders' Party won by a landslide, with 56 percent of the vote. The communists captured 17 percent, but the Soviet occupation authorities insisted that a coalition government must include the communists. Thury was supposed to be the seventh person on his party's parliamentary list, but his name was crossed out at the last minute by Zoltan Tildy, the party's leader and the first president of the newly proclaimed republic. Instead, Thury was appointed as the spokesman for the Commission of Abandoned Property, an important postwar government institution closely watched for financial and moral integrity but uninvolved in politics. (Tildy never explained why he did not want Thury, a man whose transparent honesty and straightforward speaking style were likely to attract voters, to run for parliament. A few years later, after the communist dictatorship sent Tildy and other top Smallholder leaders to jail, Thury said he was grateful to Tildy for removing him from politics.)

Uncle Levente kept his word about tickets for the trial of the two Arrow Cross criminals responsible for the deportations. Though he had to pull all kinds of strings — which normally he did not like to do — he got second-row seats for Mara and Anna.

But, as I found out years later from my mother, the two sisters could not sit through the trial. After an hour or so of watching the prosecution presenting its case, they got up abruptly and left the courtroom. Uncle Levente hurried after them.

Once outside, he asked what happened. One sister, trembling, said that the two infamous officials "looked frightened," and she felt sorry for them, and the other sister said she felt the same way. "But those killers sent your mother to the gas chamber in Auschwitz," Uncle Levente cried out in anger.

The two sisters had no response other than that they were going home. "You are much too tender-hearted," he told them. "Those killers do not deserve to be called human beings. In fact, they are not." The sisters walked out, and he returned to the courtroom.

Nevertheless, when the two men were executed four months later, in April 1946, Uncle Levente did not use his ticket to witness the event. "All his life my father sided with the victims and against those in power," his son explains. "He must have been afraid that he might feel sympathy for the men being hanged even though they were evil and he hated them."

At the first family birthday celebration after the war, Endre, my mother's first cousin, took Uncle Levente aside, and confided to him his plan to emigrate to Israel. Endre said he concluded that he could no longer live in Hungary, among people who murdered his eldest son or stood on the sidelines when such murders were being committed. Uncle Levente said he understood, and he sympathized.

Then something snapped in Endre. "May this land sink to the bottom of the sea," he cried out. "May this nation disappear from the face of the earth." In a language redolent with nineteenth century Hungarian poetry — which he loved — and raising his voice, Endre cursed the country of his birth and voiced his certainty that the

Hungarian nation was fated to die. He said he was not going to be present for the funeral. Nor would he mourn. Shaken, Levente said nothing.

I do not remember witnessing a similar confrontation in all the many family gatherings I attended.

Catching the drift of Endre's words and realizing that the exchange was no longer the kind of intimate one-on-one huddle routine in the family, several relatives approached Endre and pulled him into another room. I later learned that they reminded him that it was the first family reunion since the war's end and that harsh words were inappropriate, particularly with Levente, who did so much for the family and other Jews during the war. Stubborn and angry, Endre insisted that regardless of what the one Christian in the family did for the family and other Jews during the war, he could not help saying what he said.

At the time no one argued with Endre. The consensus was that he was too distraught to listen to reason. But a few days later one of Mara's brothers suggested to him that he should think about apologizing to Levente. Endre refused, arguing that he loved and respected Levente whom he was proud to call his relative and that he did not say anything that would insult him personally, of course not, and he would never do that.

Other family members at the gathering were deeply troubled by Endre's words, and Shumi, Mara's eldest brother and head of the family, apologized to Levente.

"A father whose child was killed can say anything that's on his mind," was Levente's calm response but verging on tears, Shumi later told me. "Nobody has the right to argue with his feelings. Endre doesn't need to apologize to me or to anyone else."

One angry outburst of Uncle Levente's I remember occurred when the two of us were out for a stroll about a year after the Soviet takeover of the country. A Soviet military truck slowly made its way uphill, and we saw that the soldiers sitting in the back were eating cherries from a hacked-down tree limb so large that it hung over the bed of the truck. Uncle Levente raised his fists and shook them, shouting at the top of his voice: "You cut down a limb and you killed next year's crop, and the crops of years to come!" Paying no attention to the passersby who stopped to watch, he cursed the soldiers with words that had a biblical flavor. His parting shot employed the nastiest phrase in his vocabulary: "You Nazis!"

Even if the Russian soldiers did not understand the Hungarian words, they could not mistake the meaning of Uncle Levente's fists and his tone of voice. But they did not stop to settle accounts with him; nor did any of the passersby report him to the authorities. People guilty of far less serious offenses against the Red Army were shot, and as a child of seven or eight I knew that one had to be very careful not to show any hostility to Russian soldiers.

Cutting off a healthy limb from a live fruit tree is "a sin," Uncle Levente explained to me calmly after the truck disappeared from sight. The soldiers violated an ancient code cited in the Bible that forbade cutting down a fruit tree even in time of war, he said, then muttered to himself something about foreign occupation as the original sin, and every subsequent violation flowing from that sin. When we reached the garden gate of his apartment building, he turned to me and said, sheepishly, "Please don't say anything to your mother or your aunt."

Between 1948 and 1953 Stalin ordered the countries that came under Soviet domination to follow the example of his purges in the 1920s and 30s. Yugoslavia's Josip Broz-Tito was cast in the role of the arch-traitor Leon Trotsky, and veteran communists who had fought Franco and Hitler were executed as fascist agents working for Anglo-American imperialism.

In addition, the secret police of each East European state approached potential supporters of a Western plan to "liberate"

Eastern Europe. Agent provocateurs organized cells for the purpose of taking over the government once Western armies struck. When a sufficient number of people were recruited — in Hungary, that number was no less than ten but no more than twenty-five — the secret police "uncovered" the conspiracy. At times, the press reported the subsequent trial, albeit briefly. The person who emerged as the leader was usually hanged; others received long prison sentences. They all confessed, of course.

⟿

In 1951, some 100,000 Hungarians who had belonged to the pre-war upper and upper-middle classes were removed from their apartments and houses in Budapest and other cities, and sent by train to remote locations in the poorest parts of the countryside. The deportees included rightists and centrists, Nazi sympathizers and Jews characterized as "former capitalists." The knock on the door came between two and four in the morning, and people were told they had one hour, sometimes two, to pack a few suitcases and put them on the truck waiting for them outside. What was left behind, including the apartment, became state property, and given to reliable Party members as a favor. I remember waking up at night to shouts of "Move," "Get going," and "Stinking Fascists." My parents told me to go back to sleep but I overheard their talk discussing which family might have been taken away. In school, we noticed when a classmate was missing but said nothing. It was dangerous to discuss who was being deported. But everyone knew what it meant when the classroom teacher read the roster and noted that someone "moved away."

Some of the victims swallowed poison upon hearing the knock; many more committed suicide later, when they found they could not cope with life in a stable or an abandoned village hut with the roof caved in. Still others died of untreated illnesses or because of the heavy physical labor required to earn a living.

There was no appeal to the deportation order, and the only public mention was a sentence buried in the back of the official Party paper about "the removal of anti-state elements" from the cities to the countryside. Similar deportations took place in Romania and Czechoslovakia, but on a much smaller scale. Nowhere was Stalinist terror more merciless than in Hungary.

During the several months of the deportations, Uncle Levente got up at two every morning, shaved, and put on a warm suit. He told his wife that he did not want the secret police to surprise him in his sleep; he wanted to be ready for them. The suitcases, one for each family member, were packed and stacked near the front door.

He made himself coffee, lit a cigarette, and stuck his head out the window to survey the street. When he saw a truck stopping by a house, he tried to identify the family being taken away. I remember hearing him discuss with other family members how shaken he was seeing an invalid in her eighties — the mother of an official he disliked who was once high up in Horthy's government — being removed from her apartment in a chair and placed on the back of the truck.

Elvitték — the mundane Hungarian word that translates as "they took him or her away" — acquired a Shakespearean resonance. It was clear that "they" meant the communists, and the rest of the people paid no attention whether the victim was supposed to be an agent of the United States or the Vatican, or seen sneering during a speech denouncing Western aggression against peace-loving North Korea. The notion of resistance seemed absurd. Only one thing mattered: to survive the terror. Or as Uncle Levente often said it: "We must wait patiently; better days are sure to come." Others in the family were not so sure — and there was widespread fear that some deportees would be transferred to Siberia — but they did not argue. My mother for instance did not want to "spoil Levente's optimism. It's good that he is so hopeful."

Uncle Levente was certain that he and his immediate family would be deported, and he was pleasantly surprised and puzzled when their turn did not come. "This regime is illogical and disorganized," he said

Levente Thury in the early 1930s.

Endre Bajcsy-Zsilinszky in the 1940s.

and contrasted the orderliness of Nazi terror with the communist terror which he thought was chaotic, and deliberately so. Some people were executed — most of them believing communists from the prewar underground — while others were jailed or deported, or put under house arrest or police surveillance. With one person singled out by the secret police, he reckoned, the communists intimidated as many as a hundred others who knew about it.

Uncle Levente was intrigued when on one occasion the secret police arrested someone in his neighborhood known to be apolitical and of below average intelligence. They kept the man for a week or so, and when they let him go home, his face showed signs of the beatings he received. In a daze, the poor man told everybody he knew that he had not been informed of the reason for his arrest. At a family gathering Uncle Levente analyzed the case. He thought that the point of the arrest was that it is impossible to predict what the regime would do to any given person and that the uncertainty itself created yet another layer of fear.

He tried to be nonchalant about the terror. He was shadowed, perhaps around the clock, though he could not always be certain, he said. At times, however, particularly during the days preceding March 15, the anniversary of the 1848 revolution against the Habsburgs, his shadow seemed to want to make himself conspicuous — as if the authorities had wanted to make sure he knew that he was under surveillance.

On one occasion, with rain coming down in sheets, Uncle Levente went out to his covered balcony and saw his shadow standing under a tree on the street, near the garden gate, without an umbrella. "Why don't you come in and get dry," he called out in his usual congenial manner. "I'll make you coffee." The man turned the other way, pretending that he did not hear the invitation. His son said to me years later when we were speaking of those times, "My father refused to live in tragedy."

The Onslaught on Truth

For Uncle Levente, the journalism he practiced between the two world wars focused on unmasking the lies perpetrated by the Nazis and their sympathizers, as well as the ruling class under the Horthy regime. "Telling people the plain and often unpleasant truth was Levente's objective as a writer and editor," Miklos Vasarhelyi — a leader of the post-communist Free Democrats and the spokesman for the revolutionary government of 1956 — told me in the 1990s. "He was the yeast in Debrecen society when I was growing up."

But once the communists seized power, they branded him "a right-winger" and "a semi-fascist," and he was not allowed to publish, except for articles on non-political subjects once in a great while. He often wondered aloud how a journalist believing in telling the truth could write in a system based on manufacturing lies and deception.

At family gatherings on his brother-in-law Mishi's farm just outside Budapest, Uncle Levente felt he could speak out of reach for the recording devices of the secret police. His arguments had the language and the structure of articles he would have written. He called the Party's constant redefinition of the past "a relentless onslaught on truth," and he detested the intellectuals, some of whom he had known before the war, who carried out the Party's orders. "Those bandits rob us of the truth and foist upon us their barefaced lies," he said. I thought a lot about his words, so much so that I quoted them in papers I wrote as a college student in the United States in the late 1950s and then as a journalist. "The communists keep twisting and turning their lies in the hope that in the end 'the broad masses' are so confused that they will not want to believe anything or anybody, and eventually people no longer feel a need to know what really happened," I wrote, based on my uncle's analysis. "Debasing the gold standard of truth is a tawdry scheme of corruption, both corrupt and corrupting, designed to make people lose their sense of who they are and what they can believe in. The Nazis mindlessly repeated their doctrines. But the communists think they can eliminate truth as a principle of intellectual inquiry, as well as root out the individual's interest in establishing the truth."

The dictatorship the Soviets forced on Hungary in the late 1940s made people repeat at compulsory weekly assemblies in the workplace, neighborhoods, and schools the equivalent of a prayer praising a wise, all-knowing, and all-powerful deity they never saw and who did not leave his mysterious ancient castle, the Kremlin, in faraway Moscow. When a speaker mentioned his name, we were expected to applaud enthusiastically, and after no more than fifteen seconds everyone got up and chanted in unison "Stalin, Stalin" for a minimum of thirty seconds. When a speaker mentioned the name of the Hungarian communist leader, Matyas Rakosi, we did the same, but half way through that celebration we switched to another rhythmic chant, "Stalin, Rakosi," which we kept up for at least another fifteen seconds. Whether in speeches or print, Stalin was always called "The Great Leader," and Rakosi "Stalin's best Hungarian disciple." An individual's deviation from these rituals prompted an immediate interrogation by the Party secretary and at the very least a stern reprimand in the first instance, and a summons to the secret police on the second occasion. People who did not get up from their seats to chant the leader's name disappeared within a few hours after the offense, and everyone in the country heard of a case in which such a reactionary was never seen again.

Stalin did not travel, yet his was a brooding, malevolent presence palpable throughout his empire. His photographic likenesses showing none of his pockmarks and wrinkles stared at us from the walls of every classroom and government building, from above the empty shelves of the food stores where we stood in line for bread and in the movie houses that showed films only from the Soviet Union and the people's democracies. (I remember how surprised I was when as a refugee in Austria I saw for the first time unretouched pictures of The Great Leader.) On his birthday, respectable poets wrote poems about his moustache, and they were recited at the assemblies. He was also declared The Great Thinker of Our Time, and he made occasional pronouncements on arcane academic subjects such as comparative linguistics, fruit tree genetics, and hydrology, and the respected professors he singled out for "ideological mistakes" promptly disappeared in the gulag. Sarcasm disguised fury in his choice of words that also made it clear that he knew next to nothing about the subjects he discussed, which left us wondering what his motives for his pronouncements could have been.

In high school we had to memorize Stalin's oration at Lenin's funeral that blended Karl Marx's turgid prose and the mystical poetry of Old Church Slavonic. Walls and banners, newspaper articles and loudspeakers in public places endlessly repeated his strangely abstruse aphorisms, which Uncle Levente thought had barbed hooks: a note of hidden self-mockery that might have been unintentional, for instance in the slogans, "Ours is a militant peace" and "True peace will come only when the peoples of the world take their destiny into their own hands."

But just exactly what did "militant peace" and "true peace" mean? "Some things cannot be *fully* explained," the Party's agitprop secretaries declared at meetings. "Some things have to be understood *instinctively*." Whenever they cited "the Great Leader of Peace-Loving Humanity," they raised their voices and spoke with the solemnity of medieval theologians discussing Christ's incarnation. On occasion, someone asked earnestly: what did the despised "mere peace" and "bourgeois peace" mean? Was that the status quo or the same thing as the Cold War which the Party accused the imperialists of inventing and waging? And why were our imperialist enemies "worse than the Nazis"? The answers came in a hushed tone and with an air of confidentiality: "We know what we mean. But we must keep the enemy in the dark."

Stalin was fond of the word "objective," which was supposed to mean a higher, scientifically determined truth, the distilled essence of history and politics cleansed of sentimental impurities and intellectual sophistry. Yet truth as proclaimed under Stalin did not exist; it was the Great Teacher himself who insisted on its frequent, ritual deconstruction.

From one day to the next, Stalin decreed heroes to be villains, and his ideologists revised doctrines taught nationwide in compulsory sessions at the workplace and issued new slogans painted on the walls of military installations and schools, factories and government offices. There was no truth other than the one that the latest issue of Pravda revealed, and slavishly repeated in its counterparts in each people's democracy. While the past kept changing, the brilliant future of "the withering away of the state and the advent of communism" receded, and speakers at meetings suggested that we might not live to see it. They gave no explanation, except for dark hints about "the persistent strength of the enemy" and its "unceasing nefarious schemes against us."

Every few years Stalin had the volume on the history of the Bolshevik road to power rewritten. By the middle 1930s, he was the co-leader, with Lenin, of the abortive 1905 uprising as well as of the victorious 1917 revolution. It did not matter that people were still around who could recall that in 1905 Lenin and other leading revolutionaries scarcely knew of Stalin, or that in the period between Lenin's triumph in 1917 and his death in 1924 there were some half a dozen Bolsheviks credited with greater popular appeal and more achievements than Stalin. John Reed's *Ten Days that Shook the World*, which Lenin praised as the best history of the revolution, mentioned Stalin only briefly, "on a total of two occasions," as Uncle Levente liked to point out. All the books that quoted Lenin's description of Stalin as "coarse" and "dangerous" disappeared from the stores and libraries, as did any writing that cited the political testament Lenin left behind warning the Party against Stalin. After Lenin's death, Stalin had that testament dismissed as forgery, and he had himself proclaimed as the successor Lenin's designated. In the world of unreason Stalin fashioned, it made perfect sense that he eventually liquidated the old Bolsheviks who had originally backed him.

As children in communist Hungary, we were obliged to call Stalin "Our Wise Father," "the Greatest Teacher in History," and "the

Architect of Allied Victory" in the Second World War. Every year our history textbooks were reissued, first to hint, then to declare with gradually increasing emphasis, that Stalin was far more than Lenin's "closest associate" and "most faithful disciple." By the time Stalin died, in 1953, Lenin was cast in the role of John the Baptist preparing the ground for the messiah Stalin.

Since apparently close-up photographs of Lenin and Stalin together were never taken, separate ones were spliced, while paintings of the two suggested that they had been the closest of partners. One such document captured them in a relaxed moment, sitting on a park bench; another showed them at the top of a staircase of the Supreme Soviet, surrounded by an admiring multitude of workers and peasants. The two icons were reproduced endlessly, and after a while you no longer remembered which one was supposed to be a photograph and which one a painting, and it took a rebellious mind to suggest that both pictures immortalized moments that never were.

Stalin was a master weaver of deception. Josef Goebbels' device of hammering home day after day the same Big Lie seemed crude compared to Stalin's shape-shifting and shadow-boxing that owed a debt to the thousand and one tales of the inventive East indifferent to logic and contemptuous of the plain truth. Stalin inspired (or coined, as some Russians believe) slogans expanded into doctrines that bombarded our minds with bizarre inconsistencies: the Communist Revolution was all-powerful and its global victory was within sight, yet we were told that "The Enemy lurked everywhere." More than 99 percent of the people, and not just "The Broad Masses," voted for the Party — a great victory — yet every citizen had to be watched closely for any sign of deviation from "The Party Line." The Party was the infallible "Vanguard of the Proletariat," yet its leaders had to be constantly purged because some of them served as "The Paid Agents of Imperialism" and "The Enemies of the People." Soviet society eliminated all differences of class, yet every day the class struggle was getting sharper.

Unlike other tyrants, Stalin had no soft spot for old friends and is not known to have responded to any of his victims' appealing for his mercy. He was unmoved by expressions of loyalty — perhaps he did not believe that anyone could be loyal to him. According to a story that made the rounds in Hungary, when the Great Leader of Humanity was informed that one of his purge victims in the 1930s, a Red Army general convicted as a German spy, shouted "Long live Stalin" just before he was shot, Stalin muttered an obscenity.

It was always a shock to listen to "Stalin's favorite song 'Suliko,'" reverentially described as such and broadcast nearly every day throughout the Soviet empire while he was alive, and seldom if ever played since then. Written to accompany a maudlin nineteenth century Georgian nationalist poem, "Suliko" is a soft, mournful Oriental melody, an allegory filled with beautiful nightingales and whispering leaves. Its theme is a search for a beloved whose grave cannot be found. Could he have had such a favorite song? No one I knew could believe that. Or did he for some reason want us, his hapless subjects, to think he was the type of person drawn to that kind of sentimental mush? But what was his reason? Was there one reason?

Stalin kept us in the dark about himself and his next steps in the Soviet strategy to turn the world communist. He reduced us to fatalism — humankind's most primitive faith — that allowed no option other than total submission to "the infallible mastermind," "the protean champion of the working class," and "the hero of the march of history." He outwitted everyone — not through any master plan that experts and amateur analysts on both sides of the Iron Curtain were busy trying to understand, but by following his own imperious, ever-changing, and unpredictable whims, the dialectic of which no rational analysis could decode.

At the time of my high-school graduation in June 1956, I heard about a test, said to be a favorite of Stalin's, applied at college entrance examinations I was about to undergo. After the formal questioning was over, one of the examiners would take the applicant aside for a little personal chat, seemingly off-the-record. After a few exchanges on subjects such as soccer or theater, the examiner would launch his spiel in a confessional tone. "I sometimes think that this great socialist experiment of ours is perhaps a trifle too ambitious," he would say. "We are trying to do too big a job in too short a period of time, and our enemies are watching every mistake we make. Of course, mistakes are inevitable."

Then the examiner sprang a surprise. "What I sometimes fear," he said, lowering his voice, "is that one day we will make a big mistake, a really big mistake, and our enemies will move in on us and topple our socialist system." Then he turned to the applicant and asked off-handedly: "Tell me, what would you do in such a situation? Would you accept the verdict of history and wait until the forces of socialism gather their strength again? Or would you go into resistance?"

The applicant who sensed a trap and hesitated giving an immediate answer was labeled an opportunist — and failed the test. If the applicant answered that he would accept the verdict of history, he was dismissed as an idiot — and failed the test. But if he thought he was smart and said proudly that resistance was the only correct thing to do, the applicant branded himself a potentially dangerous enemy: the person who struck such a heroic pose was marked for life in the personnel files maintained by the Interior Ministry.

As usual, there was only one correct response. "What are you talking about?" the applicant should have said, puzzled, or, better still, angry. "There can be no return to capitalism. The gains of our socialist system are irreversible."

I told Uncle Levente about the test I heard about in school. "How devilishly cunning," he said. "I could see how Stalin himself might have devised it." Then he pondered if the generation that grew up in the shadow of Hitler and Stalin could ever throw off the memory of such hateful fathers. Defying a tyrant requires intransigence and reck- lessness, qualities not useful in the give-and-take of democracy, he said. He asked: could it be that those growing up under the century's evil twins and learning to hate both become not only devotees of truth but develop an excessive, inordinate concern with thinking and doing the right thing — or as the Russians phrase it, "the correct thing?" Have the obsessions of the hateful fathers rubbed off on all of us, booby-trapping our minds?

Like a caged tiger, Uncle Levente would often pace his living room, cursing the communists and shaking his fists. I once overheard Aunt Mara telling my mother that she was afraid that one day he might storm out of the apartment and unburden himself to the first acquaintance that happened by. He vented his anger in the course of the monthly family gatherings, where his brothers-in-law Mishi and Shumi enthusiastically agreed with him, and nobody sympathized with the communists. Aunt Mara sighed and sighed, gripping his hand from time to time, saying, "Calm down, my dear, please calm down," and on occasion my mother tried to divert him with a request to pass judgment on her hazelnut-and-coffee layer cake, or the new glaze she developed for a chocolate torte. He responded by kissing his wife on the cheek, or tasting his sister-in-law's creation and expressing his admiration by kissing her hands and forehead. Then he went right back to where he left off his political analysis. He also talked to me, a frequent visitor, as we lived only a few blocks from the Thury apartment. I listened avidly, and I learned more from him than from my teachers. For instance, he told the truth about the communists having been a puny, insignificant minority in Hungary during the Second World War and in its immediate aftermath — rather than constituting the great popular anti-Nazi force that postwar communist propaganda presented. He had vivid memories of the communists refusing to get involved in rescuing Jews or even declaring rescue a worthy cause — despite the fact that many of the communists were of Jewish origin. (The first point has since been made in rich detail by Charles Gati in *Hungary and the Soviet Bloc*, and the second was discussed by Randolph Braham, in *The Politics of Genocide*.) From time to time I noticed that Uncle Levente held back. He did not want me to do something foolish such as repeating dissident views in front of others or, as he sometimes said, following his example of "useless passive resistance."

In the mid-1950s, in my junior year in high school, I wrote a critique of the communist interpretation of nineteenth century Hungarian poetry that described the best poets as proto-communists. Uncle Levente read the paper carefully. "It's well written and well argued, though here and there, it is a bit overwrought," he said, and he identified the passages he liked and disliked, and explained his reasons.

"Now let's burn all the pages immediately," he said after our discussion. "And you promise me that you will not write such essays again lest you find yourself not only thrown out of school but in jail, and no one will be helped by that."

Uncle Levente was reluctant to "write for the drawer" because he feared a "house search," a favorite practice of the secret police, Nazi and Communist. They relished waking up a suspect before dawn and going through his personal items, contemptuously dropping letters and photographs on the floor, laughing at the discomfort of the family asked to sit down and not move, and cracking jokes about hoping to find dollars stashed away in underwear or pieces of forbidden literature one could not buy in the bookstore.

Nevertheless, at times he could not resist the temptation to remove the plywood case of his portable typewriter, a treasured relic from the early 1930s or maybe late 1920s, and to punch out a few pages that he thought might add up to a book one day. He joked that the secret police would get tired of reading his manuscript which dealt with philosophy, cited Kant and Spengler, Huizinga and Freud. No mention of Marx and Lenin, or the contemporary world. The thirty double-spaced pages he left behind take the reader on a Socratic stroll as the author speaks of "the extension of the ego" as a basic instinct, which leads to the creation of culture; and about "the stable, horizontal worldview" of the Christian Middle Ages and "the emphatic verticality of Gothic architecture" which he thought "defiantly built on the present" and "presaged the Renaissance."

The manuscript is both an extension of the prewar debates of his friends about Hungarian history and a flight from concerns hermetically Hungarian. There is a hint that he freed himself from the shackles of the dictatorship by recalling the fate of martyrs who dared to disagree with the Church in the sixteenth century. Like a prisoner trying to escape his prison by denying that his cell has walls and bars, he first announced that time was the basic reality that replaced matter in twentieth century thought. Then he dismissed time as insubstantial and illusory.

He sneaked in a few of his personal convictions, such as "one's overwhelming need for truth" and the ineluctable impulse for "an internally consistent, comprehensive *Weltanschauung*" which he went as far as to declare "an instinct." Mentioning in the abstract the possibility of the death of a nation, he recalled being shaken as a child by a nineteenth century Hungarian poem prophesying how the nations of the world will stand around the gravesite of the Hungarian nation and mourn. Adding darkness to darkness, he noted: "Now I know that a nation dies in moral and material filth."

"I see my father as a moral philosopher," his son sums up.

But in a communist dictatorship one could not withdraw from politics; philosophy had to be in the service of "the socialist transformation of society," and no private life or intellectual escape was permitted. Being apolitical itself was a political act, and not taking sides in the great ideological conflict of communism versus capitalism was nearly as treasonous as embracing the capitalist cause. Stalin and his pronouncements constituted articles of faith that could not be bypassed. As Illyes put it in 1950 in a poem not published until 1956, when it became the "Marseillaise" of the Hungarian revolution, not sung but its words often quoted:

> Tyranny got there first when you lie down together,
> it is in the nose and in the mouth,
> on your plate and in your glass,
> in the cold and the dark,
> outdoors and inside your house.

At one point in his youth, Uncle Levente was fascinated with mathematics, and he remained friends with numbers. Sometime in the early 1950s he decided that he would devise a system to win large amounts of money in a game of chance known as "Toto" and played routinely by hundreds of thousands of Hungarians, avid soccer fans. Each week people bet on the outcome of twelve soccer games, and those with the highest number of correct guesses won. The fewer the winners, the larger the payoffs. Naturally, the state pocketed a significant portion of the pool, though the percentage was not disclosed.

Uncle Levente put his calculations on sheets of typewriter paper and stacked them according to categories. Eventually, the stacks covered the living room floor. With his brother-in-law Mishi, he bought hundreds of tickets, and the two of them spent countless hours filling them out, according to the mathematical formula Uncle Levente developed. Both of them were convinced that they would make a fortune, or at least this is what they said.

A few times they did win, but the award was disappointingly low, barely paying for the many tickets they had to buy each week to follow the formula. After several months, they concluded that the state pocketed a much larger percentage of the money than they had thought possible. So their formula could not pay off, and they stopped gambling. But reading books on probability theory and working out a formula kept Uncle Levente's mind busy. In retrospect, it occurs to me that Uncle Mishi might have talked his brother-in-law into the lottery venture for that reason.

A year or two later, the two of them launched another venture: a chicken farm. They reckoned that even if they didn't make much money selling chickens, at least the family would be well fed. But the chicks got ill, many died, and the project was eventually reduced to a few tough old hens the brothers-in-law grew fond of and would not slaughter. Distributed within the family, the eggs were most welcome because they were seldom available in the stores.

Family members tried to secure jobs for Uncle Levente. For some time he was a night watchman for a construction company owned by the state, as was virtually every business. He had to make sure that people did not steal bricks, lumber, or other material from a fenced-in site in a rough section of the city known for its thieves and murderers. He did not seem to mind the danger. He said he enjoyed the required hourly walk around the site, and of course he read a book when staying in the tiny booth where he had a telephone to call the police in case he noticed someone trying to break in. When asked what he thought of his job, he smiled and said he was living through his youth again: staying up all night walking and reading, and hovering between law and lawlessness.

Eventually he lost the job because the personnel department — or perhaps the ever-vigilant secret police — discovered that he was "a class enemy," which was a term the regime reserved for those incorrigibles who had been born into privilege and power, and therefore opposed "the dictatorship of the proletariat."

Then a cousin managing a coal and firewood depot hired him to hand over notices to people specifying the time of their next delivery. As everything else in those days, coal and firewood were scarce, and people were delighted when someone rang the bell and handed them the notification. "I like bringing joy to people," Uncle Levente said at a family gathering, and he was proud of the modest tips he received.

He also enjoyed his dealings with the rough characters in charge of delivery. He gave them names from Hungarian literature and history, the equivalents of Sir Lancelot and the Ancient Mariner, which they accepted gladly and boasted about them in the taverns they frequented. But eventually his job was eliminated, after an order came down from headquarters to use the mail instead. Or as his son, my cousin Levente, heard it, his legs could not take the strain of walking all day long. Or perhaps the secret police intervened again. We will never know the truth.

His wife Mara earned the money needed to make ends meet by selling custom-made sweaters to actors and actresses, a privileged class similar to athletes. The business was illegal because she had a license to sell only sweaters she knitted herself, but no license for what she actually did: having private individuals do the dyeing and the knitting in their homes. Uncle Levente and Aunt Mara lived in fear of the law, and my mother worried about the strain but accepted their argument that there was other way of making a living. In retrospect it appears likely that the higher authorities, undoubtedly aware of the sweater business, chose not to prosecute. Surely it was another way to keep the family off balance.

The stores sold the yarn in basic colors and in balls. To have them dyed in fashionable hues, the yarn first had to be turned into skeins. Uncle Levente decided that he would be in charge of that transformation. Ensconced in his favorite leather armchair in the living room, he turned a contraption called the skein-winder, a square wooden frame with the yarn winding on pegs, which pivoted around a wooden base. At first Aunt Mara worried that he would come to hate the mechanical motion as numbingly mindless. But he said he enjoyed turning the wheel and making "finite skeins out of seemingly infinite lengths of yarn." It was a kind of meditative exercise that reminded him of the theologies of the East as well as of Mahatma Gandhi spinning cotton. "I am in touch with eternity," Uncle Levente said, only half in jest. "I am a helmsman of a wheel of life even though the circle I control is a square."

Uncle Levente took pleasure in the small joys of life. For example, he enjoyed leisurely strolls under the stately, spreading horse-chestnut trees of his street. Every May, he lingered by the lilac hedges that pressed against the wire fences. To an observer who did not know him, he was an image of timeless contentment: an old gentleman with thin legs sticking out of his loose shorts, contemplating the beauty of the candle-like blooms of the horse-chestnuts or taking in the sweet scent of lilac panicles.

He liked shopping for provisions at the neighborhood grocery store, and if any of the suppliers were around he did not miss asking them about their crops. (Hungarian farmers habitually complain about a crop that was lost or mostly lost, but Uncle Levente was an appreciative audience.) He engaged the butcher, a witty man, in a back and forth about the national soccer tournament. Conversation was in fact about politics because each soccer team represented a political force: the military, the secret police, the trade unions, or a section of the capital city known for its nationalist views. Customers understood the symbolism and appreciated comments such as the soldiers being walloped by those in charge of state security. It was impromptu political cabaret, and not particularly dangerous since the talk was overtly about soccer, the great national pastime. He stopped off in the barber shop even if he did not need a haircut. From time to time he also visited a neighborhood furrier though he never bought anything there.

The greengrocer, the butcher, the barber, and the furrier had been members of his wartime labor battalion, which they never referred to when someone else was present — and someone else was usually present. I do not know if they ever discussed the old days, but family members living close by knew of the link because the four men extended their affection for Uncle Levente to his family. When there was a shortage of some food item, my mother always sent me to "Levente's grocer." On one occasion, the grocer whispered to me as he handed over a bag of potatoes or onions: "I admire your uncle. You are a lucky child to have such an uncle." But the four of them knew that he did not like a reverential atmosphere, and they learned to appreciate the casual, chatty tone that came natural to him.

But as much as he tried to live a quiet, contemplative life, he was clearly not born for it, which was one reason he did not become a pastor like his father and paternal grandfather. He needed to be engaged politically, debate his political and philosophical beliefs, and write polemics.

From time to time I heard Uncle Levente express his shame that Hungarians had not done more to stop the deportations during the war and that there were not enough Gentiles who condemned anti-Semitism before and during the deportations. He was heartbroken over his compatriots' apathetic or opportunistic acceptance of Nazi ideology. He saw tragic flaws in the Hungarian character, including the refusal to face reality and using pride in being Hungarian as a cover-up and an excuse.

He did not like to discuss what he had done during the war or why he had done it. "I did the minimum," he said among friends. "I should have done the maximum." A few times I overheard him say words to the effect that *not* doing anything seemed to him impossible. "I did what I did because I could not do otherwise," he once said, with uncharacteristic churlishness, to a young daughter of a friend who confronted him with a direct question. "For me, that was the only thing to do." He refused to be drawn into analytical discussions about motives and means, and he declined to be honored during the three years before the communists seized power and put a stop to honoring non-communists for anti-Nazi activities. Once in the early 1950s I even heard him reply to a question from a new acquaintance that he had done nothing during the Nazi occupation except trying to save his own skin.

I was in high school when I found a letter from September 13, 1945, signed by Major-General Edgcumb representing Britain on the Allied Control Commission that supervised Hungary. It was hidden in one of the tin boxes my mother collected in the pantry. Written in a most gracious language on behalf of His Majesty's Government, the letter commended Levente Thury's "courageous action in the highest possible terms" and "devotion to the cause for which the United Nations have fought this war." It listed the news service he ran, his maintaining "contact with highly-placed pro-British groups in Hungary," and placing himself "in extreme danger" by "actively associating with resistance groups under the spiritual guidance of Endre Bajcsy-Zsilinszky." The final paragraph offered "as a small token of recognition" a payment of 125,000 pengo "as a symbol of the recognition and gratitude of Great Britain."

Worried that I stumbled upon such a dangerous secret, my mother said that her brother-in-law entrusted the document to her care, that I should not have read it, and that I must not mention it to anyone, including Uncle Levente "who does not need another headache."

Having received a copy of the document from Cousin Levente in the 1990s, I tried to obtain his father's file from Britain's MI-5, as well as our Uncle Mishi's, a recipient of a similar letter from Great Britain which Cousin Levente and I had discovered together in another tin box, buried under a loose brick in Uncle Mishi's chicken coop. (The two brothers-in-law used the British awards, adding up to a substantial sum in Hungarian money, to buy a piece of farmland outside Budapest.) Even though a senior CIA official put in a word for me, I got only as far as a telephone conversation with his counterpart in London who agreed to look into the matter. He eventually informed me that yes, he checked and found the two files containing reports from the two Hungarian gentlemen, secure in the archives of British intelligence, but that the law does not permit their release until the year 2045.

I asked for one favor.

"And what might that be," intoned a cultured, mellifluous voice at the other end of the line.

I asked if he could tell me if two files are thin or thick.

"They are thick," the reply came after a chuckle. "Your uncles did good work."

Sparks off the Cobblestones

"He covered his tracks as carefully as an Indian," says his son who, like most Hungarians, had read and re-read in his teens Cooper's *Last of the Mohicans* and Karl May's books about Winnetou. "He never told me what he had done, and to this day I don't know the details."

But Uncle Levente could not escape his past, and I witnessed him confront it on a few occasions. One day we were walking together when a man I had never seen before waved to him excitedly from across the street and rushed over, dodging traffic. The man embraced Uncle Levente and kissed him on both cheeks. "Is everything all right with you?" he asked. Uncle Levente said, "Yes, yes, but what about you?"

They kept gripping each other's shoulders and asked each other again and again: are you in good health, is your family all right, are you making a decent living?

But the man, well dressed and self-confident, was far more insistent with his questions than Uncle Levente. "Is there anything I can do for you," he pressed, again and again. "Could I help you find a good job? Do you live in the same apartment? May I come to see you?"

Uncle Levente said that he needed nothing, but that unfortunately these days it was not a wise idea for him and his old friends to get together. "You know why," he added, making a face. The man paused and said light-heartedly, "Yes, I understand, but perhaps soon the time will come when a visit and a long talk will be possible again. We must talk. I must hear you out."

During the brief moments of the meeting, it seemed as if the steel heel-plates of their shoes had thrown sparks off the cobblestones, the color of ashes. But the thrill of a chance reunion in a big city burned out faster than such sparks. As the two men parted, after another hug and exchange of kisses, their faces looked as old and weary as the cobblestones that were once again as ash-gray as always.

I watched them from a few steps away so as not to intrude, and only later on did I realize that my uncle, though usually a model of courtesy, had neglected to offer introductions. "He was one of my people," Uncle Levente said with a little sigh after we resumed our walk, and I knew that he did not want to say any more. I knew that the man had to be one of the Jews he had helped during the war. Mutual loyalty seemed to bind them together — a bond that resembled the one between father and son, or maybe the one between inspired teacher and star student. I also knew without being told that Uncle Levente did not want the man to visit him and then get into trouble with the secret police. Or it occurred to me later that perhaps he *was* in the secret police — he was elegant enough and spoke as if seated on top of the world.

Even though I witnessed two or perhaps three such encounters — they were so similar that they merge in my memory — I could not tell whether they made Uncle Levente feel better or worse. But I knew he was hurt that people who had been his friends before and during the war and then turned communist would not call him or speak to him if they met on the street. "What cowards," he used to say, and he would not ask them for help, such as securing a job, even though their ranks included members of the cabinet and leading writers and journalists.

In retrospect, it does appear probable that one or more of the people he had saved during the war were responsible for the fact that alone among the top dozen or so leaders of the Smallholders' Party who did not cooperate with the communists, he was neither imprisoned, nor deported to the countryside. Nor was he dragged into one of the Stalinist show trials of the late 1940s and early 1950s, that relied heavily on torture to force false confessions.

Nevertheless, the secret police kept an eye on him. They summoned him for meetings, for which he prepared himself by reading a tattered old Bible inherited from his grandfather. He read and reread the psalms he loved and knew by heart, and he looked up the story of Jacob, a survivor of misfortunes but a trickster and thus most unlike him, and he thought about the passages at length while looking out the window or pacing the living room. "What a smart man Jacob was," I once heard him say. "I wish I could be like him."

His secret police interrogators reminded him that they could send him to Siberia for spying for the British during the Second World War. They could also take away his son. But they were prepared to be compassionate. They said they could not understand that as an anti-Nazi he did not at least sympathize with what the Party was doing. He told family members, Shumi and Mishi first of all, that his response was that he was a tired old man — and he did look at least ten years older than his age, never having recovered fully from the Gestapo interrogations. He did not want to take part in public life, he told them, he had lost interest in politics. He just wanted a small, modest nonpolitical job, like a night watchman's. He wanted to be left alone.

But they would not leave him alone.

Was the smart, articulate young intellectual, the kind who would have been his friend and ally in the old days, an agent provocateur? The man came from a small town and brought with him an old clipping of an article Thury had written in his newspaper in the 1930s. The visitor claimed that the article — which attacked a newly appointed prime minister for being out of sympathy with the poor — changed his life. He was about to join the extreme right, but the article convinced him that he ought to be in the ranks of the Smallholders' Party. But now with the communists in power, he did not know what to do.

The visitor and his enthusiasms sounded genuine. He kept asking questions. What could one do to dismantle the communist regime? Was there a way to affect political change, perhaps gradually? What did his host think could be done?

Uncle Levente was evasive, as he was with other, similarly insistent visitors. He wondered: which one of his old friends who stayed out of the Party but had a good job served as a police informer? What should he think about the son of a colleague from Debrecen who appeared out of nowhere and asked for advice on how to cope with the dictatorship he hated so much that he was ready to organize a resistance movement? Was there a way? Or should one give up and cooperate with the regime? "I can't tell which of my visitors is Rosencrantz and which is Guildenstern," I once overheard him say to his favorite brother-in-law, Mishi. "But what I can't stand is that they cast me in the role of Hamlet."

By nature, he was trusting and open-minded, and he liked exchanging thoughts with all kinds of people, in all stations of life. He hated to be in a position of suspecting motives. He did not like to hold back, yet he felt he had to. Wasn't everybody certain that Hungary had become riddled with informers during the communist rule? Weren't the cynics right when they said that one half of the nation spied on the other half, and that one half of the spies watched the other half? He said he now understood that it was inevitable that a traitor should have penetrated Zsilinszky's anti-Nazi resistance movement and betrayed its plan for a military uprising. Hungarians are good at soldiering and spinning out theories but are lousy plotters, he said, and he pointed out that in the thousand years of Hungarian history every single conspiracy failed. As did every uprising.

During the 1956 Hungarian revolution, Uncle Levente got together with his friends from the Smallholders' Party's old guard who had survived the Stalinist terror and they started planning for a return to democracy. He argued for caution rather than confrontation in dealing with the Soviets and their local hardliners. He did not believe that the West would intervene. His son told me: "Though he did not say it aloud — he didn't have the heart to say that — he knew the struggle was hopeless."

But he was awed by the spontaneity of the uprising and its anonymous heroes who fought the communists on the streets. The revolution's energy and world-remaking fervor buoyed him. He conferred with old friends about setting up an independent newspaper. But they did not have enough time for getting started in the two weeks between the students' pouring out into the streets to demonstrate against the Stalinist regime and the massive, second Soviet intervention that put an end to all the high hopes.

The defeat deepened his gloom. Wasn't the revolution another flash in the pan or, as it is said in Hungarian, *szalmaláng*, meaning the multi-colored but short-lived flames of a fistful of straw on fire? The past four centuries of Hungarian history featured long periods of apathy interrupted by revolutions, one in each century. There was no master plan for any of the revolutions; they thrived on a momentum that at first seemed unstoppable. Total desperation, rather than careful calculation, was the driving force. But after the fire died down and the heroes were jailed or killed, life for the survivors had the taste of ashes. Insistence on cultivating the glorious memories only led to melancholy, the cherished national neurosis.

Uncle Levente did not try to talk me out of leaving the country, and he too thought that my participation in the revolution, however modest, would lead to a short-term imprisonment. He predicted executions and a Stalinist reign of terror, at least for the first few years. "Harsh times are ahead," he said.

Going to America occurred to him too, but he said he feared he would not have the physical stamina required for escaping across the border to Austria. Nor did he think that at his age, sixty-one, he could start a productive new life abroad. Far more important, his wife Mara was firmly against leaving Hungary, then and always, and their son was only sixteen, not yet entitled to a vote in the family council. I knew my uncle well enough to understand that regardless of the persecution he faced, he would not wish to live anywhere else but in the country of his birth. He would much rather keep waiting for a better day — wait and wait. "Honor is the only true power an individual has," he told me when I went to say goodbye to him. "Honor is what we should be left with after everything else is lost."

Uncle Levente failed to find a way to fight the communists. "They pinned me down," he used to say. "They tied my hands. They gagged me. Then they said that I should be grateful that I am allowed to live." Once in a while a newspaper would agree to publish an article of his on a topic such as new developments in the treatment of juvenile diabetes, an area in which he became an expert while keeping a close watch on his son who was afflicted with the illness. He longed for the spirit of resistance during the Second World War when he was writing and actively engaged in fighting the enemy, and when he had many friends who did the same.

He was not willing to make the kind of compromises demanded by Janos Kadar, the man who presided over the suppression of the 1956 revolution and the execution of hundreds of rebels, including his erstwhile comrade, Prime Minister Imre Nagy. For two years, Nagy refused to join Kadar's government, or to acknowledge publicly that he had "made mistakes" during the days of the revolution. A lifelong communist who had spent many years in Moscow before World War II, he died as a Hungarian patriot, executed in secret in 1958 after a secret trial. Like Zsilinszky, Nagy refused to escape his fate, would not plead for clemency, and ended up being acclaimed "the last romantic." What could be more romantic than to be the last of a species, and especially the last of those who pursue romance rather than deal with reality? And when the next "last romantic" makes his (or her) appearance, that will only confirm the vitality of a fine tradition.

Uncle Levente had offers of "a comfortable small job" if he cooperated with the authorities. But he saw no acceptable role for himself in a Hungary dominated by communists, Hungarian or Russian, Stalinist or Leninist, orthodox or reform. He did not live to see the miracle of the Berlin Wall coming down and communists recycling themselves as democrats who champion the multiparty system, but it is unlikely that he would have believed their sincerity. He would have probably cited the Hungarian equivalent of the phrase, turning a sow's ear into a silk purse, which he once used against repentant Nazis asking for forgiveness.

He could not decide whom he disliked more: the communists who were believers or the opportunists who joined the Party to make a good living. After the post-1956 communist restoration, he saw nearly everybody selling out. He felt that the nation lacked pride, honor, and love. Contemptuous of the East and disappointed in the West, Hungarians decided after 1956 that they were beyond nationalism and communism. They had seen everything, they said, and nothing could surprise them any more. They ran out of illusions and causes. They no longer believed in believing.

Privately, the poet Illyes spoke of "the Russification of Hungary:" Byzantine intrigue on the top; unbridled opportunistic philistinism in the middle; a muzhik-like acceptance of the status quo among the masses, along with the rise of new skills worthy of Gogol's characters in circumventing the rules. Truth has disappeared as a standard; the moment of half-truth is embraced as the best that one could hope for. "This is not the Hungary I used to be proud of," Illyes told my cousin Levente and me when the two of us visited him in 1980. "My old friend Levente would agree with me."

Zsilinszky's Chosen Death

Zsilinszky's martyrdom awed Uncle Levente and left him with questions that never ceased to trouble him. Wouldn't Zsilinszky have been more valuable to the nation if he had escaped the Arrow Cross and stayed alive to take on the next invader, the Russians, and their Hungarian stooges? The Smallholders' Party and the rest of the non-communist left had no one of his stature to stand up for democracy and independence. But could he have been successful against Stalin and his ruthless Hungarian minions? Wouldn't he have been the first to be eliminated — jailed, banished, silenced or killed? What would have stopped the communists from doing to him what they did to so many of their opponents?

Zsilinszky deliberately chose a martyr's death, believing it was the only honorable way out of a situation that admitted no solution, Uncle Levente argued on one of the occasions when Zsilinszky's widow, Maria, visited the Thury family. I felt honored to be invited at age eighteen.

In a measured, dispassionate tone, he explained that once the three top military co-conspirators were hanged, Zsilinszky reached the conclusion that he must share their fate and that escaping would mean betraying his comrades. Posterity, Uncle Levente argued, should accept Zsilinszky's own explanation as the truth and nothing but the truth, as Zsilinszky was a man whose perceptions, however changing through his life, reflected his constant search for truth. Uncle Levente reminded us that Zsilinszky also told his fellow prisoners: he was as convinced as nine months earlier when firing at the Germans who had come to arrest him that if he could no longer help his nation while alive, he might still help as a martyr.

Uncle Levente believed that Zsilinszky did the right thing by refusing the opportunity to escape from Arrow Cross captivity. At least one person must be different, Uncle Levente said, one person must set the highest standard and shoulder the responsibility for the nation that others for one reason or another dare not or will not. This exceptional quality made Zsilinszky an inspiring leader, while the rest, including himself, remained "mere followers."

Uncle Levente looked up to Zsilinszky as a man who had the courage to lose his life in a hopeless situation in the expectation that others, perhaps the next generation, would draw strength from his example. "Our friend found the right way to die," he concluded. "He proved worthy of the heroic past he admired."

In a few words Maria Zsilinszky invoked the final scenes of her husband's life: the offer of rescue by the soldier from Tarpa, the last words under the gallows, and the hangman's suicide. All of us in the room listened in silence to what amounted to a ritual, a widow's way of lighting a candle of remembrance.

Now, nearly half a century after that evening in the Thury living room, I find myself within the circle of the legend, and I feel privileged that Maria Zsilinszky sent me a book about her husband, an anthology of writings that the communist regime at last allowed to be published in 1969, and in which she inscribed an affectionate dedication.

Uncle Levente said he envied Zsilinszky's fate. In an article he wrote in the late 1940s or early 1950s — which was finally published in that 1969 anthology — he mourned his friend as "the brilliant star of the Hungarians" and called him fortunate to be able "to dream his eternal dream" in his grave in the village of Tarpa.

"His death was a chosen death," Illyes wrote in the same anthology. "It was not suicide. Someone who commits suicide looks at his life as having no value, and he gives his life up for nothing." But Zsilinszky gave his life "for *something*, for *somebody*," and that was what Illyes called "a community" — the nation.

It seems to me that Zsilinszky was a man of destiny, whose inner voice, changing over the years but never hesitant and always rising above political exigencies, impelled him toward an inevitable conclusion. His decisions flowed from the passionately activist essence of his character, and his life and death reflected the fate of his nation. His conspiracy, trial, and execution seem uncannily preordained — as if carefully scripted and staged — and part of an historic collective tragedy that is as much a defining theme of Hungary as slavery followed by redemption is Israel's.

But have I come to these conclusions myself, or did they originate with Uncle Levente? I can no longer tell. Like his son, I find the copyright line blurred. The thoughts have become part of a family legacy.

Onions in the Holy Language

Uncle Levente was an earthy man who looked back upon the kitchen garden of his parental home as hallowed ground. He worshipped the genus *Allium*, better known as the onion, and talked about the ardor of chives, the understatement of leeks, the earnestness of garlic, and, of course, the incomparable verve of the common, basic, indispensable onion. "Concealed in an onion's many layers is the secret of good health," he intoned. Every day he ate at least one large onion, either raw or doused in vinegar. It was a treat watching him prepare a snack, starting with the selection of an onion ("what an image of beauty," he cried out), then a thick slice of bread ("the crust should be as brown as the color of good soil"), and finally a slab of very fatty bacon, almost pure lard. (He did not take sides in the national controversy whether it tasted better pickled or smoked, but he insisted that it must have plenty of paprika). If someone pushed the buzzer of the apartment's front door, he or she was invited to join the feast, and it was impossible to turn him down. He did the cutting and slicing at a slow, deliberate pace, wielding his penknife, which he kept razor sharp, and offered his guest the meatiest — and the most appreciated — piece.

In our family, he was the only male who cooked. He enjoyed chopping up vegetables and stirring big pots of soup or goulash. He was fond of *cholent*, the celebrated Hungarian Jewish stew of beans, potatoes, chunks of smoked goose, and, above all, onions that was eaten Friday night and the leftover put back in the oven to bake at a low heat, to be served for Saturday's midday meal.

He could argue passionately about food. On occasion he would even criticize my mother Anna, the family's acknowledged champion in cooking and baking, because of "a mistake" in her recipe for pickles, which I think might have had to do with her overuse of chunks of bread and, on occasion, not enough salt. The one time I saw him being almost rude to his wife Mara, an indifferent cook, was when she tried to hush him. "This argument is between Anna and me," he said, sternly. "You don't know enough about pickling to have a say in the matter."

He loved his family, which was his wife's family because he had no blood relatives, except for some distant cousins in the countryside who surfaced once in a decade. He was often asked to be the best man at family weddings, and he relished the role that he performed up to the highest standards, spicing dignity with humor, and taking upon himself the responsibility of making friends with the relatives of the person joining our family. He had a knack of saying the right things and, somehow, he avoided hurting all the multitudinous sensitivities of the women such as his wife and my mother and certain cousins who took pleasure in taking and then nursing an offense, and preferred that reconciliation come in stages, in the course of many months if not years.

On occasion, he went downtown to have coffee with Mishi, his favorite brother-in-law, or tea and cakes with an old friend or two. He carefully balanced the two wings of his favorite bow tie, blue with maroon stars, which matched his bluish-gray plaid suit with maroon strands. Both tie and suit were made before the Second World War. His broad smile suggested that all was well with the world and the times. When asked how things were going for him, he never complained. One of his stock answers was, "I am young and handsome, and my broker just informed me that I have become a millionaire."

When on the street he ran into one of his young relatives dressed up for theater or a party, he suggested "a diligent exploration of the great Hungarian democratic night." He was elaborately courteous and irresistibly charming when introduced to a person in whom a family member indicated a romantic interest. "I recommend romance as the antidote to everything," he once told me after seeing me a few times with the same girl, and his brown eyes sparkled.

In the summer of 1956, his wife's youngest brother Bedi, a kib-butznik in Israel since 1929, received a visitor's visa to Hungary, an unprecedented favor seen as a sign of Nikita Khrushchev's destalin-ization. It was the first and last time the two brothers-in-law met, and Uncle Levente was eager to hear about Bedi's life. "Tell me what the soil is like in your kibbutz," he asked Bedi. "Do your onions taste as good as the Egyptians'? Tell me about the banana trees you planted. But I'd like to hear your answer first in the holy language." Bedi gladly complied, and Levente listened intently, with eyes half-closed, as if in a daze, softly repeating those Hebrew words he recognized. "Fundamentally, in terms of character, he was a cheerful person," says his son, Levente junior. "The only time I remember him looking des-perate was when he could not cope with some health problem con-nected with my diabetes."

Yet in the end, Uncle Levente succumbed to melancholy, a mood that overwhelmed many thoughtful Hungarians through the cen-turies. He did not want to wait any longer for what he called "the mir-acle": Hungary escaping from the domination of the Soviet Union. In his last year he indeed did become the tired old man he tried to per-suade the communist secret police that he was. From what I heard later from Aunt Mara and Uncles Shumi and Mishi, one day he reached the conclusion that as he had "nothing worthwhile to die for, he had nothing to live for."

My mother's letters to me quoted the doctors; he gave up, they said after he was hospitalized because of his damaged spleen and liver, he lost his will to live. They said that his physical condition was not life threatening and did not justify his precipitous decline. Uncle Mishi, who was closest to him, refused to believe the doctors' diagnosis. He told his sister Mara that he would confront Levente and talk him into fighting for his life. When years later I asked what happened, Mishi said that the response was enough to break one's heart and that he could not talk about it. He had tears in his eyes. (A few years later, Mishi asked to be buried next to Levente and Mara, and he was.)

Uncle Shumi, who also tried to talk to his brother-in-law, told me that he begged Levente to think about his wife and their son, and the rest of the family, all of whom loved him and needed him. His answer was that he appreciated everyone's feelings, but that he no longer had the strength to go on. "I have lived long enough," he told Shumi. "Enough."

"It was as if the flame of a candle had blown out in my brother-in-law's soul, and in its place there was only darkness," Shumi told me a few years later. "Levente was one of us, a beloved member of our family, but he did not share our stubborn Jewish insistence on the precious primacy of life and on not giving it up regardless of the circumstances. At times we need to remind ourselves that he was not Jewish."

"In his last days he was possessed of a vision," his son recalled. "His face was yellow from kidney failure, and he no longer looked like himself. Maybe he was already another person. He called out the names of the people he was fond of to come and board the ship he said he had just acquired and was waiting for us outside. Our ship has arrived, he declared. He was very concerned about keeping everyone happy once on the ship. He thought of himself as the biblical Noah, and his ship as the ark. But did he actually say that, or did I think that myself? I can no longer differentiate between what he said or thought and what I say or think. I guess all this means a good relationship with my superego — or was he my superior ego?"

My mother Anna liked to reminisce about how anxious her brother-in-law was in wanting to gather "all the right people" aboard the ship. He asked her to make sure that everyone in the family was notified and had suitable quarters. "I want you to be in charge," he told her. "That way I can be certain that everybody will be happy." He suggested that she telephone me to say that I should come too, even though by then I was in America, which was, in those days, as far away from Hungary as the moon. She assured him that she would do as asked. "Good," he said, "I know I can always rely on you."

My mother felt greatly honored that her brother-in-law chose her to be in charge, and she thought of it as an assignment to be taken seriously. "Levente was so very convincing," she explained later. "He seemed so purposeful and insistent." Only after she got home from the hospital did she realize that he was delirious when talking about the ship and that she did not need to make any phone calls. It occurred to her that once again her brother-in-law sensed an impending catastrophe and again he wanted to rescue people, and of course he began with his family.

When I received a note from my mother about his death I went to a synagogue and said Kaddish for him. It seemed to me the right thing to do; today it seems that it was the only thing to do. (A few years ago I was delighted to read in a book, *Responsa from the Holocaust*, the ruling by Rabbi Ephraim Oshry of the wartime Kovno ghetto that it is not only permissible to say Kaddish for a Gentile who saved Jewish lives but it is a *mitzvah* to do so.) That was the first time since my leaving Hungary that a family member died. I could not share my grief with my relatives or with people who knew my uncle. It was one of those rare occasions when I felt like an émigré who left his heart in the country of his birth. I still cannot think of a greater loneliness than mourning alone, surrounded by people who suddenly seem like strangers because they did not know the person who passed away yet was so very much with me.

A week later I received Uncle Shumi's detailed letter describing Uncle Levente's last days. He was getting weaker and weaker, the letter said, and when he felt that his time had come, he asked to say goodbye to members of the family. They came to his hospital room one by one, and he had something kind and light-hearted to say to each. He also told his wife to remember him to relatives abroad, in Israel and the United States, naming those he had known and leaving brief messages for each of them. Finally he asked for Shumi and Mishi. He told them to hold his hands and recite the Kaddish for him. Others might think the scene strange and puzzling, but to me it is a parable, a vignette of Jewish life in Hungary: two nonobservant Jewish brothers who had not used their Hebrew since praying at their father's funeral nearly forty years earlier trying their best to remember a string of tongue-tripping words foreign to them, so they could comply with the last wish of their brother-in-law, a Protestant drawn to the burnished words of Jewish tradition and the warmth of a Jewish family.

"In his darkest moments he felt he lived a mostly useless life, accomplishing nothing," Uncle Shumi later told me. "But he died the way he wanted to." His was a chosen death, I now think.

His funeral, in 1958, was attended by a large crowd. In addition to the family and friends including colleagues from before the war, scores of people from the neighborhood came, including, of course, the grocer, the barber, the butcher, and the furrier, and others from their labor battalion, as well as strangers no one remembered but who identified themselves, some of them tearfully, as grateful to Mr. Thury who had saved their lives. One of the scores of letters of condolence his widow and their son received came from Jozsef Antall, then young Levente's high-school teacher of history and years later the country's first noncommunist prime minister. "As a scion of the historic nobility, Levente Thury used his pen to improve the lot of the Hungarian peasant, the nation's gold reserve," he wrote. "He was a journalist who fought for the Hungarian people, tricked and disinherited a thousand times." Antall identified "the great Hungarian tragedy": in the twentieth century, the elite did not combine effectively historic continuity and the spirit of innovation. "The nobility that upheld the 1848 revolution perished on the battlefield or in Habsburg prisons; it lost its economic footing, and the new elite — the new middle class — that rose suddenly danced to foreign music, regardless of who played it."

Though the national journalist association offered to pay for the funeral including a marble tombstone, Shumi, as head of the family, refused. "You ignored Levente for the past ten years as if he had been no longer alive," he said to Peter Veres, a senior official of the association and famous in Hungary, who had once contributed articles to Uncle Levente's newspaper in Debrecen. "So why should you care now that he is indeed dead?" Even though Hungarian custom calls for attending the funeral of someone who was no longer a friend at the time of his death, his friends from the 1930s and 40s who became communists did not show up — perhaps on command. Or they no longer needed such a command.

Standing in the back of the crowd were two strangers who stayed close together — "as if one had been handcuffed to the other," as Shumi described them. Family members whispered to one another: Who are those stocky middle-aged men with the expressionless faces? No one had a clue. When at the end of the funeral everyone queued up to say goodbye to the widow, the two strangers were the last. They expressed their condolences. While they did not give out their names, they subtly identified themselves as the government officials whose assignment included "talking to Mr. Thury from time to time." One of the men assured the widow that he personally respected the departed; his partner nodded but said nothing. Aunt Mara gulped and turned pale but surprised herself by managing to say "thank you."

The two men were the secret police officers in charge of the Thury case. For years they interrogated him, threatened him with imprisonment, and pressured him to bow to the inevitability of communist victory around the world. Once every month or two, they called him for a meeting, usually over a cup of coffee in an espresso bar. Or if they felt the need to tighten the screws, they summoned him to one of their fortress-like villas surrounded by nine-foot-high wire fence and kept him there for a day or two. Occasionally, they pushed the buzzer to his apartment, unannounced, and looked around, checking what was on his desk, opening the drawers, and picking up a book or two from the shelf. With mock courtesy, they addressed him as "Mr. Professor," and from time to time they feigned respect for his "great learning." At other times, one of the pair threatened to take his son and send him to a correctional institution "to make a good communist out of him." The other said nothing, only nodded at times. They kept prodding him to talk, and again and again he had to list all the people he had spoken with since their last meeting. The two officials attended the funeral to close his file.

Reveries in a Leather Armchair

When I think of Uncle Levente, I see him sitting in his favorite leather armchair, the gift of Great Britain's intelligence service. With hands cradling the nape of his neck and his thin legs crossed at the ankle, he looks at Zsilinszky's portrait hanging in the place of honor, above a bookcase. The drawing shows a man handsome in a classical way, with a robust nose and chiseled features. "What would you do now?" Uncle Levente asks his old friend. "What should I do? What course of action does honor suggest?"

He takes long puffs from his cigarette. With his mind somewhere else, he forgets to flick the ashes into one of the numerous ashtrays around him, and the ashes drop and scatter on the parquet floor. Eventually, he wakes up from his reverie and reprimands himself for his absentmindedness. He gets up, looks for the broom, and sweeps up the ashes, so as not to upset his wife who does not like a messy floor, who objects to his smoking because of its effect on his weak lungs, and who is too busy earning a living to concern herself with a friend of their youth, a ghost from Shakespeare's "undiscover'd country."

Alas, the present lacks the principal prop of my reverie: the armchair fell apart long ago, though Levente junior, respectful of well-crafted objects and the spirit (he says) they acquire over their years of service, had repeatedly repaired it himself, replacing the springs and patching the flaking leather until it began tearing and curling around the tufts and along the seams. Now he sits on a plain wooden chair in the same spot once favored by his father, and the living room is his studio where he sculpts, mostly ceramic heads and torsos. He calls each of them a *golem*, after the giant clay figure shaped in sixteenth century Prague by the kabbalist Rabbi Judah Loew (who according to family tradition was an ancestor of ours). According to the legend, the rabbi put in the clay figure's mouth a parchment inscribed with the Hebrew word *emes*, meaning truth, which gave it the breath of life. The *golem* walked, performed chores, and protected the Jewish community, doing whatever the rabbi asked of it. But the *golem* could not speak, and it lacked a soul. One day it went amok, smashing whatever got in its way. People rushed to the rabbi for help. He was in the synagogue, in the middle of a prayer. He hurried out to the street and called to the *golem*, ordering it to tie his shoelaces. With the *golem* on its knees, the rabbi took the parchment out of its mouth. The creature collapsed, breaking into hundreds of shards, and the debris was collected and stored in the attic of the synagogue, where it remained and gathered dust over the centuries. Levente junior treasures a tiny jar filled with that debris, which he obtained during one of his many visits to Prague.

His ceramic creations, which he calls "only one degree more imperfect than us human beings," watch us from all around the room. They are hung on the walls and strewn on the floor. The expressions on their faces suggest that they long for something. They could be waiting for the breath of life, Levente junior says, if not for a soul. Why shouldn't a *golem* expect such a miracle — just as a devout Jew awaits the Messiah and just as Levente senior waited for things to turn for the better?

The year is 1996 and my cousin Levente and I try to imagine what his father would say about the confusing new constellation that has replaced the one he knew and thought hopeless. The Red Army withdrew, and for the first time in centuries no major power threatens Hungary's independence. The Soviet Union is gone. However, the communists who no longer call themselves communists are still very much in evidence, many of them wealthy entrepreneurs and top executives in Western-owned corporations; in fact, they won Hungary's second free election. What would Uncle Levente say about their leader, Prime Minister Gyula Horn? As a young man Horn joined those who crushed the 1956 revolution and went on to help eliminate the resistance that remained. Advised by some of Washington's smartest spin-doctors, he now projects an image as a champion of democracy and the multiparty system. Since 1989 Horn has piously denied doing harm to any of the rebels in 1956 or later. (The files on what he did after the revolution are said to be "missing.")

What would be Levente senior's reaction to Horn and other leaders of his so-called Socialist Party laying annual wreaths on the tombs of the executed revolutionary leaders of 1956? How would he interpret their expressionless faces and stiff bows? Until the late 1980s the graves were unmarked, and their location, a weedy lot in the outskirts of Budapest where the corpses had been dumped, was one of the darkest secrets of the People's Republic. For three decades, the "liberal" communist regime surrounded the site with barbed wire and armed guards, and no information was given out on what was being protected. (Though many people thought they knew, and they were right.) Visitors were not allowed to approach within hundreds of yards. As recently as the late 1970s, repeated appeals by widows to Party Secretary Kadar were left unanswered. Letters on their behalf signed by American leaders asking that the Budapest government allow family members to visit the graves were returned to their senders by the Hungarian ambassador in Washington, explaining in a note that such requests are "irreconcilable and incompatible with historically established intercourses between representatives of states." Hungary's "liberal" communists crafted a dialectics of denial that would have made Stalin proud: they calculated that if they kept refusing to discuss the issue of the graves, eventually the public (and even the bothersome Western press) would accept the fact that there are no graves. If there are no graves, no one died, and if no one died, no one led the revolution. If no one led the revolution, the revolution did not really happen.

Uncle Levente might have said, damn it, there must be a curse on my poor homeland. But he would add, as individuals we must pursue our own lines of truth and refuse to succumb to the threats and blandishments of people trained in the arts of deception. Truth, I can imagine him quoting his friend Illyes, is our "language of loyalty" and our "password of hope." In another mood he would laugh and joke about the power of irony that he liked to call "God's snicker" and the one reliable inevitability in history.

Blessed Be He Who Was Not There?

Man cannot win a suit against God.
If he insisted on a trial with Him,
He would not answer one charge in a thousand
Wise of heart and mighty in power
Who ever challenged Him and came out whole?

The Book of Job

When the endless winter of 1944-45 finally yielded to spring, the stomach-turning stench of thawing corpses drowned out the sweet scent of hyacinths. By April, as the last German units fighting in Hungary retreated across the Austrian border, the ice broke up on the Danube that swells into a river in Germany and then collects tributaries in five more countries before it empties into the Black Sea. The current carried thousands of corpses, and at times pairs of them were caught in eddies and whirled together.

Some of my relatives walked down to the riverbank, once the promenade for Budapest's most elegant citizens, to say Kaddish, the prayer for the dead, in remembrance of Imre, a cousin of mine. Throughout the fall of 1944 he had been hiding with his mother and two younger brothers in an apartment that belonged to an army officer, his father's labor battalion commander. But at age sixteen Imre could not stand being cooped up. He left for a walk one afternoon and never returned. Someone in the neighborhood later told his father that a roving Arrow Cross gang captured Imre, which meant that he was probably taken to the Danube. Born deaf, he could not hear the shots that thrust him into the river.

I remember Imre as a cheerful extrovert who did not mind playing board games with those of us half his age, and he had a talent for explaining with gestures and facial expressions what he was unable to sound out. In the years that followed I sometimes wondered how differently the war must have appeared to him, shut off from sounds still in my ear: the relentless thuds of artillery fire that at times seemed as though they would never stop; the staccato whimper of a horse I first saw gallop and then collapse in gobs of blood on the cobblestones of our street, and the high-pitched bickering by the hungry crowd that gathered quickly, waiting for the animal to stop kicking so they could carve up its body for food; the muffled, arrhythmic sobbing of my closest relatives, huddled around Aunt Clara who lived to tell the story of how some of our family's oldest and youngest members were sent into the gas chambers in Auschwitz.

The wartime sound that rings in my ear most often — especially when I am in a synagogue — is the piercing cry of Moshe Mannheim, a devout Jew who addressed himself to God from the sidewalk of his native town of Debrecen. I did not hear him myself, but I listened to his story, first as a child and later as an adult, as told by my Uncle Shumi who was haunted by it for the rest of his life.

A rabbi and a descendant of rabbis, Mannheim was a stocky, high-cheekboned, mustachioed replica of a storybook Hungarian farmer. At age eighteen during the First World War, he enlisted in the Austro-Hungarian army and twice received the empire's highest decoration for exceptional bravery under enemy fire, also making the leap to officer rank. After the war he compiled the first Hungarian-Hebrew dictionary while teaching religion in the Jewish high school in Debrecen, the country's second city. He made friends with my mother's eldest brother, Shumi Schwarcz, one year his junior, though Shumi was neither a synagogue-goer nor an enthusiastic ex-warrior. Seeing no reason for the dietary laws, the daily prayers with their repetitious phrases, and the countless rules and ordinances of the Orthodoxy he was born into, Shumi nevertheless sought meaning in Jewish tradition.

Moshe on the other hand was a scholar and a fighter, an ideal debating partner and unlike other Orthodox Jews who would not waste time arguing with someone nonobservant, he reveled in the challenge of Shumi's questions, and he applied rationalism, Shumi's highest standard, in justifying Jewish beliefs and observances.

Moshe never got angry or raised his voice, even though Shumi asked such questions as: Why worship our origins? Why worship? Why must we spend our days in fear of violating rabbinical prohibitions such as the mixing of meat and milk? Why so many prohibitions? Strolling under allees of Debrecen's cherished sycamore trees or sitting on a park bench in their shade, Shumi told Moshe that he could not understand how a modern, enlightened Jew in civilized, progressive Central Europe could remain bound by words that one man heard, or thought he heard, more than three thousand years ago in the Sinai wilderness, at the extremity of polytheist Asia facing animist Africa.

Shumi was even more skeptical about the wisdom of the talmudic rabbis who amplified and extended the rules that came down from Mount Sinai. Shumi argued that we are no longer caged in a sunless ghetto or make a meager living plying a trade on the highways, equally fearful of bandits and gendarmes who could be lurking behind the next bend, ready to attack us. Mankind is moving toward the light of tolerance and the rule of law, he said, and these days in Debrecen passersby find nothing unusual in seeing — and overhearing — two Jewish citizens, one with a hat and the other without, engaged in a debate in a public place. Life is reasonably good here on this landlocked island, Hungary, where people go about their business feeling no need for a thunderous vision handed down from a desert mountain or for tortuously phrased rulings issued from rabbinical houses taking their cues from Jerusalem.

Yet in what he called his weak moments, Shumi said to me, he conceded that his arguments, usually anchored in his favorite subjects of geography and ethnography, were feeble and niggling when measured against the elemental force of Moshe's credo: "Our faith provides the key to all that is worthwhile in the world. Our faith defines us. It is *us*: you and me, and our parents and grandparents and their rabbis. If we deny our faith, we deny our own selves."

During the Second World War, Moshe qualified for an exemption from anti-Jewish laws on account of his outstanding military record from the First World War. Unlike the rest of Hungary's Jews, Moshe did not have to join a labor battalion, and his wife and their two children were not deported to Auschwitz or Bergen-Belsen — favors for which they thanked Regent Miklos Horthy, the head of state. For Horthy, himself a much-decorated admiral of the Austro-Hungarian Navy during the First World War, bravery under enemy fire was the supreme virtue, and he stubbornly insisted on honoring all war heroes even if they happened to be Jews, regardless of furious protests from German and Hungarian Nazi leaders.

A few days after the Russians drove out the German and Hungarian armies from Debrecen in October 1944 and Shumi found his way back from a labor battalion to what used to be his home, the two friends met by chance on Market Street, the town's broad, busy main thoroughfare. They were overjoyed seeing each other alive. But within seconds their conversation turned somber.

Shumi said he did not as yet know the whereabouts of his mother, and his wife and their five-year-old daughter. Moshe said his wife and their two children, a daughter and a son, died in the final days of the Nazi rule, in the last Allied bombing raid which flattened their apartment building. He happened to be out on an errand at the time, and now he wished that he too had died with his family.

After Shumi expressed his condolences, he added that he suspected that his family might have perished in Auschwitz. But as long as he had not heard from an eyewitness, he could not and would not give up hope that they might be still alive. He said he was prepared to wait for a long time. He had to have proof.

Moshe shook his head. "But my dear Shumi, there is no hope," he said softly. "By now we know that in Auschwitz the oldest and the youngest were killed right away."

"But what about our faith?" Shumi burst out, unable to accept what he had just heard. "How could our God allow such a thing to happen?"

Something snapped in gentle Moshe. Ignoring the crowd that quickly collected, many of whom knew who he was, he began screaming. He called God a murderer, a criminal who cut down innumerable family trees, and an enemy of the Jewish people. He said he wished he had never chanted a blessing. He regretted thanking God for Creation, for the Torah, for sustenance, for his children, and for all the many wondrous divine gifts that an observant Jew must express gratitude every day. Finally, shaking his fists in the direction of the heavens, he cursed God, again and again, at the top of his voice, pronouncing the opposites of the blessings in The Eighteen Benedictions, the centerpiece prayer in synagogue liturgy.

Moshe's rage stunned Shumi. He did not try to interrupt because, he later explained, the curses seemed to him akin to a prayer, and he had been taught not to interrupt a prayer for fear of canceling its effectiveness. "Besides," Shumi added, "he could not be stopped." Only later did it occur to Shumi that the townspeople around them who stared and listened must have thought the rabbi mad and that he should have found a way to remind his friend that the two of them were not alone.

But what made Shumi's insides turn into stone was the realization that he had been foolish in persisting in his hopes. For the first time he understood what others did not know or were reluctant to break to him: his immediate family was no more. Nevertheless, he found the strength to address his thoughts to Moshe. "Your loss is much greater than mine." Shumi said. "You lost your God, as well." The two bereaved men hugged and kissed on both cheeks, and each went his way.

On two occasions Moshe attempted suicide. Shortly after his family perished, he approached a German soldier he saw on the street and said that he was Jewish and ready to be shot. The German replied that he would not dirty his hands with Jewish blood. Moshe's second try came weeks later: he lay down on a train track. The conductor spotted him, and the brakes worked though he broke a leg.

Moshe's life story however has a bittersweet denouement.

A year after war's end he met a woman seventeen years younger than he, who had just returned from Auschwitz. They fell in love and married. A year later, she gave birth to a girl who was given the names Eva Terez, after the daughter and the wife Moshe had lost in the war.

Toward the mid-1960s, Eva married one of her father's students, and the couple took advantage of a weekend group excursion to Vienna and arranged to emigrate to Israel. Then Moshe's second wife died after a long illness, and in 1968 Moshe petitioned Hungary's communist authorities to make an exception in his case — he was seventy years old and lived alone — and disregard the state policy of punishing families whose members left the country illegally and permit him to leave for the land of his forebears. Eventually, after interventions by influential friends and the usual bureaucratic delays, his request was granted.

After the loss of his first family, Moshe stopped praying, and he avoided the synagogue. Except for fasting on Yom Kippur — which he did at home "as an act of solidarity with fellow Jews," he explained — he refused to have anything to do with the laws of Orthodoxy. But in Israel he felt the tug of small pressures from his family that included an observant young nephew, a particular favorite, who reminded him of the son he had lost.

One more time Moshe fell in love and married. His third wife, a soft-spoken widow a few years younger, longed for tradition, though she said nothing, afraid to tear up old wounds. Nevertheless, Moshe understood the dialect of her silences. Little by little, step by step, and with plenty of initial reservations, Moshe returned to the faith of his youth, first keeping the Sabbath and celebrating other holy days, then attending synagogue services, and, finally, following all the many hundreds of rules and customs of Orthodoxy.

In his eighties, Moshe went back to school and qualified as a scribe of religious documents. When he realized that he was going blind, he devised a contraption with several lenses that enabled him to pen tiny, flawless Hebrew letters, their tips suggesting flames, and their base evocative of roots. He specialized in the amulet *mezuzah*. On a scrap of parchment smaller than his palm, he copied the biblical text about the Almighty and His readiness to shield His people from all harm. Rolled up in a scroll thinner than a pencil, the parchment is placed inside a metal or wooden tube, which is nailed to the right side of the doorpost. Tradition maintains that the *mezuzah* has the power to protect a home and all who live there.

In 1992, at age ninety-four and at peace with his God and with himself, Moshe was gathered to his ancestors. At his request, he was buried in Jerusalem; his two grandsons, whom he liked to call his sons, said Kaddish for him.

"Despite everything that happened to him, my father was a happy person, always in a good mood, and especially when among his family," his daughter Eva wrote to me in response to my query. "He had serenity — perhaps because he had returned to the faith, which to him was the natural way. In retrospect, the [three] decades he lived without religion seem unnatural."

Moshe of Debrecen, Moshe of Sinai

Moshe's story may be read as a parable of faith triumphing over despair, love over anger, and life over death. Yet for me, all the loving words I read and heard from members of his family about his miraculous restoration of a private world that was once whole cannot undo a single one of his curses. If I close my eyes, I see Uncle Shumi reenacting that moment of his awe on Market Street, a stone's throw from the house where his mother Roza lived prior to her deportation in 1944; within view of the Calvinist church where Hungarian rebels proclaimed the dethronement of the Habsburgs in 1849; and a short walk from the Soviet military headquarters where Raoul Wallenberg was first detained, in 1945, before his transfer to Moscow's Lubyanka prison.

Now that Uncle Shumi is buried in our family cemetery in his native village, I am an heir to his memory of Moshe's curses. Since childhood I have imagined them as a string of explosives that might have set the air on fire. I can see that fire burning whenever someone cites the biblical passages on Moses — whom we call Moshe *rabbeinu*, our master — coming upon the thorn bush which "burned with fire" yet "was not consumed" and, later on, climbing Mount Sinai, "the mountain burning with fire up to the heart of the heavens."

Moshe in Sinai and Moshe in Debrecen stand at the antipodes of Jewish history. We may define all other times by the way we can relate them either to the fires of Sinai, or to the fires of the crematoria. Their fearful symmetry haunts my mind.

As His people, we were closest to Him at Mount Sinai after we accepted, through Moshe's mediation, His sovereignty over us. But He has not spoken to us since then. His gradual distancing Himself from our fate reached its farthest extremity in the six years of the Second World War. Moshe on Market Street spoke for those of His people who during that war rescinded or at least suspended their unquestioning submission to Him contracted at Mount Sinai.

The God of Our Fathers abandoned us at the time of our greatest need. Though the rabbis cite as precedents the expulsions in the Middle Ages, the auto-da-fes in Spain, and the pogroms in Poland and Russia, none of them prepared us for the magnitude of the Nazi Final Solution, for its meticulous planning and thoroughness, for its merciless fury. We read that at Mount Sinai the Creator of the Universe spoke in the midst of thunder and lightning so we would choose His law. But His withdrawal during the Second World War forced some of us to hold back our unconditional assent and to be reluctant to assume the traditional supplicant's stance that the Orthodox prayer book worshipfully compares to "a slave praising his master before he dares make a request."

Can we bring ourselves to acknowledge that in ignoring our pleas, He betrayed us? Those who believe with intact faith object to such a thought; some object vehemently, refusing to concede any possibility of a break in our intense, intimate, and exclusive relationship with the King of Kings, affirmed by every generation for some four millennia, ever since Abraham chose the One God and smashed his father's household idols. Much like Job's three old friends who suggested that he must have done something grievously wrong to deserve the disasters visited on him, many devout Jews perceive the Holocaust as God's punishment for the failure of His people to observe His laws in their totality.

The inescapable fact is that during the Second World War, God turned His back on us. He offered no exemptions for those who kept His law and studied His Torah with unflagging dedication. He ignored their constant pleas, just as He ignored the desperate cries from the skeptical, the atheist, and the apostate.

There must be an explanation — the moral grammar of Jewish thought demands it.

No straying from the true path — and no true path —— can justify the destruction of one-third of our people. We read that at Mount Sinai, even after the multitudes committed the ultimate sin in denying the One God and reverting to the worship of the Golden Calf, the Almighty allowed Moshe to talk Him out of acting on His "hot anger" and annihilating His people.

The question, as impertinent as it is practical, is whether we should add yet another blessing for Him who, in the words of The Eighteen Benedictions, "sustains the living with kindness," "supports the fallen," and "releases the confined." Should we also say: Blessed be He who was absent?

Could He, omnipresent and eternal, absent Himself from any place, at any given time? (Kabbalists long ago invented the evasive, poetic metaphor of "God hiding Himself," and twentieth century theologian and storyteller Martin Buber offered honeyed words of explanation about "His eclipse.") God's absence in wartime Europe raises doubts about the meaning of our covenant which began with Abraham, received confirmation when Moshe was addressed from the burning thorn bush, and concluded with the alliance at the foot of Mount Sinai which was to last for all time.

If He was absent some six decades ago, is He with us now? Can we recapture the intimacy of our relationship so that we can once more take a leap of faith? Might there be a time when one of us can hear His voice again? And will we — can we — trust in Him then? Or are we to live off the handed-down memories of Sinai as if the twelve years of the Nazi era amounted to an episode of no special importance and our relationship to God should have nothing to do with it?

How Darkness Flared

Human beings we called angels came to our help when He did not. They appeared when they were most needed, albeit they rescued only the fortunate, random, precious few. For those of us so chosen, they salvaged some of our faith in goodness and justice, or, as many survivors like to say, "our faith in humanity." Memories of our benefactors also made postwar normalcy — which we welcomed or we told ourselves to welcome — seem ever so bland and insubstantial. No one could measure up to those righteous heroes of wartime; no brilliant project of reconstruction seemed comparable to the drama of their actions.

But am I justified in using as antique a word as "angel," tangled in the silk cords of myth and theology?

Hungarian Jews used that word — *angyal* in Hungarian and *malach* in Yiddish — in referring to rescuers. The word places on a pedestal the men and women who exempted themselves from their pursuits of self-interest and suspended their instincts for self-preservation. They were, as ancient rabbis said, immune to the temptations of the Evil One, the cunning, merciless *Yetzer Ha'ra*, a life force we so often recognized during the war as real. Angels conducted themselves as if the natural laws of planet earth, such as the fear of death, did not apply to them. They grew wings, as it were.

What made them soar while others cowered and crawled?

Several of the angels I have written about spoke of being overwhelmed early on in their rescue work by feelings and convictions they could not explain, then or later. "I did what I had to do almost unconsciously," Pastor Gabor Sztehlo confessed in his memoirs, a statement that speaks in varying measures for his fellow rescuers as well.

Some of them shrugged when hearing an admirer praise their courage. They insisted that theirs was simply a natural response to what the times and the circumstances called for. "What I did seemed the only thing to do," said journalist Levente Thury. "I could not do otherwise."

Success spurred them on. Once engaged in rescuing people, they could not stop themselves. They were pulled into a vortex of action and found that obstacles diminished or vanished, and the seemingly far more powerful enemy retreated. While the war drained other people of energy and optimism, the angels had both in excess. Unlike their demoralized protégés and the passive Gentile majority, most of the rescuers were certain that the remaining Jews of Hungary would be saved and that liberation was only a few days away.

They seemed to have been invested with a force greater than themselves. It was almost comical how scrawny little Mr. Kanalas, an otherwise disreputable janitor, could chase away, by the power of his words alone, two gangs of Nazi thugs thrilled by the chance of hunting down their quarry. Erzsebet David — a weak and indecisive woman though a most competent, conscientious official of the state — discovered the courage to violate her oath of office and forge Christian birth certificates.

These extraordinary beings did not spend much time weighing the likely consequences of their rescue work. Rational analysis cannot fully account for their successes, and especially for the Nazis' failure to stop them. I am also at a loss to explain their sudden appearances as well as the undeserved melancholy of their exits.

They were not drawn to the scent of mortal danger as are many adventurous people. At times it seemed as if they had had access to another world — they were visionaries more akin to William Blake than to Winston Churchill. They also shared one notable feature: their actions ignoring their mortality offered them the best times of their lives. They seemed to be convinced that they were doing what they were meant to do on this earth, and all that happened to them before the war was only preparation and what followed the war amounted to no more than an afterthought.

Were they like the rest of us? Or did their personalities include something strange and unusual?

The ordinary and the preternatural blended differently in each of the five rescuers. An American college teacher of Raoul Wallenberg's thought that the young Swede "had extremely normal instincts." But to some Jews in Budapest, Wallenberg had a passionate commitment to his protégés that suggested a role assigned to him in the divine scheme: he was the harbinger of the Messiah who was on His way, they believed, to save what was left of Hungarian Jewry, the last intact Jewish community on the continent. A child rescued by Pastor Sztehlo now remembers him as "a pure spirit" and as "a special person who performed real miracles"; while his cousin Sara Sztehlo found him "entirely down-to-earth" and "a marvelous but ordinary man."

They were people like us, yet they were also as unlike us as a human being is different from a *golem* — a creature shaped to resemble a man. Molded from clay, it is endowed with the breath of life by means of magic incantations, such as those uttered by Rabbi Judah Loew of Prague, a sixteenth century kabbalist. While a *golem* is less than human and depends entirely on its master for instructions on what tasks to perform, angels at times seemed superhuman, possessed of a spontaneous inventiveness and relying entirely on themselves in standing up against all odds.

After stepping out of their original selves, they acquired second personalities. While seeming to take leave of their senses, they remade themselves in response to what they saw as a moral emergency. In the process, they discovered they had powers they had been unaware of.

They accomplished what others with far more authority and resources could not or would not. They made the darkness flare.

But why were there so few angels, in Hungary and elsewhere in Europe? Why didn't more righteous Gentiles step forward?

What is surprising is that there were any rescuers at all. They not only risked their lives day after day but they defied a spectacularly successful *Zeitgeist* of pillage and murder, a master race marching in ecstatic lockstep, believing in its absolute right to enslave or to eliminate "lesser races." Even to some of their staunchest opponents, the Nazis seemed unstoppable — the ineluctable future, just as the Nazi marching song declared, with a refrain that proved hypnotic for far too many: "The future belongs to us."

Could we understand these angels as having been sent by the God of Compassion and Grace suspending His absence and indifference? Could they have served as His emissaries, recalling the biblical angel who stopped Abraham, with knife in hand and son Isaac tied up, from sacrificing his son?

In centuries past, the appearance of such exceptional individuals would have suggested divine inspiration. But nowadays it takes a most loyal subject with a belief in His absolute monarchy to advance such an explanation. Or did the angels fool not only the state authorities but God as well? Just as Pastor Sztehlo set up thirty-two houses of refuge rather than a single one as his bishop had instructed him, some of the other angels too kept expanding their enterprises. Again, it seemed as if they would not and could not stop.

Jewish tradition maintains that each angel is assigned one task and one task only. To keep playing God carries the risk of competing with Him or appearing to compete with Him by arrogating some of His omnipotence, which suggested to the ancient rabbis that angels run the danger of believing that they are on the same level with Him. Thus the power that an angel assumes could amount to a challenge if not a rebellion.

Perhaps the argument should be reduced to one over language. What eyewitnesses and deep believers have been moved to call "angels," psychologists and sociologists diagnose as "altruistic person-ality types," and students of history and political science identify as "charismatic individuals" and "brave dissidents." But these are abstract and rational characterizations. Why not use instead the word "angel," a felicitous anachronism that occurred to someone unknown and was accepted enthusiastically two generations ago?

The Invisible Tattoo

Throughout the centuries since the liberation from the gods and taskmasters of Egypt, our rabbis have been telling us that every Jewish soul who ever lived or will ever live was present at Mount Sinai. It is a thought as lyrical as it is didactic. Its message is that to accept a binding obligation as all-important as the covenant with the Ruler of the Universe, all the generations needed to be at the foot of the moun-tain and vote by acclamation. That is how we became His people and He became our God.

"We have never been the same since the day on which the voice of God overwhelmed us at Sinai," the Polish-born theologian Abraham Joshua Heschel wrote in 1955. It was "like no other event in the his-tory of man." What Rabbi Heschel said about Sinai can be said about the death camps as well. "Nothing can ever be the same again," my relatives said over and over again after the war. Two generations later, many Jews including those non-observant are possessed of the same feeling: each of us was, in a yet undefined and perhaps indefinable way, present in the death camps as well.

Of course the Nazis intended that all of us end up there. As the years pass, we tend to forget how very close they came to winning the war in Europe and northern Africa, and that they were within a breath of conquering the British Mandate of Palestine. Given more time, they could have tracked down every Jew in the Old World. But for those of us who escaped that fate and others born since then, imagining ourselves in those barracks surrounded by fences of high-voltage wire is an act of will. It is the mind's pilgrimage to the site of our unbearable terror that tightens the throat like a noose and makes the heart hammer the chest. In comparison, all our current disaffections seem petty, as do our critical decisions about marriages and mortgages. We return home with invisible numbers tattooed on our arms. "Auschwitz is the anti-Exodus because it is a journey from freedom to slavery," says Michael Berenbaum, an American-born rabbi devoted to the study of the Holocaust. "In Sinai the key relationship is between God's command and human responsibility. In Auschwitz, it is the Nazis who play God."

No experience since Sinai has held us in its thrall as have the death camps. While each year at the Passover Seder we dutifully obey the rabbinical command and think of ourselves as if we ourselves had left Egypt, many of us are visited by the recurrent nightmare of being marched into the gas chambers. At Mount Sinai, each of us gained something immeasurable; in the death camps many of us lost something irretrievable.

The part of me that burned up in Auschwitz was my grandmother Roza's unquestioning surrender to God's justice and loving-kindness, as well as her abandon in chanting unselfconsciously the prayers that praise Him with such oriental extravagance. I find I cannot return to the orchard of her perfect faith where she had once walked with her husband, my long-departed grandfather and model farmer after whom I am named. I cannot claim their legacy of absolute obedience to Him and to the rabbis assigned to interpret His words. For me, it is a strain to repeat prayers such as "Praise God in His Sanctuary; praise Him in the firmament of His Power. Praise Him for His mighty acts; praise Him as befits His abundant greatness." At times I mumble when a prayer cites His "infinite mercy," and I cringe when reading Job's slavish avowal, "though He slay me, yet will I trust in Him." Silently, I have added questions when reciting The Eighteen Benedictions: Where were You when Your people were packed into cattle cars? Why didn't You respond when we called out to You? What was on Your mind when the poison gas began to disperse? O my God, God of Our Fathers and Mothers, You failed Your people.

Nevertheless, I cannot bring myself to repeat any of Rabbi Moshe Mannheim's curses, not even in cold print, not even for the purpose of a quote.

Analyzing "the coherence of curses and blessings" in the biblical narrative, the American scholar Robert Alter wrote in 1976: "Again and again, we become aware of the power of words to make things happen. God or one of His intermediaries speaks: man may repeat and fulfill the words of revelation, repeat and delete, repeat and transform; but always there is the original urgent message to contend with, a message which in the potency of its concrete verbal formulation does not allow itself to be forgotten or ignored."

Repeating, deleting, and transforming words from the potent message of The Eighteen Benedictions, Moshe's curses are still as valid now as the reasons that prompted their spontaneous combustion more than fifty years ago. Surely he was not the only Jew who angrily confronted God for deserting us. Others in other parts of the continent must have cursed Him in one form or another, though perhaps not so publicly and elaborately, and witnesses might not have kept and handed down the memory as Shumi did.

After liberation many Jews expressed their disenchantment with their faith and God. Some converted, or in the earthy talmudic phrase, "cut their roots;" others turned their backs on the dietary laws, the synagogue, the holy days, even the community. Still others cut a deal: they would observe some or even all the rules, even though they no longer believed in God or dismissed the traditional presumption of a special relationship with Him.

For Shumi, Moshe's curses confirmed his need for a permanent dialog with and about the deity — what Buber called "the I-and-Thou relationship." After Shumi moved to Budapest and lost touch with Moshe, he found other knowledgeable Jews to spar with. But Shumi never returned to the Orthodoxy of his parental home. He could not, as he was a questioner, not a worshipper. Nevertheless, in his last years he made elaborate arrangements to ensure that he would have a proper Jewish funeral — and he did, thanks to his nephew Levente's devotion to him.

Moshe's curses cannot be unsaid. They hover over every prayer I recite; they are invisible footnotes to each page of Talmud I study. Theirs is a darkness that smolders and flares.

Moshe Mannheim volunteered for the Austro-Hungarian army in World War I, became an officer and received a number of decorations for bravery.

Rabbi Mannheim in the 1940s.

A snake of a thought is coiled on the tree above my head. It hisses: Could it be that He is our invention, as much as we are supposed to be His? Could such an unwritten, clandestine reciprocity account for the longevity of our contract? Nevertheless, I praise Him. Tradition obligates me, and fellow-Jews expect me to join the chorus as a matter of course. How could I refuse the honor of being called up to say the blessings before and after the weekly Torah portion is read in the synagogue? Why should I deny myself the honeyed glow of ritual? Why should I stray from what strikes me as the natural way? If I don't praise Him, I miss the burnished phrases and their antique resonances. Whenever I fail to join the prayers chanted in unison, I am aware that I do not live up to my forebears' standards. I feel diminished, and at times ashamed.

When saying Kaddish I recite the long list of praises extolling Him and His magnificence and His compassion. In my family tradition, the Kaddish is the most important prayer because, my ancestors believed, it helps the soul free itself from a used-up body and enables it to seed itself in another not yet born. On his dying day, the Baal Shem Tov, as unafraid of death as he was of a dark forest or hungry wolves, said: "I can see a door opening while another is closing."

At my mother's funeral, in November 1995, I added a personal prayer I think might have resembled the one said to have been composed by my maternal ancestors but not passed down to my generation. (The ideas in the prayer I had long been familiar with, and the words came to me as fast as I could jot them down, during the flight back to Hungary, suspended between the New World and the Old.) I asked *Riboyno shel Oylam* to return my mother's soul again to this earth soon because she loved life here despite all the hardships she faced. Because she did good deeds. Because she felt she still had much to give to others. Because she was afraid that she did not pay back all her debts. Then I asked the God of Abraham, Isaac, and Jacob to return her soul in our family, so that one day soon there would be among us again a child with the talent of her hands and with all the love that lived in her heart.

Dafke

I do not pray three times a day, though I envy the devout who do. However, I love saying the blessings that connect us to the Creator and to a newly launched creation such as a pear sapling or the first tomato of the season. Blessings also link that moment to other similar moments that passed long ago and to those that are yet to come.

But it is not because of Him that my heart pounded faster when in the synagogue I cradled the Torah scroll in my arms and led the procession at my daughter Malka's *bas mitzvah*. It is not because of His command to remember slavery under the pharaoh that many of us revel in the harsh taste of horseradish during the retelling of the Passover story each year. The observance of traditions repeated faithfully for so many centuries is for our sake as much as His. Because we treasure them for their solemn, stately beauty and their archaic, half-suppressed, and half-forgotten magic. Because they remind us that we are all part of the people we became in Sinai. Because vaulting over the fences of time and space and spurning the entries on our birth certificates and passports, we turn into our ancestors — and they into us.

When pronouncing the curses, Moshe did not deny His existence; instead, he struck back at Him for violating His covenant with us. A gentle rebuke came from the Yiddish poet Jacob Glatstein, born in Lublin, Poland, adjacent to the death camp Maidanek and some two hundred and fifty miles north of Debrecen:

> We received the Torah at Sinai
> and in Lublin we gave it back
> Dead men don't praise God
> The Torah was given to the living.

Similar thoughts might have occurred to Isaac, after the shock of his escape from Abraham's knife, directed, or so Abraham believed, by God's command. Whatever Isaac's own response might have been — anger, gratitude or emotional exhaustion — it did not merit a single word in the Torah. Nor does the Bible hint at how Abraham felt. The story concludes with God's angel expressing satisfaction with

Abraham, and that pronouncement clangs like a knife dropped on granite: "Now I know that you fear God." Was the silence that followed a premonition of His future withdrawal and absence?

But a few passages later the Bible tells how one night Isaac's son Jacob refused to submit himself to God, wrestled with an Angel of God, and in the end won. Jacob's reward was a glorious new name, Israel, meaning "he who wrestles with God and prevails." The name implies that it is not only permissible but meritorious to fight God. Yet in the Book of Job the Bible warns us: "Who ever challenged Him and came out whole?"

Just as the anguish and the triumphs of intense Abraham, passive Isaac, and pugnacious Jacob lose their depths of meaning without their ultimate faith, our lives are incomplete without the one Supreme Being they chose as our God. But could it be that all our prayers through the generations have disappeared in an emptiness as vast as space? My heart sinks when I consider the possibility that no one listened to the Kaddish for Cousin Imre — or for Moshe, or Shumi, or my mother Anna. Could it be that the Almighty has become not only mute but deaf as well? Perhaps we should turn into a permanent question the bitter statement by the Talmud's Rabbi Eliezer following the destruction of the Temple in Jerusalem nearly two millennia ago: "Is the gate of prayer closed, and is the gate of tears the only one left open?"

Nonetheless, it cannot be that He is not. Jacob Glatstein, please accept a postscript to your poem:

> Moshe Mannheim cursed God in Debrecen,
> and in Jerusalem he returned to the faith
> Love lights the way to the Torah
> The newborn call the dead back to life.

For some of us shackled to memories of the Holocaust as our irrevocable experience of awe, faith is an exercise in applying the word *dafke* — an irreverent, dissonant, and quarrelsome Yiddishism, bleached of its passion when translated, usually as "despite," or "nevertheless," or, simply, "but." To grammarians, all four words qualify as disjunctive conjunctives suggesting an apparent oxymoron or a Zen *koan*, but as Jewish as the notion that nothing is as whole as a broken heart. I picture them as thorns of negation stippling a stem crowned by an inexplicably splendid bloom, tradition's flawless thirteen-petalled rose of faith.

Alas, thorns yield no harvest of bloom, neither fragrance nor fruit, nor shade — and a thorn bush is memorable only when set on fire. Similarly, negation offers no comfort. It leaves us dry-mouthed and sour-stomached. In contrast, the origins of our faith anchor and sustain us, just as forking roots burrowing far down in the earth braced and nourished the mottled trunks of Debrecen's sycamores that towered over Moshe and Shumi. For me, the example of faith upheld and ritual observed — albeit with gritted teeth because the event commemorated showed no evidence of divine mercy — will always be the Kaddish for Cousin Imre in the spring of 1945, on the Danube riverbank.

However, the forking roots of Jewish thought join faith and doubt, affirmation and denial, submission and defiance, strategic silence and thunderous pronouncements, desert starkness and extravagant ornamentation, appropriate prayers chanted at precisely defined times and lapsed observance following disappointment in the deity. We can live a wholesome life as Moshe's curses echo in our ears, while our tongues *dafke* confirm the covenant Moshe sealed. A Jew is entitled to cleave to both.

Bibliography

Robert Alter. Biblical Narrative. Commentary magazine, May 1976.

Per Anger. With Raoul Wallenberg in Budapest. New York. Holocaust Library, 1981.

Lars G. Berg. The Book That Disappeared. What Happened in Budapest. New York. Vantage Press, 1990.

Randolph L. Braham. The Politics of Genocide. New York. Columbia University Press, 1994.

Maria Ember. Rank Akartak Kenni (They Wanted to Blame Us). Budapest. Hettorony, 1992.

Mario Fenyo. Hitler, Horthy, and Hungary. New Haven. Yale University Press, 1972.

Charles Gati. Hungary and the Soviet Bloc. Durham. Duke University Press, 1986.

Jacob Glatstein. Selected Poems of Jacob Glatstein. Translated by Ruth Whitman. New York. October House, 1972.

Daniel Jonah Goldhagen. Hitler's Willing Executioners. New York. Alfred A. Knopf, 1996.

Moshe Elijahu Gonda. A Debreceni Zsidok Szaz Eve (Hundred Years of the Jews of Debrecen). Tel Aviv, no publisher or date indicated.

Abraham Joshua Heschel. God in Search of Man. New York. The Noonday Press, 1993.

Gabor Kadar & Zoltan Vagi. Zsidok es Nem-zsidok, Szolidaritas es Embermentes a Veszkorszakban (Jews and Non-Jews, Solidarity and Rescue during the Holocaust). Budapest. Holocaust Fuzetek, 1998.

Emil Koren. Sztehlo Gabor Elete es Szolgalata (Gabor Sztehlo's Life and Service). Budapest. Az Orszagos Evangelikus Muzeum, 1994.

Kati Marton. Wallenberg. Missing Hero. New York. Arcade Publishing, 1995.

Laszlo Peto. Vegtelen Menet (Endless March). Sao Paulo. Livraria Landy Ltd., 1982.

RW. Letters and Dispatches, (Raoul Wallenberg's Correspondence) New York. Arcade Publishing, 1995.

Gabor Sztehlo. Isten Kezeben (In God's Hand). Budapest. A Magyarorszagi Evangelikus Egyhaz Sajtoosztalya, 1984.

Jeno Thassy. Veszelyes Videk (Dangerous Land). Budapest, Pesti Szalon, 1996.

Karoly Vig, editor. Kortarsak Bajcsy-Zsilinszky Endrerol (What Contemporaries Wrote About Endre Bajcsy-Zsilinszky). Budapest. Magveto, 1969.

Photo Credits

Prologue, p. xxxiii
Hungarian soldiers look at the corpses of eight Jews they shot on the bank of the Danube in 1944. Photo — U.S. National Archives, courtesy of the U.S. Holocaust Memorial Museum Photo Archives.

Conscripts of Hungarian Labor Battalion VIII/2 laying track in 1942 in Huszt, Hungary (now Chust in Ukraine). Photo — Adalbert Feher, courtesy of the U.S. Holocaust Memorial Museum Photo Archives

Chapter 1, p. 11
Ferenc Szalasi, the Fuhrer of the Arrow Cross movement, swears in as Hungary's new head of state on October 16, 1944. Photo — Magyar Zsido Muzeum es Leveltar, courtesy of the U.S. Holocaust Memorial Museum Photo Archives.

In 1938 Hungary's Regent Miklos Horthy crosses a bridge on horseback. Photo — Yad Vashem Photo Archives, courtesy of the U.S. Holocaust Memorial Museum Photo Archives

Chapter 2, pp. 54 and 74
Portrait of Raoul Wallenberg in his office at the Swedish Legation in Budapest in late 1944. Photo — Thomas Veres, courtesy of the U.S. Holocaust Memorial Museum Photo Archives.

On November 1, 1944, at the Jozsefvaros train station in Budapest. Jews stand on the platform, about to be deported. Raoul Wallenberg (on the right with his hands clasped). He is flanked by a Hungarian gendarmerie officer named Lullay and a Jew holding up a Swedish protective passport. Photo taken by Thomas Veres — courtesy of the U.S. Holocaust Memorial Museum Photo Archives.

Hungarian Jews, rescued from deportation by Raoul Wallenberg at the Jozsefvaros railroad station on November 28, 1944 walk back to the International Ghetto of Budapest. The photo was taken by Thomas Veres from Wallenberg's car as they drove past the group. Photo — courtesy of the U.S. Holocaust Memorial Museum Photo Archives.

Ambassador Per Anger of Sweden in his office, in front of the portrait of his friend and colleague, Raoul Wallenberg. Photo — courtesy of the U.S. Holocaust Memorial Museum Photo Archives

The publishers wish to thank Inger Crickenberger of the United States Holocaust Memorial Museum for her research assistance in locating these photographs.